TRIBAL CULTURE IN INDIA

TRIBAL CULTURE IN INDIA

Dr. Narayan Mishra

KALPAZ PUBLICATIONS
Delhi-110052

Tribal Culture in India
(Tribal)

Rs. 720

ISBN: 81-7835-219-2

Published in 2004 in India by
Kalpaz Publications,
C-30, Satyawati Nagar, Delhi-110052
E-mail : Kalpaz@hotmail.com

Laser Typesetting at : Shree Vaishnavi Creations, Delhi
Printed at : Mehra Offset Press, Delhi

Contents

Preface

I studied Anthropology under late Professor L.P. Vidyarthi and Dr. M. Roy in early sixties. These eminent teachers inspired and initiated me for doing the field-work. Most of the empirical facts for these papers were collected from the tribal areas of Chotanagpur but a few from the Garhwhal area of U.P., while the rest are based on the library work. The present volume is a collection of fourteen papers written for various seminars and journals. The theme of each paper may not be fresh by now, but they were relevant when they were researched and published. I hope, all of them are useful even to-day. Since most of them have been withdrawn from the circulation by now, I have tried to put them together in the form of a single volume to fulfil the wishes of my well-meaning friends and students.

It is vivid from the perusal of various titles of the papers included in this volume that twelve out of fourteen papers are based on my personal field-work on various topics of anthroopological singnificance in the contemporary period of which was spread over thirty years of time and only two are based on purely library work" Ecological setting and Demographic pattern of Anjan", "The Hindu Jajamani system in Tribal village of Chotanagpur". The leadership Pattern of a tribal village", "The sacred specialists of a Tribal village", Bhagat cult and Social mobilization", and "Occultism and Kamru-cult in Chotanagpur" are some of the papers based on my personal field-work carried out for the Pht hesis in and around Anjan,a tribal village of Chotanagpur during 1965-70. The paper "Tribal indebtedness and indigeneoces Banking System" is based on collection of empirical facts from the village of pugu near Gulam. Similarly "Habitat and Economy of Netarhat" is based on the field-expedition in 1970-80. I undertook the field-work at Kothal-gate near Rajpur in Dehradun in 1986 and wrote a paper "Role of voluntary organisation the Garahwal area". "Wild animal as a source of joy and sorrow for the natives of Palamau" is an outcome of my several trips to Betla and other elephant affected areas of Chotanagpur. Some of the materials collected in these trips helped me in writing "Problems of Rural areas in Chotanagpur". The paper" A Socio-psychological study of the University students" is based on a survey of the students of Ranchi University conducted with the help of a scheduled cum-questionnaire drafted for this. In the mid-fifties and early sixties when researchers on the village studies were at its apex, I studied intransitively and published a paper "Village studies in India". Similarly "Theoretical Anthropology and E. B. Tylor" is another paper based on the Library-work.

I will consider my efforts amply rewarded if the thoughts which emerge from this volume stimulate some young anthropologists to hursue them. The members of my family particulary my son, Keshav and daughter, Jaya helped me a lot by way of suggestions and assistance. Shanti, my wife and Dibya, my daughter also helped me very much by providing physical confront during the period of editing the book. I thank each of them for their help and support.

This volume is dedicated in the memory of late Professor L.P. Vidyarthi, my teacher and guide who taught me the very alphabet of Anthropology and under whose feet I learnt whatever I know about it.

Dr. Narayan Mishra

I

Tribal Culture in North—East India

Far away in the north-east of India, in Arunachal there lives a tribe known as *the Apa Tani* who has a very special interest for anthropologists. The Apa Tanis have developed a form of intensive cultivation without the use of the plough or of cattle, and have been able to support for generations a population which is almost as dense as that in the alluvial plains of Bengal. For intensity of cultivation the only area with which the valley in which the Apa Tanis live can be compared is the Hunsa valley in northern Kashmir, which almost lies at the foot of the Rakaposhi peak, where also fertility has been maintained for centuries by an unusually skilled community of peasants. (Howard 1945, 173-74.)

The Apa Tanis live in seven villages in the open valley of the Kele river (27° 34' N. lat., 93° 51' E. long., average elevation 5,000 ft.), which drains into the Rangandi, which on its part flows into the Subansiri. Their number, according to the census of 1961, was 10,745 persons living in 2,520 horses altogether. The valley is an open oval-shaped one, only about 6½ miles long. The story goes that, at one time, all this land was a marsh, inhabited by lisard-like reptiles of large sise. The Apa Tanis cleared the marshes of these animals and eventually settled down to found their villages. Prof. Christoph Von Fiirer Haimendorf, who has written an excellent account of them, believes that they came from the north by crossing the longitudinal valleys of the Khru and the Kamla, and then crossing the watershed which divides these valleys from the Ranga and its tributaries. In physical appearance and in matters of religious belief, they are not different from the Dafia or the Hill Miri who surround them, although their economy, and consequent social or political organisation, have become very different from those of their neighbours.

The seven villages of the Apa Tanis are arranged in three groups, which act in certain respects as titual units. According to the census figures, the number of houses in each village is as follows : Hang, 514 houses; Hari, 368 houses; Bela, 672 houses; Haja, 433 houses; Duta, 160 houses; Mudang-Tage, 180 houses; and Mishi-Bamin, 193 houses. (Haimendorf 1962, 64.)

Agriculture

As it has been already said, the Apa Tani cultivate without the plough, their principal implement being the hoe, with the aid of which they level the ground, build terraces and balks or ridges between fields, and use the land is a gardener treats a small plot of garden land. In this respect, the only other people with home they can be compared are the Newars of Nepal who also carry on agriculture in terraced fields by means of the hoe alone.

Each village contains, more or less, three kinds of land. At the bottom are the flat rice-fields which are irrigated by drawing water from the river Kele or small rills which flow into it. Then come the higher fields which are fit for drier froms of cultivation. Besides these are the village groves of bamboo and pinetrees, with a little land which can be spared for pasturing a few cattle the Apa Tanis bring from the plains. Their principal wealth, however, consists of the mithan *(Bos frontalis)*, which is semi-wild and left free to grase in the more distant forests in the hills, which belong to a particular village, and which may lie two or three miles away. Each such forest is also used by the villagers for collecting, hunting or trapping.

It is neccessary to measure accurately the amount of land which each family in the village utilises; for, only when that is done will it be possible to calculate and compare the carrying capacity of Apa Tani agriculture with those froms of agricultural production.

In the matter of husbandry, the Apa Tanis display an industry and a skill, compared to which even some of the best farmers of Assam or Bengal appear to be almost clumsy rustics. Every ounce of water is carefully carried from one field to another, so that all may share in the wealth which nature has generously provided in the valley. The paddy which is grown in the low fields is of the transplanted variety; and weeding is done, not once, but several times so that none of the plant-food may run into waste.

Water is not allowed to flow unchecked over a field while irrigating, as that might sweep away the finest layer of clay from the top. We found that along the boundary of the field inside a shallow drain had been dug which would carry the water without disturbing the top layer of surface clay. The slow spill-over from these drains actually waters the field. Moreover, when water has to be drained from one field into another, which may belong to one's neighbour, a peculiar device is adopted. A hole is made in the blak and a bamboo pipe of short length carries the water to the next lower field. What is important is that a flat board of wood is temporarily set up in front of the pipe at the lower level, so that when the water comes pouring in through the bamboo pipe, its force is broken and it is cscattered in the from of a spray. It is thus not allowed to wash up, or dig a hole in the lower field.

Terracing and levelling of fields has been carried down to the from of an art, for which a very large amount of human labour is expended. Lumps of earth are often carried by means of a wooden board on which they are placed, and which is then drawn across the field with a roap by one member of the family and deposited in the required place. The final work is done, of course, by means of the hoe.

The balks are also made with great care. They are like a parallel-piped in cross-section, the top of which is used as a path from one field to another. The sides of the balk appeared to us to be remarkably free from grass; and on looking carefully it was discovered that the small, thin walls of the balk had been sown with millets, which had been gathered before we had gone there on a visit. In fact, every yard of land which can be utilized is thus made good use of. Prof. Haimendorf says in his book that even the millet *(Eleusine coracana)* is also transplanted from seed-beds where they have been previosuly sown.

Another interesting feature of Apa Tani villages is that bamboo groves and pine trees are all carefully fenced in by thoroughly well-made, strong fences, so that no animal, whether mithan or plains cattle or even pigs can breakthrough them into the plots where vegetables or tobacco are grown. Every piece of handwork carried the evidence of care and industry which had been bestowed upon it.

Even in such a densely inhabited valley, each village appeared to have been able to preserve much of its forest wealth, and we were told that it was a custom among the Apa Tani to first plant a tree when he needed to cut down another for any purpose whatsoever. We do not know how far that is true; but without some custome of this kind, it would indeed be difficult for any community to conserve its forest welth. The bamboo which is grown by fencing all round is reared for its special qualities.

Trade

The Apa Tanis as farmers have developed a high form of individualism. the fields are personal property, expect for certain patches which belong either to the clan or to the village as a whole. Land and its possession is the aim of every Apa Tani farmer; and mithan, which is used s currency, is used mainly for the purchase of land. if a man is captured by the Dafla, or if a Dafla is imprisoned by the Apa Tani, the compensation or ransom has to be handed over in the shape of mithans, swords, Tibetan bells, pieces of Assamese silk-cloth, and so on.

Indeed, in order to secure wealth in the shape of all these, is always the ambition of an Apa Tani; and they have proved to be one of the best traders in this part of the world. They carry on trade with the Dafla and the Miri, their immediate neighbours, as well as with the distant plains of Assam, from where they buy iron and salt, or plains cattle and pupies, which are needed for certain sacrificial ceremonies.

After the opening up of roads through Apa Tani country since Independence, they have proved to be most adaptive and enterprising. Their trade with the plains of Assam has increased, some ot the young men have gone to school or have become motor drivers and mechanics of shopkeepers, and a whole world of new opportunities seem to have opened up before them in the district town of Hapoli, of which they have readily taken advantage.

Villages and Houses

Apa Tani villages are densely crowded; the streets are not straight, and two rows of houses face each other on both their sides. In the middle or so of the village, there is an enormous block of flat stone, brought from the hills with great care. This is known as the *lapang,* and is used by members of a clan for sitting and gossipoing. This is also the meeting-place where members of the clan assemble to come to fromal decisions of any kind. Prof. Haimendorf observed that more than one clan may use a common *lapang* for sitting, while in very large villages there may be more than one *lapang. (op. cit., 65.)*

The houses are all built on stils, which are fairly high, so that one has to climb up by means of a ladder. In front, facing the street, is a verandah, and the entrance into the house is on the narrow front of the house which opens into the verandah.

As garbage and filth go on accumulating underneath the platfrom, it can be gathered and used in the fields as excellent compost for manuring.

Besides the *lapang* or sitting platfrom, another important feature of the villages is a small shrine, called the *nago,* which is an isolated hut, and is used by a group of clans as their temple. There are many rituals and ceremonies which are connected with the *nago,* and which help to strengthen the bonds of unity among the Apa Tani *(Ibid.)*

Social Authority

The family is, of course, the primary unit through which

all agricultural activity is conducted. But in a crowded agricultural community, where peace has to be maintained so that life and industry can be carried on properly, it is necessary to have some from of effective social control. The Apa Tanis depend very much upon the council of clan elders for this purpose. They do not have a highly centralised authority, but an infromal one, called *buliang,* in which all men of influence on account of their experience of character can and do participate.

The *buliangs* are of three kinds. The first consists of elders and the aged who guide by means of their wisdom and tact. The second group consists of te middle-aged, who are actually active and responsible for carrying out the decisions of the council. The third consists of young people who serve as messengers and assistants. The divisions are, however, not rigid or permanent; one can pass from one group to another without going through any fromalities.

Among the young men and women, there is another intitution known as the *patang*. It is a kind of club or brotherhood, the members of which join one another in common labour. There is no bachelors dormitory as in many other Indian tribes; but the bond which is cemented by the *patang* is not less strong than that fostered by other kinds of youth organisation.

To what extent can a village be looked upon as a social unit? Prof. Haimendorf says that the unity of a village community is expressed by the simultaneous observance of religious feasts and days when all abstain from work, which is also a ritual matter. There are processions and ceremonial visits from one village to another, in which all clans cooperate on equal terms. There is, however, no centralised authority, which is a source of weakness when a conflict arises between the war-like Daflas and some Apa Tani families. Even if there are raids and captures, the Apa Tanis do not unite in order to ward off what should be regarded as a common danger.

Social Divisions

We have already alluded to the clan organisation which

is ofgreat importance among the Apa Tanis. There is, however, another kind of division in Apa Tani society which has been described as a division into patricians and commners. It has been observed that there is a broad physical distinction between the two. All Apa Tanis belong to the Indo-Mongoloid stock; but the 'patricians' are fairly tall and fair-coloured, with long noses, while the commoners are smaller in sise, with more pronounced Mongoloid features akin to the Daflas.

The Apa Tanis used to practise slavery even when they were first visited by Prof. Haimendorf in 1945. With the extension of the Government of India's influence in that area. slavery has, of course, disappeared; but those who are interested in its details may read its details in Chapter IV of the book referred to.

Society is divided into the *mite,* the patricians, and the *mura,* the slaves or commoners. A *mura* can never aspire to rise in the social scale and become a *mite*, that is, completely forbidden. Every *mite* household may have a number of slaves attached to it. One can become a slave by capture from, say, among the Daflas. If one is in debt, may also reduce oneself inot the position of a *mura* unitl the debt is cleared off, or ransom is paid. The slaves are, however, treated as dependants and join the master and his family in common labour in the fields.

The slave addresses his master as 'father', and is indeed taken into the clan of his master. He is also free to carry on any trade with the plains of Assam, and if he can gather enough money, he can free himself and then set up his own household and enjoy a status like that of the free-born. Slavery is thus not a permanent phenomenon, and is looked upon more as the result of an individual's fate and ill luck, from which he can be retrieved either by dint of his own enterprise or by the help of friends.

Young men who from the *patang* working groups may be either *mite* or *mura* with no discrimination whatsoever. A householder is not to have any sexual privilege over the slave at all. But if a girl belonging to the *mite* group has an intimacy with a *mura,* it is condoned to a very large extent.

If the girl admits that the father of her illegitimate child is a mura, then she has to become a *mura* herself, subject to the same rules which govern the life of other *muras*.

Besides this division of Apa Tani society into *mite* and *mura,* there are some other distinctions made between those who practise specialised occupations and the rest. Pottery is manufactured by four *mura* clans in the village of Mirchi-Bamin. If a girl belonging to any of these clans marries in another village, she may not manufacture pottery any longer. Women of other villages may marry into these clans, and learn pot-making.

Pottery is made by hand from a lump of clay which is shaped roughly by hand and then the walls are thinned by beating with a wooden beater outside, while inside a piece of rounded stone is held as an anvil.

There were only three blaksmiths among the Apa Tani when they were first visited by Prof. Haimendorf. One belonged to the *mura* section, the other two were praticians, who had slightly lowered themselves in social estimation by their new enterprise. Now a days, Apa Tanis obtain most of their hardware from the plains of Assam.

The castration of pigs is done by women alone, this being known as *kenna.* Those who do so are debarred from participation in feasts and ritual ceremonies. A *kenna* is not supposed to marry, but if a man lives with such a women he is also degraded. Childern born to the *kenna* belong to the mother's clan. Only one of the daugthers becomes a *kenna,* the rest do not suffer from social disabilites. If a *kenna* dies, the man with whom she lived regains his normal ritual status, so that, 'untouchability' attaches itself only to the occupation, and to nothing more.

Conflict and its Resolution

Conflicts arise in the Apa Tanis peaceful society on account of various reasons, and there are different ways of settling them without involving the rest in the conflict. If, for instance, there is difference of opinion about how water for irrigation should be distributed, the simplest way is to draw out another channel from an existing stream so that none becomes the loser.

When larger issues are at stake, naturally, the solutions are likely to be more complicated. The Apa Tanis have highly developed sense of individuality and of personal honour. It has also been said that particular persons from among the Daflas. Prof. Haimen dorf relates a case which happened a few years before his first visit among the tribe.

A Dafla had come to live in the house of a freed slave, who originally served a rich man named Ponyo Tamar of the village of Hang. This Dafla had at one time taken part in the capture of a mithan belonging to Belo Lampung, another influential man of village Hang. One day, Lampung caught hold of the Dafla and kept him confined. Ponyo Tamar looked upon this capture of a man living in his slave's house as a grave personal insult, and offered a ransom of five mithans to Belo Lampung. But Belo Lampung killed the Dafla. This enraged Ponyo Tamar and he seized two cows belonging to Belo Lampung and slaugthered them close to the latter's house. For fear of aggravating the trouble, Lampung ignored the loss, but Ponyo Tamar was not satisfied and, according to the custom among the Apa Tani, he challenged Belo Lampung to a *lisudu.*

Lisudu is performed for the vindication of one's honour. What Ponyo Tamar did was that he slaughtered three mithancows of his own before Lampung's house, gave away the meat to the villagers for a feast, and also destroyed some other valuable property such as a sword and a Tibetan bell. In retaliation, Tamar killed ten mithans, and Lampung answered by killing twenty. On the following day Tamar slaugthered thirty mithans, and Lampung answered by killing sixty. Tamar than caled upon his kinsmen and gathered eighty for killing and distribution of meat to all the villages. At this point the *buliang* or council of elders interveried, and induced Tamar to sacrifice not more than sixty, so that the *lisudu* would end in a kind of drawn game. The quarrel or challenge to Ponyo Tamar's prestige was thus repaired, and normal relations were gradually restored in the village. *(op. cit., 111-12.)*

The animals which are slaugthered in this manner are

not always the property of the contestants. They are often contributed by the kinsmen of each contestant, belonging both to the maternal and paternal lines. When the competition crosses a reasonable limit, and there is danger that this would render someone completely bankrupt, it is the kinsmen who ask the *buliang* to step in and stop the fray.

While this author was in Apa Tani country, he heard of a case in which interference had come from the new generation of educated young men. Many of them have joined the school in Hapoli, and when message was carried to them by their mothers that two of their elders were becoming involved in a competition of killing mithans for the sake of prestige, they rushed back to the village, went on arguing with both parties, and eventually succeed in preventing this senseless slaugther merely for the sake of personal prestige and honour. A new element of more rational values is thus developing among the new Apa Tani generation through their education and contact with the larger world outside.

Lisudu is resorted to between inhabitants of the same village. But when trouble arises between two separate villages, there is another method by means of which peace is once more resorted. This is a pre-arranged ceremonial battle called *gambu sodu*. The partisans of an aggrieved person challenge the partisans of another to meet them in battle on an appointed day. Both sides come prepared with bows and arrows, spears and swords. The rule of the game is that they would shoot at one another from a distance, and if there is any casually, the aggrieved party on each side would have to bear the compensation. So those parties personally refrain from fighting, for, as Prof. Haimendorf remarks, if any of them fell, then who would pay compensation ? In the *gambu sodu* some damage may be done to gardens, bamboo groves or granaries, but no general destruction ever takes place. There is also no open combat between the partisans on both sides by hand to had fighting. If, by chance, there is a casualty the battle is at once brought to an end, and the parties retire as they consider that what has been done is enough. Normal relations are then restored.

(op. cit., 113-14)

It is in this manner that the Apa Tanis have developed some more or less civilised froms of conflict which would work off ill-feeling and yet not disrupt the peace and harmony of the villages, which is so much necessary in order to carry on their agricultural and trading pursuits.

This does not, however, mean that there can be no violent conflict between the Apa Tanis and their neighbours who may belong to other tries. The Daflas, for instance, are organised more effectively for war than the peace-loving, industrious Apa Tanis. Prof. Haimendorf gives us an account of a *buliang* in Bela, who was a balanced and peace-loving person, but who had once led a raid on a Dafla village in which 13 men were killed and 17 women and children were captured. He remarks that "when throughly roused, Apa Tanis seem to be less mercenary than the Daflas, and may prefer to kill or ensalve captive enemies rather than huggle over ransoms." (op. cit., 129.)

He also makes a very significant comment about the institution of *lisudu.* As mithans slaugthered in a *lisudu* are widely distributed between the villages and residents of other villages also, and as the rich alone are so sensitive about their prestige and position *as to* challenge others to *lisudu,* wealth is thus widely dispersed, and prevents the accumulation of too much of it in the hands of a few prominent persons. *(Op. cit.,* 113,117,140.)

Mechanisms for Fostering Social Solidarity

Quite apart from the *lisudu* undertaken for the enhancement of the prestige of a person in his village, there are several religious ceremonies, like *un-pedo,* or feasts like *padre-latu* in which two or three mithans are sacrificed and the meat distributed among one or two villages belonging to the donors own group. These rituals and feasts are a part of the Maran celebrations, and wealthy peersons who do not spend part of their wealth for such purposes often compelled to do so by the pressure of public opinion.

Mloko is another, and perhaps the most important, festival observe by the Apa Tani. This occurs in the month of March/April, and is perfromed every year by one of the three groups of villages inhabited by the tribe. "Hang perfroms the Mloko one year, Bela and Hari the following year, and the group consisting of the villages of Haje, Data, Mudang-Tage and Michi-Bainchi in the third year." *(Op. cit.,* 141.)

The sacrifices of pigs, chicken and a dog take place at the clan sanctury. Inter-village visits take place, while gifts are also exchanged. There is a set of well-defined rules by means of which the *buliang* representing the particular ward or clan of another village receives a portion of the sacrificial meat from another village. These rules tend to cement firmly the ties which bind together one Apa Tani village with another.

Family Sex Life and the Individual

We have so far spoken mainly about the collective life of the Apa Tani, whether it is in connection with economic, social or ritual activities. These are indeed of great importance in the very homogeneous siciety and culture which the Apa Tanis have built up for themselves. But, after all, it is finally by that test that the worth of a culture has to be measured.

We have already said in connection with the agriculture of the Apa Tanis that there is strong sense of personal property, a desire to grow rich by the possession of more mithans and its investment in land. But there are again other social mechanisms, or approved ways by means of which wealth is dispersed, and accumulation does not inflict the injury which it could upon the rest of the community if it were unrestrained.

One of the features of this free growth of individualism obviously consists of the comparative freedom from restraint which individuals enjoy in their sexual life. Prof. Haimendorf had made the observation that boys and girls begin to have their experience of sex even as early as when they are eight or ten years old. *(Op. cit.,* 95.) We have also seen that, although the Apa Tanis are divided into the patricians, *mite*, and slaves or commoners, *mura,* young men and women belonging to both sides can from a common working group, the *patang*, without any discrimination whatsoever. And when intimacy in work develops, it may lead to intimacies in other fields also. This is not frowned upon even if the partners belong to the *mite* and *mura* divisions. So much so that when a *mite* girl bears a child and names a particular *mura* as its father, all that happens is that she slides down into the status of a *mura*. The chief taboo in such relations in between members of the same clan; that is considered highly reprehensible.

Polygamy is permissible, but occours in less than one per cent cases in one village where it was counted. (*op. cit.*, 94.) It is, however, not favoured, and the kinsmen of a wife whose husband proposes to take another may be subjected to grievous insult if he actually tries to do so. But, of course, the rich and influential people can take care of themselves.

The break-up of a marriage is considered to be damaging to the wife and her kinsmen. But no serious view is taken of a husband who seeks satisafaction with other girls when his wife is pregnant. So long as the mistress is not taken in as a wife, the relations of a man with her are more or less, ignored.

This lack of stringent inhibitions on sexual relationship naturally has produced a type of personality of a more open, extrovert kind than is usual in another society dominated by jealousy, of extremly rigid rules of sexual behaviour.

Summing Up

On the whole, one can say that the Apa Tanis have succeeded in producing a culture which is very different from the culture of the tribes which we have considered so far. They have chosen a piece of land for their settlement which has been richly endowed by nature, but they have augmented it by the intelligent care and enormous industry which has been bestowed upon the land, its water and forests. Their whole social and religious organisation-the latter being comparatively less importnat than the fromer-is geared to the demands of peace. They are not oppressed very much by poverty, as the Birhors or the Juangs are. They are not exploited as much as the industrious Saoras of Orissa; and all this has become possible because they-have built up their own culture and wealth in comparative isolation from other Where they have established close relationship with others, the Apa Tanis have done so on their own terms. Even when the more militant Daflas have tried to raid their villages, lifted cattle or made captives for securing ransom from their kinsfolk, the Apa Tanis have developed means of defence which have so far proved effective for their purposes.

GEOGRAPHICAL BACKGROUND

Location of Santal Parganas

With an area of 5489.3 sq. miles or 14129 sq. km., the district of Santal Pargana occupies a transitional position between humid Bengal Plains in the east and th Sub-humid Bihar Plains. Geographically, the district stretches from 23^0 40' N to 25 ^{0}18' N latitude and from 86^0 28'N E to 87^0 57' E longitude. The length and the breadth of antal Parganas are almost the same, i.e., 160 km. The greatest lenght of the district is 192 km. from the Ganga in the north-east to the river Barakar in the south-east. Politically, the district is surrounded by a number of district of Bihar and West Bengal. In the west are situated Giridih and Monghyr, in the north-west and north are the districts of Bhagalpur and Purnea, and the Dhanbad district of Bihar lies in the south-west. Similarly, four administrative cenits of west Bengal lie towards the east namely, Burdwan disrict in the south, Birbhum in the south-east, Murshidabad in the east and Maldah district in the north-east.

Culturally, Santal Parganas is situated at the cross-roads of the traditional Bengali culture in the east and the predominant Anglika culture in the west and as a result of its cultural situation the district has developed an intermingled cultural landscape. A significant aspect is that it displays tribal traditions. A straight line joining Jamtara in the south-west to Rahmahal in north-east may be thought of as a cultural divide separating the Bengali traditions and culture from the rest of the district.

The district consists of six subdivisions and forty-one anchals or blocks. The density of population in 1961 was

188 anchals or blocks. The density of population in 1961 was 188 persons per sq. km. and according to 1971 Census it was 226 persons per sq. km. This shows an overall increase of 16.81 per cent in the density of population between the years 1961 and 1971. Dumka is the district Headquarters of the Santal Parganas, occupying a central position in the district. An exclusive area within the district is reserved for the tirbals. This is known as the "Dumin" area. The following table gives a list of the administrative units :

Subdivisions	*Anchals or Blocks*
Dumka	Dumka
	Ranishwar
	Masalia
	Jama
	Jarmundi
	Saraiyahat
	Ramgarh
	Gopikandar
	Kathikund
	Shikaripara
Jamtara	Jamtara
	Narayanpur
	Nala
	Kundahit
Deoghar	Deoghar
	Madhupur
	Mohanpur
	Sarwan
	Palojori
	Sarath

Subdivisions	*Anchals or Blocks*
	Karon
Godda	Godda
	Poreyahat
	Pathergama
	Mahagama
	Meherama
	Boarijor
	Sundar Pahari
Rajmahal	Rajmahal
	Barharwa
	Pathna
	Barhait
	Borio
	Sahebganj
	Jaljhari
Pakur	Pakur
	Maheshpur
	Pakuria
	Ampapara
	Litipara
	Hiranpur

Tribal Concentration in Santal Parganas

Out of a total population of 3,186,908 (1971 Census) in Santal Parganas, the tribal population is 1,154,281. It shows a fairly even distribution in the district. both within he Damin area and outside of it. The subdivision level break-up of tribal population is as follows :

Subdivisions	*Total Tribal population (1971)*
Dumka	3,57,287
Jamtara	1,35,807
Deoghar	80,765
Godda	1,70,110
Rajmahal	1,87,194
Pakur	2,23,118

It was observed in the field survey that the tribal people occupy both the high lands and lowland areas. But the most significant aspect of the spatial distribution of tribal population is that the Santals normally occupy the lowland areas which shows their acquaintance with the people of different non-tribal cultures; on the other hand, the Paharias mostly inhabit the highland and the flat tops of the ridges in order to maintain their separate identities.

Ethnologically, the Santal Parganas are one of the most important cultural districts of Bihar owing to the variety of races found in it. The hilly country is inhabited mainly by the Santals, Paharias and other aboriginal tribes. The undulating region is inhabited by semi-aboriginal races with a smaller proportion of aboriginals and a fair sprinkling of Aryan settlers.[2] Racially, the tribes belong to the Negroid group and most of the tribal people including females show identical physical characterisitics. It was during the Aryan onslaught that the non-Aryan Negroid people called Dravidians found shelter in the Chotanagpur highlands including the Rajmahal region. Physical barriers in those days and even during the contemporary British administration largely impeded the inroads of Aryan ideas and cultures thus putting the Dravidian people in isolation. The Negroid-Dravidian people cut off from allsides by physical barriers, developed their own system of belief which gradually gave rise to tribal inconography. The advent of the British people and traditional Bengali culture from the east brought a radical change in the belief of those tribal people of Negroid stock which occupied relatively lower areas and hill slopes.

The dominant tribal people in Santal Parganas according to 1971 Census are the Santal, Oraon, Mal Paharia, Mahli, Sauria Paharia, Munda, Kora, Lohara and the Kharwar. For subdivision and anchal level figures, Appendix III may be seen.

Damin-i-Koh

To prevent encroachment on tribal areas by the lowland samindars of Bhagalpur district, which were constantly attracting reprisals from the highlanders, a tract of country measuring nearly 300 miles in circumference was separated and marked off by large masonry pillars. All the land situated within those pillars was kept under official control for which the Government was declared to be head proprietor and the hill people were infromed that their rights in it would be respected so long as they conducted themselves peacefully. But the hill-men only cared for the highlands and the lowland tract included within the pillars called *Damin-i-Koh* or *skirts* of the hills and the valleys running into the hills could be made available for other settlers mainly the Santals. The hills within the Damin-i-Koh are still inhabited by the Malers or Sauria Paharias who may be allowed to designate themselves as the real Paharis.

The Damin-i-Koh has always been regarded by the Government as reserved for the aboriginal races of the district and the intrusion of non-aborigines or foreigners called *Dikku* has always been kept within the narrowest limits. It is, therefore, laid down that foreigners must not ordinarily be permitted to hold land within the boundraries of the Damin and any one who may be improperly admitted is liable to be evicted unless there is good cause to the contrary. This legal geographical region purposely meant for the Paharias includes portions of Rajmahal, Pakur, Godda and Dumka subdivisions. The region geographically lies at the foot of the Rajmahal Hills but almost the whole range is between the Ganges in the north and the Brahmani river in the south. The tract consists of hills surrounded by flat country, with fertile valleys lying between rarallel ranges.

The average altitude is from 250' to 1500' and on the tops of the hills, especially towards the south, there are extensive tablelands.

History of the Mal Paharias

The story of the Mal Paharias, their capacity and abilities to adapt themselves and also their increasing control over the nature is full of contradictions. There are divergent views regarding their origin, movement, migrations and above all, their relations with the tribal and non-tribal people. Scholars have made extensive studies to depict the historical cultural traits of this peculiar tribal people whose origin, if chronicles are to be belived, dates back to the *Vedic* period. This is evident from the under-mentioned studies taken by various scholars and historians of international repute.

Professor Wilson referring to the position assigned to the Mala in Kalidas's poem the *Meghadoota,* places it in Chattisgarh. Colonel Woilford assigns them to Malabhum in Midnapore. In the *Vishnu Purana* there is a reference of the Malavas who were supposed to be the people of Malwa, the country to the north of the Vindhyan range, between Bundelkhand and Gujarat. These were the prototypes of the Rajmahal Paharias. It was not until 1795 that infromation regarding the Maler Paharias, their customs and ethnic peculiarities came to be known from a monography by Lt. T. Shaw. He was succeeded by Dr. Buchanan and Colonel Walter Sherwill who after having surveyed the hills confirmed Shaw's infromations.

One of the authorities holds the view that ethnologically the Mal Patharias seem to have been related to the same stock as the Maler. Buchanan also describes them as a distinct branch of the Maler. Ball confroming the findings of Dalton, agrees to the view that the Mal Paharias were altogether distinct in appearance, custom and language from the "Asal Paharias" who inhabited the Rajmahal Hills. Ghosh (1935) has further stated that in and around 1807-1814 the southern Paharias denounced all kinship with the northern Paharias[5] and constituted a distinct tribe.

If chronicle is to be believed, it may be said that Megasthenese, the celebrated Greek emissary who visited India in the 4th Century B.C. during the reign of Chandragupta Maurya found a distinct race in the north of Rajmahal Hills who appeared to be identical with the "Malli". But it is not clear from his writings when and where from the people had come.

O'Malley. divided the Paharias into the Maler or Male Paharias or Sauria Paharias who inhabited the area north of the Rajmahal Hills and the Mal Paharias who occupied the hilly and wooded country in the south and west of Santal Parganas. The word 'Male' is derived from the common Dravidian word 'Mala' meaning mountain. This shows that the original meaning of the name would be hillmen. He further outlined: "A clue to their origin is found in the tradition of the Oraons that their original home was in the Carnatic, hence they went up the Narbada river and settled in Bihar on the banks of the Son. Driven thence by the Muhammadans, the tribe split into two divisions. One of these, now represented by the Oraons, accended the Son into Palamau and turning eastward long the Koel, took possession of the north-western period of Chotanagpur. The other branch following the course of the Ganga, series in the Rajmahal Hills and were the progenitors of the Maler. In these hills, hemmed in by the Ganges on the north and east, and shut off from the outer world by thick forest on the south and west, the Maler have remained almost untouched by outside influences to this day. They have no characteristic of language on common with the races which surround them, from which too they differ in physiognomy, in their social habits, in the way of froming their villages and houses, and in their methods of cultivation"

As regards the origin and traditions of the Maler, Lt. Shaw recounts the myth: seven brothers were sent from the Heaven to people of the earth. The eldest fell sick, while the remainder were preparing a great feast. It was arranged that each was to take of the food that he preferred and go to the place he had chosen to live in. One took goat's flesh and went to a distant country and his progency were the Hindus; another from whom the Musalmans were descended took flesh of all kinds except pork. It is not stated what the third took but he originated the Kherwars. The fourth took hog's flesh, went north and from him sprang the Kiratis; a fifth become the ancestor of the Kols. The sixth took food of all kinds and went far away and it was not known what had become of him till the English appeared, when it was concluded that they were the descendants of the Omnivorous brother. The seventh brother was named Maler who was the eldest and fell sick but soon he became an outcaste and was left in the hill.

Commenting on the differences between the Mal Paharias and the Maler, Sakar has suggested that the Mal Paharias might have separated from the parent stock between the years 1778 and 1819 and the available cultural data also supports the close relation which once existed between these two tribes. Another difference which has become apparent after a close examination and investigation is that the Maler are beef eaters, while the Mal Paharias differ from each other. The language spoken by the Mal Paharias worship the cow. Linguistically, the Maler and the Mal Paharias shows considerable Bengali influence which in itself is some fort of mixed-in character. This is evident from the writings of Grierson in 1903.

Risley (1892) supporting the view of Droses has mentioned that Mal Paharias and the Malers seem to have common origin because both the tribal people can understand each others language but their dialects are different.

Bradely-Birt has observed that the Mal Paharias have not preserved any tradition of their earlier migration and the available records throw very little light on their early migration. He believes that it is in the Rajmahal area that the Mal Paharias first spring into being. He also supports the idea of Lt. Shaw regarding the origin of the Maler.

Crooke has called the Mal Paharias as the wildest, a most backward of th Bengal aborigines who had no tradition of their own and had been gradually pushed eastward by the pressure of other tribes until they were brought to a stand in the hilly regions. This wild tract of hill and forest offered them an impregnable sancturay but they might have commanded for many centuries the great trade route along the valleys of the Ganges. Even the powerful Moghal rules dared not interfere into their affairs. It was during the British period that they were subjugated.

It appears from the above historical analysis that there is no definite and accepted chronological sequence in the historiography of the Mal Paharias. Most of the scholars who have tried to analyse the history of the Mal Paharias believe that they to have migrated from the south especially during the Aryan inroads. They took shelter in the hill country or Rajmahal where gradually they developed into a distinct group. Most of the writers are the English people who came in contact with these people for administrative purposes. Indian writers have written very little about the Rajmahal tribes.

There are altogether eighteen tribes in Santal Parganas but nine of them are dominant because their population exceeds 1000 in different subdivisions (*see* appendix III). Basically Santals, Sauria Paharias or Maler and Mal Paharias are the most dominating tribes in terms of their numerical strength. According to 1971 Census, the total population of the Mal Paharias is 46,395 and their major concentrations occur in the Dumka, Godda and Rajmahal subidivisions. However, on personal investigation it has been found that major concentrations mainly occur in Dumka and Pakur subdivisions which contradicts the Census reports indicating that the Mal Paharias are more or less unifromly distributed throughout the district.

Another interesting contradiction between the Census information and field investigation is that very few families of the Mal Paharias are found in Rajmahal and Godda subdivision. It is believed that this discrepancy has occurred in Census records because of the ignorance of the enumerators who have little knowledge or experience of tribal culture, and have often declared the Santals or Sauria Paharias as Mal Paharias in the Census froms. Geographically, their concentration lies between 24^0N and 24^045 'N latitudes and 86^055'E to 87^048'E longitudes. During the field investigation it has been found that there are only 19 Mal Paharias villages in Barhait anchal, 2 villages in

Borio *anchal* and one each in Sundar Pahari and Taljhari anchals. One important aspect of their concentration is that the majority of the Mal Paharias inhabit the top of the ridges though a considerable number do live in the lowlying areas mostly at the base of the ridges.

A brief analysis of the physical build of the Mal Paharias is desirable here. They are a Hinduised section of the tribe. They have slender build and are dark skinned with short hair, but some of them are taller and more robust than their counterapart Sauria paharias. They have a nasal index of 92.9, cephalic index of 75.8 and a facial angle of 66 per cent.[12] The common stature of the Mal Paharias is 157.7 cm. They have adopted the languate of the Aryan neighbours, speaking a corrupt from of Bengali. They cultivate the hill summits which often consist of miniature tablelands, especially in the south and south-western ranges, and are divided into terraced fields.

Delimitation of the Area Under Study

For an intensive study of the Mal Paharias the smallest units of the administrative hierarchy have been taken and the boundaries of the study are have been made to geographically correspond with the boundaries of administrative anchals or blocks. These include Dumka, Kathikund, Gopikandar, Masalia, Ramgarh, Shikaripara and Raneshwar anchals, in Dumka subdivision and Litipara, Amrapara, Hiranpur, Maheshpur and Pakuria anchals in Pakur subdivision. Sample villages have been selected from some of these anchals (Kathikund, Gopikandar, Shikaripara, Amarpara and Maheshpur) for a proper appraisal of the socio economic and cultural conditions of Mal Paharias in their true from.

Cultural Pattern

The geographical-cultural pattern of the tribesmen shows marked distinctiveness particularly in their habit, dress and religion. The tribesmen in different communities have their own distinct sets of beliefs based on their relative isolation from the people in the plains. The tribal people who moved into dense forest, descended across the mountains and settled on the wellprotected valleys during the great Aryan invasion have developed their own way of living. Centuries of experience, adaptation, exploitation and war have made it possible for the tribesmen to achive further moral reflinment. The tribal behaviaeer today may be the result of their desire to preserve their identity, and thus they try to live apart from the plains folk as they are afraid of being reduced to insignificance.

The members of tribal communities have a clear knowledge of their distinct social identity and are set off from the neighbouring people in speech by at least a difference in dialect. They recognize regular linguistic differences which are seen in their habit, dress and religion. The tribesmen in their mythology have a creation of myth that sets them apart from all other people. They have created unique cultural characteristics for thesmelves and have succeeded in preserving their social customs, artistic traditions and religious beliefs to a large extent.

The tribal way of life manifests increasing tendency to adjust with the harsh environment which hardly bears any territorial productive complexes. The tribesmen in India generally reside in the remote forested areas and also on the tops of the ridges and plateaus. The distance itself speaks of differences and gaps between the tribal and non-tribal communities. This has also increasingly influenced the socio-economic organisation of the tribal people. Life in the remote and forested as well as inaccessible areas is hard and is full of struggle for survival. The tremendous diffculties of the enviroment have not been able to suppress the initiative and adventurous spirit of tribal men. During centuries of experiences and exploitations of the physical environment, they have developed some sort of adaptive skill and uncommon vigour, which seems to be responsible for the tendency to achive self-sufficient agricultural economy. However, they have witnessed rapid erosion of their primitive administrative powers particularly along the peripheries of their cultural landscape. In some of the outlying areas there are instances of radical changes in their social-political-economic organisatin. For example, there is an increasing tendency to adopt socialism for party and equality.

The overall way of life of the tribesmen is primitive. They build up small huts just over the higher sites close to their agricultural fields where they grow mostly coarse grains. The agricultural fields appear as isolated patches in the midst of the forests. The agrarian organisation of the tribals follows in the wake of their primitive organisation. The tribal way of life and the nature of the country they live in has moulded their agrarian organisation to a great extent. When the Hos migrated to Singhbhum in course of their wandering, they decided to settle in the Kolhan, perceiving an abundance of fertile virgin soil covered with dense jungle and traversed by the various rivers and streams. They set themselves to clear the jungle for residence and cultivation. Once settled to an agricultural life, the Hos often suplemented their food by the produces of forests and sputs and chase. Fishing is another important diversion from the monotony of their traditional uneventful occupation. However, agriculture is the principal occupation of the tribals.

In all their activities sporadic or regualr, there is a felling of solidarity and cohesion, an idea of mutual obligations or participation in the same economic undertaking. Thus, this spirit of mutual help prevades all possible spheres of their agricultural life like ploughing of fields, weeding, transplating and harvesting. The rhythm of their work is sustained by songs and so tedium is avoided. The most interesting aspect of the tribal way of life is the system of primitive organisation that reflects in their desire for separation from neighbouring people. On the whole, the tirbals are poor and they strive hard to sustain their livelihood. However, by nature a tribal is in lasy communiar with nature. Labour is the hillman's abhorrence, but necessity compels him to cultivate a small portion of land for his actual existence, beyond this triffing labour he never exerts himself.

The tribals' habits seem to be rigid and inflexible and lack fluidity. The tribals discourage their youngesters from adapting such habits which may prove harmful and suicidal for their traditional primitive identities. Conservatism is reflected in their way of living, modes of culture and also in the pattern of the inter-tribal relationship. The felling of inheritance is strong among tribesmen who constantly strive to preserve their cultural identities. They lead a very simple life. Most of their household implements are made of bamboos and of various grasses. The baskets and mats of various shapes and sises mde of split bamboo and leaves of the palmyra and datepalms serve as containers for storage and carriage. Besides baskets and mats, there are domestic utensils mostly earthen pots of assorted sises.

The tribal dress is again primitive in nature and reflects an overwhelming influence of nature. The males generally put on a piece of markin cloth in the from of *dhoti* around their waist and a small piece of cloth on the shoulder while the grown up females mostly use *loongi* and *panchi* (a long piece of cloth) which they wrap on their bodies. The tribal childern wrap a peice of small cloth just sufficient to cover the lower part. But on the threshold of the tribal and non-tribal culture, sophistication in dress has stripped off the traditional dress particularly among the tribal youth. The spread of education and political consciouness has also led to changes in the pattern of their dresses.

Each period of history has been marked by a particular set of ideas which were born out of the changing experience of life and which might be called the 'soul of culture'. The character of this change from time to time and the outward form of the social organisation also got reogranised in confromity with the changing circumstances. Thus, the tribal religion was evoloved which is mostly borrowed from other religions. The worship of the natural features and elements was a charactieristic feature of tribal religion before the advent of the Christian missionaries. These missionaries began the process of baptising the simple and oridinary tribals who largely belived in animism. There was a wave among the tribals to accept Christianity. Hindus it may be said, were largely responsible for the rapid expansion of the alien Christianity because they exploited the tribals and tried to reduce them to insigneficance. The christians, on the otherhand, tried to bring about their social uplift through reconciliation and persuasion. The basic religious concept was and attempt to conserve the fund of general meanings in terms of which each individual interpret his experience and organises his conduct.

Sinha has emphasised that the ideological system of the tribals covers man to supernatural, man to nature, and man to man relationship. The gods are classified into those that are benevolent and those that are malevolent. The gods are portrayed as being more interested in personal loyalty than in any demonstration of ethical or moral virtues. Rituals are perfromed mainly to avoid sickness and death. There is some sort of belief in reincarnation but it is not associated with *Karma* as in Hindu Philosophy. The entire universe is believed to be animated by spiritual beings. Man, nature and the supernatural are all bound within a common boundary of relationships.

The Habitat of Mal Paharias

The Mal Paharias maintain a distinct habitat from the other tribals of Santal Parganas. This evident from the nature of their psychology in association with the physical aspects of the region occupied by them. The Mal Paharias mostly occupy the hill tops, though a few sporadic Mal Paharias settlements do occur on the plains. The forest hill topography has affected their material life to a great extent. The roofs are thatched. The dwellings lack windows and provision for sanitation.

Most of the dwellings of the Santal occur in the plains ewith varied shape ranging from square to rectangular. Walls of the dwellings are made of bricks or stone slabs joined with mud. The roof may be thached or tiled depending upon the availability of meterial and the economic condition of the Santals. The houses of the Sauria Paharias are identical with those of the Mal Paharias.

The Mal Paharias follow the Santal tradition of decorating the lower part of the plinth of their dwellings with white or coloured daubs and paintings and also put the same decorative marks on the outside wall of their dwellings, preferably on the lower parts. Most of the Mal Paharias dwellings are small and one-roomed (*see* Chapter 3).

Dress and Ornaments

Cloth is one of the basic requirements of human beings. It seems, howerver, to be a secondary rwquirement of the tribals. The forest hill environment hs a profound influence on the nature of dress of the Mal Paharias, who give very little emphasis on their dress. The shephards use *gamcha,* a peice of cloth between the two legs, known as *darichucha.* The Mal Paharias youths living in the plain areas use shirts, trousers and *dhoti,* while those who live in the villages on high plateaus and in remote areas were *gamcha.* The old Mal Paharias people mostly were *dhoti* or a piece of cloth three yards in length. According the survey, Dhoti alone accounts for 49.30 per cent of all dress while *lungi* and *gamcha* account for 30.98 per cent. The share of *langot* is 16.90 per cent and shirts and trousers account for the balance 2.82 per cent.

The young Mal Paharias females mostly were *kanda dan* and *pelma angarka* which cover their upper portions. The author has noticed that females after attaining the age of 14 years use *panchi* (a *gamcha* of 2 to 3 yeards length) to cover the upper part of their bodies. They wore it diagonally. They also wear *lungi* to cover their lower portions. But the young Mal Paharias females living in the plain were *sari* and *blouse.* The old Mal Paharias females mostly wear *sari,* a part of which they use in a diagonal fashion in order to cover the upper portion of the body. The survey reveals that the share of *lungi* and *panchi* is 54.49 per cent, while *sari* and *blouse* account for 45.51 per cent of all dress.

Most of the Mal Paharias children remain naked even at the age of 4 or 5 years. The children attaining an age of 8 or 9 years wear *darichucha, i.e.,* a small piece of cloth wrapped between the two legs up to the waist. It was observed that quite a good number of children including the female children at this age use *gamcha* just cover their loser portions. They do not use any cloth on the upper part of the body. But the school going childern in the plain areas use shirts and half pants. *Gamcha* accounts for 49.62 per cent, shirt and pant 36.85 per cent, and *lungi gamcha* 13.53 per cent of male children's dress. The females being to wear *lungi* at the age of 7 to 8 years and gradually they change over to *lungi* and *panchi* as their age increases. The scholl going children at this age wear skirts, frock and *iser.* The pecentage of girls wearing *putli* or *gamcha* is 53.92 per cent, those wearing *lungi panchi* is 33.04 per cent and those having frock and iser is 13.04 per cent.

The most significant aspect of this dress study is that the rate of nakedness increases with the distance from the plain lands. Even among the Santals *lungi panchi* is mostly used by the females and the males were *dhoti baniyan* and half shirt. The Santals are better dressed and the incidence of nakendess is much less.

The author has observed that the Mal Paharia women use little ornaments. Mishra has also noted that the females give little emphasis on the use of ornaments. Silver chains or glass chains are frequently used by the Mal Paharia women. They call it *mala* or *jhunjhur.* They also use a silver nose-ring or *lolak* and *fulli.* Another name for this is *lurluri. Nathia* is a larger nose-ring frequently used at the time of marriage. Nose top or *putki* or *karlophuli* is the most common ornament among the maried Mal Paharias women. They also use ear-ring as well as *pagra* or *phutaki* on their ears. *Kaner sana* and *kan-kudi* are other names used for them. The Mal Paharias women wear bangles on their hands. Those of silver are called *sankha* or *khadu-chudi.* Other names are *baju* or *bariya,* etc.

Paisen is worn by the females on their legs. They also call it *chura* or *karima.* The hairpin is called *khil.* The names of these ornaments differ from village to village. For example, *lolak* is called *nakphuli* in Amirjola, while in Nakti it is known as *lurluri.*

Apart from the ornaments mentioned above, most of the females buy glass bangles, metal chains and steel hairpins from the local weekly markets and wear them exclusively.

Tattooing

The Mal Paharia give little importance to tattooing. A

small black tip on the forehead of both males and females is commonly seen among the Mal Paharias. Marks of snake, flower, arrow and sun are found on the forearms. Tattooing of name on the hand is a rare practice. The tattooing itself is very painful and even the adults weep at the time of tattooing. Tattooing is very common practice among the Santals and other tribes. The hands, chest and shoulder of the Santals and others are full of tattoo marks and symbols.

Religion

95.49 per cent of the Mal Paharias are Hindus in Santal Parganas. The number of converted Christians is 1.76 per cent, while the remaining 2.75 per cent belong to other religions and persuasions according to 1971 Census. There has been a greater incidence of conversion into Christianity among the Santals and the Sauria Paharias. Thus, the Mal Paharias seem to be a more conservative sect of Hindus lying on the theshold of animism. Crooke has also stated that the religion of the Paharia is of the animistic type, the head of their pantheon being *Dharmer Gossain,* the sun god, and beneath him a host of minor gods to each of whom some department of human affairs is assigned.

The Mal Paharias do not take beef, while the Santals prefer to take beef and pork. The Mal Paharias do not even touch the dead cow. They observe a *bhoj* in the name of the dead cow, while the Santals and the Maler or Sauria Paharia come and remove the dead cow from the village. The Maler prefer to eat the flesh of the dying cow.

Ceremonies and Festivals

The Mal Paharias believe in the powers and ethereal spirits who are beyond the scope of their reach and also in transmigration of soul and rebirth. Their belief in *Karma* is firmly established since they stick to the basic norms of Hinduism. The influence of environment on the spiritual idea of the Mal Paharia is evident from their tendency to worship the earth, the sun, and the seasons. It is particularly evident when they seek the support of those natural spirits whose abode has been the environment where they live. Death is conceived as the resurrection which envisages life after death. This has led to the development of ancestor worship. It has been their practie since time immemorial to worship a host of spirits alongwith their ancestor on all occasions including borth, marriage and death.

The chief deities are Sun (*Beru-Gossain*) and the Earth (*Dharti Garmi*). The author has observed that the Dharti Garmi or Bhui Deo worship is widely practised in the Damin area. It is believed that the worship initiated by the Mal Paharias, steadied the earth when it was trembling. There is a general belief that the worship of Bhui Deo yields good harvests. The *Dehri* or *Pujahar* (village priest)perfroms all kinds of rituals. The sacrifice of goat and pig (one each) and a pair of red cocks is the most common pratice of this *Bhui Deo Puja.* All males partake of the flesh of the animals sacrificed as *parsad* but not the females. The priest takes away the heads of the sacrificial animals.

In order to remain in peace from the evil spirits and animals, the Mal Paharias also worship the 'hills' once in every year, assuming a stone as the symbol of deity. This worship is also perfromed by the village priest. The nature of sacrifices changes from village to village. In some villages the people sacrifice a pair of chicken and eggs, while in others they sacrifice a pig and a pigeon. Again, the priest takes away the head of the sacrificed animal or poultry, while the villagers sitting together near the place of worship eat the cooked flesh. The females are forbidden to eat this cooked meat. People in all the villages during the *pahar puja* drink *pochai.* However, this practice was not found in Asan Pahari village.

There are a number of ceremonies associated with the Mal Paharias : to the rising sun and pray that their families may be saved from suffering and disease.

Shiva Puja is observed in the month of March when a brown goat is sacrificed on *Shivaratri* night. Both males and females observed this festival with great enthusiasm and show. They pour water on the deity made of stone. After this the marriage season begins.

The Mal Paharias also worship *Mansamai* in the month of *Sravana* (July/August). They offer a white goat, two pigeons, sugar, milk and betel. The purpose of this *puja* is to learn some sort of *tantra* (mystic power) which can be used in the case of snake bite.

Besides these festivals, there are some minor festival observed by the Mal Paharias:

Mauca Puja

A worship of snakes in the month of Bhado.

Jitia

It is observed by bringing in a branch of *peepal* tree around which the Mal Paharias dance and sing. On the next morning the branch is thrown into the pond.

Kurma

A branch of *Kurma* tree is planted at the centre of the village where the people assemble in the night. It is celebrated in the month of *Bhado* and is observed by dancing, singing and drinking throughout the night. On the following day the branch is removed and thrown into the pond. This festival is also common among the *Oraons* and the *Kol* of Chotanagpur.

The Mal Paharias celebrate Holi and Deepawali with great enthusiasm but the author has learnt that there are some Mal Paharia villages where these festivals are not observed.

It will be seen that the Mal Paharias have mixed nature of festivals and rituals. The influence of Hinduism and Bengali culture is clearly observe in the celebration of Kali Puja, Dussehra, Shivaratri, Holi and Deepawali, etc. The worship of the Sun God and snakes is also related to Hinduistic rites in many parts of the country. On the other hand, the sacrifice of animals and poultry on most occasions and the religious ceremonies of *Tat-Ariye, Gangi-Ariye, Osre-Ariye, Pun-Taddih* and *Kurma,* etc., are typical tribal festivals. The rituals at the time of these ceremonies and in different agricultural seasons keep them occupied throughout the year. The expenses involved are heavy and result in a considerable strain on the economy of the Mal Paharias, as discussed in Chapter 5.

Mal Paharia Customs and Habits

The Mal Paharia rituals are different from those of the other tirbal communities. They are a reflection of their separate religious and cultural background.

Child Birth

Pregnncy is considered to be a signification part of the cultural heritage of the Mal Paharias and is equally a happy event. The pregnant woman is given special care and is not allowed to go alone to the jungle or any other place. She continues to do all household chores until she delivers the child. It is commonly believed by the Mal Paharias that there is every possibility of miscarriage if the pregnant women is not properly protected from the influence of evil spirits.

Just before the time of delivery, a separate hut called *kuria* of *kumba* is temporarily constructed outside the main house where the child is born. The mother or mother-in-law or any other elderly women assists at the time of delivery. After the birth of th child, the mother is declared to be in the condition of *chute* or untouchable. She cannot enter the main house or do household work. The husband is equally declared to be in the condition of *chute.* He lives with his wife and the new-born babe in the *kuria.*, but cooks the meals and sleeps outside the *kuria.* The period of untouchability lasts for five days. In Nakti and Asan Pahari, this period continues for ten to fifteen days.

After this period is over, the parents and the child go to the *jharna* or spring where the mother boils her clothes, cleans them and had a bath. She also pares off her nails. The husband also shaves his beard and has a bath. The hair of the newlyborn baby is shaved by a barber. This ritual is known as *randa jagu.* Then they put on new clothes and return to the main house.

The mother is now asked to live in a corner of the house. She cannot cook food for the family. Her husband is also not allowed to attend any religious or social ceremonies in the village for a period of three months. Sometimes, this period may extend to six months. After three months the husband gives a feast called *handipoda* or *narta* ceremony. He has to arrange for boiled rice, a he-goat, two chickens and *pochai* or country liquor for the entire village. With this feast the period of *chute* finally ends.

Name Giving Ceremony

The child is given a name after the randa jagu ceremony. The name is whispered in the ear of the child either by the mother's brother of by the father. The child inherits the name of its grand-parents : a boy is given the name of the grand-father, while a girl is named after the grand-mother.

Puberty Rites

The Mal Paharias do not observe any ceremony at the attainment of puberty by the girls. It is held that during the period of menstruation, the girl remains under the influence of evil spirits who cause harm to the family if she is allowed to cook food or to touch grain.

Types of Marriage

Marriage is an important ceremony among the Mal Paharias. It is mostly aranged within the tribe and marriages outside the tribe is strictly prohibited and restricted. Sexual relationship is strictly prohibited before marriage. Monogamy is the common practice, though polygamy is also rarely practised. The bridal price is an important consideration to be paid before the marriage is performed.

There are various ways of marriage in the Mal Paharias society :

(a) Marriage by purchase or by paying bridal price;

(b) Love marriage;

(c) Marriage by adoption;

(d) Marriage by exchange;

(e) Marriage by service; and

(f) Widow marriage.

Marriage by paying bridal price of *pon* is the most common practice among the Mal Paharias in which the groom's father expresses his desire to a *sithu* or a mediator for getting his son married. The *sithu* then goes to the bride's house and meets the father of bride. When he sees the girl and feels that she is suitable, he offers some presents. If the present is accepted the *sithu* porceeds with the negotiation.

A day is finally set for a meeting between the bride's father and the groom's father at the weekly market. There is every opportunity for the girl and the boy to meet each other at this market. After the meeting, a suitable date is fixed for the marriage. The average bridal price of *pon* is Rs. 16 and in some cases it is Rs. 25.

In love marriages, the lover runs away with the beloved to his village where they stay as husband and wife till the bride's father comes and demands the *pon.* The boy pays this to the parents of the bride and arranges a feast. In some cases a lover who fails to get the girl interested in him, tries to follow her and suddenly puts vermillion on her forehead at a lovely place or in the market. He then succeeds in marrying her.

Marriage by adoption is another type of marriage in which the bride's father who has no male heir to his line. adopts a bridegroom for his daugther. The groom becomes a *ghar jamai* or *ghar-damad* (son-in-law living in the house). The adopted son-in-law then looks after the property of his father-in-law and becomes his legal heir.

Marriage by exchange follows a simple function and is arranged when a man marries away his sister and takes a bride from the same family in exchange. This involves no bridal price.

Marriage by service takes place when a boy agrees to work on the fields of the bride's parents until he has earned enough to pay the bridal price. After he has done so, the marriage is arranged.

Widow marriage is not common among the Mal Paharias. It happens when a brother marries the widow of his elder brother. Sinha sees previous initimacy as a cause of widow marriage. But it may also be the result of economic considerations.

Marriage Ceremony

As mentioned earlier, the *sithu* or the mediator plays the key role in arranging a marriage. After he has met the bride's father and the intending couple have also been given an opportunity to meet each other at the village market, the *sithu* goes to the groom's house alongwith ten or twenty people and puts a binding on the boy that he cannot marry anywhere else. This social binding is called *chheka*, and consists of a function called *chumawan*. Five days after the chheka the sithu finalises the date for the marriage by negotiation. Generally, the marriage is fixed after evelen days of this. On the tenth days a *barat* or marriage procession containing both men and women goes to the residence of the bride. They are housed in a *janmasa* or place of hospitality located a tittle away from the house of the bride. They are served with meat and *pochai* or country liquor. The *barat* moves to its destination sometime around midnight, which is called *parichhan*. The boy then goes to the *mandap* for marriage. This is a straw shed constructed in an open space. On the next morning the priest chants the hymns and puts oil on the forehead of the girl. At this oment all persons withessing the ceremony who are generally in a drunken state, start dancing and singing. The drums sound loudly. The boy puts vermillion on the forehead of the girl and the marriage is said to have been perfromed.

The bride returns with the groom to his house and stays there for seven days. Thereafter, the couple visit the bride's house. This is called *samangala* or*satopura*. After this a small feast is given and the bride and her husband remove the *mandap*.

Divorce

Divorce is permitted in Mal Paharia society but it is not as frequent as is the case with the Sauriyas. The divorce is sought owing to the barrenness on thepart of woman, lack of faith, laziness or unvompromising attitude of either spouse. The barrenness of the woman and the lack of faith or unfaithfulness are the two most common reasons for divorce.

Divorce is granted by th village panchayat which sits in the couple's house or any other place where the members listen to the couple and on their satisfaction, divorce is granted. The congregation which listens to the couple is known as *bhaiyadi.* After the approval of the divorce, the couple tear a sal *leaf* indicating their separation. This is called *pat chira chiri* (tearing of leaf). If the divorce is sought on the part of the woman, the bridal price has to be returned to the husband. In case there is a child, however, the wife is not supposed to return the bridal price.

Death Rite

The Mal Paharias perform distinct rites after a death in the family. In most cases the dead body is wrapped in a new cloth and carried on a cot to the burning place. Here it is cleaned with the water and anointed with oil and turmeric. A pyre is built of branches of sal tree. After the corpse has been kept on it, several branches of sal tree are again put on it. The females also go to the burning place to observe the rituals. The husband or the eldest son or the youngest son lights the pyre by touching a ligthed torch from the head to the mouth and then towards the legs in the south. The person perfroming these rites shaves off his hair and beard. Other relatives only shave their beards and pare off their nails. Afterwards, the entire party takes bath and returns to the village. These rites are very similar to Hindu rites in north India.

There are instances in which the dead bodies are not cremated but are laid to rest in the burial ground. A grave is dug according to the sise of the dead body and partly filled with branches of trees. The corpse is laid to rest together with the cot on which it was carried. Again branches of trees are placed on th body and the grave is filled with the soil. The belongings of the dead man are also put into the grave. In both the cases of cremation and burial. oil, eggs and *arwa* rice are thrown on the pyre and in the burial ground. If the death has been caused by sanke biting or small-pox or if a woman has died while giving child birth, the body must be buried and not creamated.

After the party returns to the village, all who had accompained the funeral procession are given *sattu* (parched gram flour) without salt to eat. The members of the deceased's family do not take salt for five days. After fives days a small quantity of a preparation consisting of *sattu* with salt, boiled rice and chicken is given to everyone. Afterweads, the family members begin taking salt. A feast in the name of the deceased is given on the tenth day or a month or a year after the death. On this day, the relatives of the deceased are invited to go to th burning *ghat* with three pieces of cloth soaked in oil, *pochai* and boiled rice. They carry with them an earthren pot containing fried rice and *pochai*. The persons who had lit the pyre shaves his head and bread and throws the eathen pot into the river. The party then returns to the village where a goat is sacrificed and fowls are offered in th name of the deceased person. *Pochai* is also offered. The meat is cooked and a feast is organised for the villagers. Obvously, all this involves consdiderable exspenditure.

Inheritance of Property

The Mal Paharia society is a patrilineal society in which the males have an exclusive right on the immovable property of their parents. Females have no right to inherit property. After the death of the head of the family the immovable property is divided among the sons of the deceased. The eldest son gets the lion's share including the house. The mother stays with the eldest son. So long as she lives, she has the right for maintenance. If she remarries, she loses this right. The income from the property must be divided equally among other legal heirs or sons but the total property stands transferred in the name of the eldest son who alone can sell the property.

Political Hierarchy

The Mal Paharia society maintains a well established territoriality, i.e., maintains a hierarchy geographically endowed within the bounds of the territorial social organisation. A village is the lowest territorial organisasion under the control of the *manjhi* or the village headman who is the custodian of the village. The *manjhi* is helped by the *pramanaik* and the gorait to discharge his duties. The villagers select the *manjhi* who nominates the *pramanaik* and the *gorait* to organise the village council.

After the death of the *manjhi*, his eldest son inherits his political status. Similarly, the eldest son of the *gorait* becomes the *gorait* of the village on the death of his father. He does not get any allowance from the Government. He is supposed to infrom the villagers about the meeting of the village conuncil.

The leadership pattern among the Mal Paharias is somewhat different from the agricultural tribes inhabiting the plains. Among the Mal Paharias, the Malers and Birhors, secural and religious powers are combined into one person. But in the case of the Oraons, Mundas, Hos and the Santals, some kind of demoratic element in the from of separate leadership (secular and religious) has been introduced.

The village council is a conglomeration of the village elders and is presided over by the *manjhi* where the *pramanaik* functions as his assistant. In the absence of the *manjhi*, the *pramanaik* looks after the functioning of the village council.

Several villages or village councils may be grouped into a bigger and rather close territorial unit to perfrom integrated social and religious functions. Such bigger territorial political units are looked after by the *sardars*. previously, *samindars* were selected from among the elders and were entrusted the task of looking after such geographical-political congregation. Now the *samindars* have been replaced by the *sardars*. The post of the *sardars* is again heriditary. Sardars are duly recognised by the Government but there is a tendency to do away with this office.

Household Articles

The author has observed a variety of household belongings and implements in the course of fieldwork. The most common implements and articles possessed by any family are brass plates, earthen vessels and brass bowls in the kitchen. Okhal or *okho* or *okhari* (used for pounding rice), *kori* (implement for digging ground), *mora* (for storing grains), dala (basket), *jijri* or *jharka* (Broom) and *ketandu (winnowing fan). Dhanki* is used to store maise and *barbatti.* It is hung from the roof by means of a rope. The household belongings also contain *chhata* (umbrella) and *kando* (a sort of chair) for the guest. The earthen plates are called sara in their dialect.

The Mal Paharia women use *kuknore* (a kindf of alkaline earth for washing their hair), *sindira* (vermillion), *esandu* (mustrd oil) and *kutme anianm* (pieces of rice) for religious rites.

The Mal Paharias use several kinds of baskets for keeping grains. They are called *dudo* (for seeds) and *angarpuri* (for basra or millet), etc. In every family there is a *mora* and *kuchri* (for storing grain). They use several kinds of earthen pots for cooking purposes which include *jagoo patli* (plate for rice); *chupi* (for vegetable); *saraki, kori* and *dilu* (a kind of cup for drinking water). The ladle used for preparing rice is called *chackodadu.*

Dabo (a kind of sickle) is used for harvesting grains and *kula* is used for winnowing the grain. The Mal Paharias sell palm juice in exchange of grains in th neighbouring villages. Each Mal Paharias family has mats *(pitri)* made of datepalm leaves and *khat* (cot) for sleeping. Other household articles found in every family include *dao* (sickle); *jhamper* (for covering the baskets), *kethra* (pig's trouhg), *ghaila* (earthen pitcher); *dabla* (dateplam broom); *agor* (split bamboo screen or door); and *tham* (plate); *lohai* (metal pot), etc. The women use *handia* (earthen pot) for storing ash. *Hanta* (steel tool) is used for digging roots. A hallow bamboo container locally termed *chonga* is usd for keeping papers, ownership documents and other papers. *Khakhorm* (a knife) is used for cutting vegetables. Regular doors are called *'Kapat'.*

Agricultural Implements

Hal or *har* (*aale)* and *far* (*pale*) are the two most frequently used agricultural implements of the Mal Paharia. Together they from the plough. The upper part of *far* is called *todda* and the lower part ise. *juwat* (jumale) is another part of the plough. The *juwat* is attached to a long piece of wood. The oxen are tied to it with *jote* (rope). *Gaiti* is another agricultural implement and is shaped like a pik. It is also called *tamni.*

Chahe (digging tool) and *khanta* (another steel digging tool) are used for *kurao* cultivation. *Kudar* or *kudal* (shaped) is used for preparing or digging the ground for cultivation. *Dauli* (axe) is used for cutting wood.

Hunting Implements

Dhrnu (bow) and *kanr* (arrow) are the two most important weapons of the Mal Paharias. They know the art of manufecturing these weapons, but they purchase iron tips for the arrows from the market. They put posion on th tips. They kill pigs, tigers, and other ferocious animals with these poisonous arrows. The Mal Paharias prepare traps for killing tigers and pigs. *Mori* toras (bird traps fitted with a roof) are used for catching birds. *Chato* is used for catcing fish. They prepare different kinds of fish *traps,* for example, *Kume, dundir* and *bena* which they use for catching *datimani, chote, pothi* and *eacha* fish from small rivers and water bodies. *Jhapa* is used ofr catching rats (*see* illus.)

Musical Instruments

Every linguistic cultural group, if it is matured enough to display its culture, develops its own music. The Mal Paharias are not an exception. They generally play *kail* (mandar), *lagra* (*digga*); *banam baam* and *dale* (*dholak*) as musical instruments. *Banshi (Bansuri), khancha (khanjari), jhalkortal (jhal)* and saranda' (sarangi), etc., are popular instruments.

Changing Cultural Pattern of the Mal Paharias

The process of moral refinement of the Mal Paharias has assumed a new dimension with the development of transport and communication. The majority of them still follow the traditional pastoral agricultural methods which is an idex of cultural backwardness. On the other hand, the transport system has brought them in contact with modern techniques. The Damin area has become a true circulation field because of the interaction between the traditional tribal animistic social organisation and the dynamic and technical modern social organisation. Hence, the level of culture has recently shown an improvement which is evident from the superimposition of the modern custom on Mal Paharia culture. The isolation which had been a significant aspect of the Mal Paharia psychology of fear of being reduced to insignificance is now being overcome and they are gradually mixing with the mainstream of Indian life.

Thus, the Mal Paharias have given up their traditional *kurao* cultivation in some areas and have adopted sericulture. But sericulture as an index of economic change is mostly noticed in only those village which are close to the transport network. The use of fertilisers by the Mal Paharias seems to be conditional as they are used only if available in the Government offices. But the villages located in the remote areas have not shown any change or superimposition of modern culture on their traditional social organisation.

In Guma-Pahari, Asan Pahari and Nijhor, the number of school going childern has increased because of the provision of educational facilities provided by the State Government. Here again, the transport system has played a crucial role. Associated with increasing educational facilities in the geographically closer villages is the impact on their dress. The school going boys now wear shirt and half pants, while the girls wear skirt and blouse. The college going students wear trousers and shirt or sari and blouse. The author has noticed a Santali impact on the women, particularly on the way they wear a sari and blouse. The religious ceremonies and festivals which follow the traditional Hindu ceremonies and festivals have become a little sophisticated. The villages exposed to the transport system are marked by modern decoration and idol worship particularly during the festivals and ceremonies. The national adult education programme has yet to exert an influence on the Mal Paharias.

Changes in market facilities and availability of modern and sophisticated materials have also made an impact especially on the Mal Paharia girls and women who now use cheap cosmetics and other articles of ornamentation. The author has found little impact of markets over the men except in a few cases where well-to-do men now wear trousers and shirts. It has also been noticed that the people of the more accessible villages are slowly getting accustomed to tea and sugar. Urbanisation, however has hardly affected the lives of the Mal Paharias.

The Mal Paharias are basically Hindus and they observe all Hindu rites and customs. The Santals who constitute the major tribal communities in Santal Parganas are largely Christians. The Mal Paharia settlements mostly occur on the hills, while the Santal settlements are found in the plains and on the lower slopes. There is no marked change in the dress of the Mal Paharias except in the more accessible villages where people now wear some modern dresses. The males generally wear *dhoti*, while the females wear *panchi* on the upper part of the body and *loonge*, to cover the lower portion. The children wear tringular pieces of cloth in the loins, Hairpin, necklace, ear-ring, nose-ring and bangles, etc., are the common ornaments of the Mal Paharia women, but the use of ornaments is rare.

Bhuin deo puja, pahar puja and worship for the seasonal harvests are the most commonly observed religious ceremonies. The Mal Paharias observe most ot the Hindu festivals with great enthu siasm. There are a number of rituals observed from child birth to death and all of them have a strong imprint of Hindu culture.. Owing to the close contact with Bengal. these customs bear a strong bias towards Bengali culture.

Previously, the village *manjhi* and his subordinates were the most important persons for all disputes and customary decrees. The *sarkar* was all-powerful and was obeyed without hesitation. Now their authority is sloly getting eroded and the Mal Paharias are turning towards the Government officials and the courts. Similarly, their food habits, utensils and occupational characteristics are also undergoing a change. This change is gradually spreading to the interior villages or those that are situated on the higher slopes or in jungles. As more and more people take to employment as labourers, service holders or traders, they will act as a link in the social change towards a more egalitarian society.

MARING

The Maring, with a population of 11,910 (according to

the Census of 1981) exhibit cultural conditions and characteristics distinct from the other tribal groups of this region. Although Capt. E.W.Dun (1881) seeks to compare them to the Kuki group of tribes, they are now generally classed as Naga. Brown (1874), however, considers the Maring to be a separate 'race' differing in origin from both the Naga and Kuki. In contrast to the Naga and Kuki, the Maring seek to locate their origin in the Kabaw valley of the east. Brown (1874) also noticed their close resemblance to the Burmese. Legend speaks of their migration and temporary occupation of some areas of Imphal town, such as Haobam Marak. Guided though it was by political considerations, the close relation between the Meitei and Maring had a farreaching influence on their culture. The fact that they had to adjust themeselves to an enviroment controlled largely by the Meitei in the plains appears significant. The names Maring is said to have been derived from two words, *mei* (fire) and *ring* (to produce). Thought distinct from the sandpoint of culture and society, their nathropomorphic similarities to the Meitei are more significant.

Their villages cover mountainous regions along the northern border of Tengnoupal district. The maximum east-west length of the area is roughly 50 km. and its width is 20 km. There are three groups of maring Red Black and Red and Balck. This classification is based on the colours they use on the border of their clothes. The villages too, fall into any one of these three groups. This classification bears testimony to an ancestral link between some villages. The following is a list of the three groups of villages:

(a) Red marking village include Khudei Khullen,Leihi, Khunou, Kambang Khullen, Kambang Khunou, Kangoi Khullen, Kengori Khunou, Panchong, Lengmeiching, Khudei Khunou (Kwarak Maring)Kharou Khullen, Sandangsemba, Leipharok, Phunal Maring, Nungkam (previously Satang).

(b) Black Maring villages include Lamlong Khullen, Lamlong Khunou, Khunbi, Langol, Laihing, Khullen, Laiching Minou, Wabaching, Thamlai, Karongthel,

Tuinem, Phunal Sambum, Khoibu, Narum, Yankhul, Khulimon, Biyang, Yamolching, Koijam.

(c) Black and Red Maring villages include Machi, Kharou, Khonou, Kamu Maring and Konaitong.

The last is a recent introduction made with the intention of projecting Marchi as their ancestral village. Otherwise too, the Machi is regarded as an original centre of the Black group of villages. There are two groups of villages from the point of view of origin, parental villages, and satellite villages or villages fromed out of parental villages. A concentration of villages is found in the north-western part of Tengnoupal district close to the valley. This group of villages is inhabited by the members of the Balck group and the newly introduced Black and Red group. Machi is the biggest village among the two groups, with a population that is well above one thousand. Because of migration the Kharou Khunou and Lamlong Khunou, which had their origin from Machi and Lamlong Khullen respectively, are located close to the area dominated by the Red Maring. Similarly, there are Red Maring villages like Phunal Maring. Sandangsenha is at a shorter distance from the capital town of Imphal. There are extensions of the hilly ranges well within the valley and these villages occupy the top of two such extended hills. In any case, these villages are much more exposed to the urban environment. Villages like Khoibu, Narum, Yankhul, Saibol have differences of dialect from the rest of the villages. Each village has a dialect of its own. The difference in dialect is just one aspect of cultural variation which, though limited in range is sufficient to warrant a separate status for these village groups within the larger Maring tribal group. Gimson (1927) was even inclined to call Khoibu Maring a separate sub-tribe.

The difference in dialect also points towards different culture contacts at different stages of their history. In all probability, the villages of Narum, Saibol, Yangkhul and even Khoibu remained well outside the range of Maring culture from the very beginning. They could at best be said to have occupied the periphery. The social organisation of the villages, though showing an overall Maring pattern of control, has many features of its own. Khoibu lengend is very explicit about an ancentral link with the Meitei and the Tarao communities. Their link with the Poi from the east is also hinted at. On the other hand, the influence of the Tangkhul, a Naga tribe, is more apparent on the people of Narum, Saibol and Yangkhul. The majority of the Maring are unanimous about their origin from the Kuli-songsong and Wasafai from the Kabaw valley in the east. The Kabaw valley, at one time appears to have been occupied by a number of tribes and sub-tribes, including the Maring, who migrated to Manipur from the east, probably to escape the wrath and torture of other powerful tribes and to seek the protection of the king of Mainpur. Another reason for their migration might have been the possibility of a population explosion in and around kabaw valley. In sharp contrast to the Tangkhul and Thadou, they rarely came in direct conflict with the Meitei kings. There were indications that the Meitei kings could count on support from the Maring. According to their tradition, some places in and around Imphal, such as Moirangkhom, Sarkhomshang, Tuidam, Yaiskul were at one time occupied by them. Like the Anol, Moyon Monsang, Tarao, Lamgang, Kabui, Miso, and a host of other southern tribes including a section of the Chin tribes of the east, they believe in the theory that they originated from a cave. Besides Kulisongsong, the other villages mentioned in their oral tradition related to their migration are Mulbi-Mulchon, Chaptam Lamal, Oklepaneng, Lepifal, Lapifai, Leikibung, Kang-Kaobung, Khungwarbung, Sikbung, Sharjibung, Ransikbung, Sik-khangrul, Chaiom, Sangathel, Khahanthra, Yangthrumtri,l Shipyal, Phengyang, Saiyal Khambikalthel, Tuini, Khumanching, Chilliching, Mokokching, etc. The Maring of Khoibu trace their descent from Mongrengfai, where they had first settled after coming out of the cave.

They are a hill-dwelling people. Their villages are generally situated on top of hills. The western group of villages are, however, situated along ridges in a more or less continuous manner. These villages lie on the western parts of the Mapithel range, which is sometimes referred to as the Heirck range. The mountain ranges are punctuated by narrow streams and small rivers. Irrigation, however, in not widespared because these do not flow deep into higher land. This is also one reason why irrigation could not be established on an extensive scale. There is not much forest cover, since most of the higher land is laid bare because of the extensive practice of shifting cultivation. The boundary of a village is defined by landmarks such as springs, steep hilly tracts, streams, collections of big trees and big boulders. Every village is provided with two main gates at two extreme ends. In some villages traces of defensive structures like stockades and barricades are seen even today suggesting inter-tribal feuds, which at one time were a regular feature of tribal life. The fortified condition of a village was lso meant for protection against wild animals. There are no restictions in the movement of persons belonging to different villages, but one must not hunt, collect firewood, or lay a trap within the territory of another village.

Their language belongs to the Kuki-Chin branch of the Tibeto-Burman family. It is believed that in their language they have an affinity with the Meitei and that there are many Meitei words which are freely used by them. Like the Meitei they use the Bengali script, but this appears to be a recent phenomenon. They have an old dialect spoken in an archaic from, unintelligible to many of their own people. All their songs. spells or prayers are in this dailect.

They can be distinguished from other tribes by their hairstryle. They keep their hair long, gathered in a bunch, somewhat like a horn rising from the front of the head. A tuft of frontal hair is tied into a *routang* (knot). A white turban called *lingkhand* serves as the head-gear. The process of making the knot is an elaborate one and every traditional-mainded Maring attaches great importance to it. The christian section, however, have dispensed with this practice. Their distinctiveness in mainly linguistic, and to some extent, cultural. By and large, they confrom to the general somatometric characteristics of the southern Mongoloid races, but are somewhat darker in colour.

Their staple food is rice. When available, meat is included in their diet. Cattle, buffalo, *mithun*, pig, chicken, birds some reptiles, and less often deer, are the main sources of meat. Pulses are not taken frequently. Some roots, tubers and vegetables like potato, pumpkin, gourd, are also taken. Chilli and coriander leaves are frequently used. While working in the *jhum* fields or collecting firewood, they look for edible roots, seasonal fruits and seeds. Big-sised beans, *yumchak* (perxia, roxburgi) are eaten regularly asa substitue for vegetables. Dried fish is a delicacy. They also use tobacco, which has both a ceremonial and a medicinal value. Yu ricebeer is a common drink. It is brewed from naturally fermented rice and also has great ceremonial value. Now a days, however, they are getting used to distilled wine. This does not apply to the Christian section, who shun all types of intoxicating drink, and prefer instead, to take tea. There is evidence to suggest that a type of tea plant is grown is some Maring inhabited areas, particularly those close to the eastern border.

The Chimkhur clan is recognised as an extended agnatic lineage. Here, the emphasis is on bonds of patrilineality. There are four major Chimkhur namely, Dangsa, Charanga, Kansouwa and Mekunga. The last named is yet to attain the structural magnitude of the other three Chimkhur. Khulpuwa. Lamthakka, Hleyowa are often referred to as Chimkhur, but they are actually branches of certain other major Chimkhur. They are divided into sub-clans, arranged in order of seniority. Each of these clans are again sub-divided into a number of lineages. Local factors like residence play a very important role in the fromation of lineages. The term *achim (mayum* in Meitei), attributed to a lineage, signifies a household. The lineages within each clan are not always the same in every village. New lineages are being added at frequent intervals. Territorial dispersion of the major clans over a period of time, has given relative autonomy to local lineal groups, thus raising their status to that of a clan. This is the case with most of the Khoibu clans. Important village offices such as the *dangsa, khullakpa* and *luplakpa* are monopolised by the Dangsa clan or Khulpu. Similarly the office of khunbu is retained by the Charanga clan. It is because of this, that they have been placed above the other clans. In the past, when *khunbu* was a more important office than *khullakpa,* the Charanga clan occupied the top position. Today Dangsa has come to the top. This type of social gradation had particular meaning in the field of rituals. One could derive political power through ritual actions. It is natural therefore, that khunbu, as the ritual head commands political power. Now, however, ritual functions have lost much of their importance.

Other than the sense of attachment that clan members feel towards each other, they hardly have any economic function either at the subclan level, or at the level of the family. By regulating marriage choices the clan continues to function as an agency of social control. It is important to note that their social system is segmentary and is essentially based on a principle of seniority, piba. The eldest son has first claim to his father's land and house, while the younger brothers have to wait till they have accumulated enough wealth for marriage and for construction of separate houses. This emphasis on seniority has an inhibiting effect. The younger brothers, having no claim to the parental property, spend all their energy in acquiring property of their own. As a result they cannot actively contributed to the field of ancillary sedentary work that is required of them. A strict adherence to this pattern of inheritance (primogeniture) leads to a fragmenetion of the household after the marriage of the sons. Individual status is ranked according to wealth. One can acquire the status of a rich man by performing 'status acquiring' rituals such as *thiltlhai, parshao, pblling,* etc. *Thilthai,* which is primarily concerned with the worship of ancestors involves lavish spending. A rich man erects a pile of stones to commemorate his name. In the past, there was a primary division of society between free men and slaves. Slaves were war captives from another community. There were reports that during *thiltlhai* before the erection of stones, slaves used to be sacrificed. The symbols of rank are also found in the dress, economic privileges and certain ceremonial privileges. Though cases of polygyny are rare these days, both monogamy and polygyny are practised and there are reasons to believe that the differentiation of status was intimately conneceted with polygyny. It was also a sign of wealth. It is customary to have a major wife, besides having 'non-major' once. The first wife is known as the major wife and is considered superior to other wives. No formal marriage ceremony takes place in the case of the later marriages. Levirate and sororate are prevalent. In the case of the levirate the deceased brother's wife is treated as the second wife. The same is the case with the deceased wife's sister. Before giving their fromal recognition, a fine, *matukna*, is imposed by the clan leaders on the second wife. This signifies the recovery of the bride price from the second wife. Marriage with the mother's brother's daugther is the first choice. If such a match is not available, it is customary to seek a girl belonging to the same line of descent. In this from of consanguineous marriage, the clans right and the father's rights over the girl are bovious.

Marriage negotiations used to be very elaborate. preliminary negotiations would begin even when the boy and the girl were living in the dormitory, It used to take three years for a marriage to be formalised. During these three years the pre-marriage ceremony, *muhngoi*, had to be perfromed three times. *Mangkot*, the bride price, used to be given at the last ceremony, symbolising the finalisation of the marriage. Feasts would follow at the bride and bridegroom's residaence. Today, however, these fixed patterns are not necessarily followed and this is one reason why marriage negotiations ae not that elaborate an affair. For example, in the case of marriage by elopement, the *nuhngoi* ceremony is not perfromed. Even when it is, the muhngoi is perfromed only once. Marriage by service, *nutul*, is also prevalent. The minimum period of service for the boy in the girl's family is three years. During this period, all his earnings would go to the girl's father. Even after completion of the probationary period there is no guarantee that the marriage will take place. Earlier. it was compulsory for every bridegroom to serve in the house of the bride for a period of six years. Divorce by mutual consent is permissible. One of the common causes for divorce is barrenness. There are, however, not too many cases of divorce. Economic considerations are implicit in the case of a divorce. Children of divorced coupples may live either with their father or their mother. Even if they stay with their mother, the sons retain their right to inherit paternal property. The most important economic unit is the family group. consisting of a man, his wife and their children, followed by the extended family. The family is patrilineal and patrilocal and continuity of residence and control of land are maintained through the lineage of the eldest son.

Although women are accorded a lower status, they assert themselves in family affairs. They are expected to be compliant, but they are not forced into extreme froms of obedience and men are rather circumspect in their behabiour towards them. Women work in the fields, as land labour in cooperative ventures, do minor trading in markets in the plains and participate in village ceremonial activities. A new mother is expected to observe certain dietary taboos for sometime immediately before and after the birth of a child. She is also expected to observe taboos regarding her movements. But she resumes lighter duties after a couble of days. On the third day after birth, a name is given to the hild which becomes his or her personal name. They do not have the custom of giving surnames. Personal names are given on the basis of the order of birth. Ritual purification is perfromed on the same day by the application of fire, yu, ricebeer and by washing. The household deity Chimthrai is worshipped. The ears are pierced after the first year. There are no special initiation rites marking the end of childhood. Adolescence is spent in dormitories in the company of the same age-group where familial control is relaxed. It must be pointed out that in their traditional social life the dormmitory has an important role to play. The dormitory system is both for boys (*kathangkhang),* and for girls (ngakakhang). Status on hte dormitory is dependent on age and seniority and the same principle is later extended to the field of political organisation.

Death is ceremonialised by mourning in which relatives and friends participate. The dead person is wrapped in a white cloth and buried with some of the personal belongings of the deceased. The medicine man, *thiem*, presides over the purificatory rituals, with the final purificatory ritual being perfromed a year after the death. At the end of the initial mourning period (two days after death) a ritual, locally referred to as *thrinthro* market by purification and feasting takes place. During the mourning period offerings are made to the dead in order to plate the spirit. Death provides the clan members an occasion to renew ties. Here the clan leader or *piba* plays an important role.

The Maring are still predominantly shifting cultivators. The land on the steep hills, called *pomlou,* is used for this type of cultivation. At Khoibu, where people are shifting cultivators, a plot is cultivated for one year only. Cultivation on the same plot is done only after a gap of eight to ten years.Clearly the shortage of land hs not yet been felt here. Land is owned individually, but no one has permanent holding rights. A family can retain its authority over a plot of land for a maximum period of three years. The village organisation is the ultimate controlling authority in this matter. In case of *chinglou or kanglou,* i.e., land on the lower slopes closer to the valley, individuals have more or less permanent holding rights. Cultivation in this type of land is carried out for twenty to fourteen years at a stretch. This type of cultivation is practised at Machi and other neighbouring villages. Although limited in certain areas, a change in the method of resources exploitation has started. In this case a system of rotation of crops in followed. Sesame is cultivated during the first year. In the second year, cotton and vegetables are grown. Paddy cultivation starts from the third year. Besides paddy, they grow maise, coriander, peas, musterd and chillies. Sometimes, separate garden plots are set aside for these within field lands. These are used for growing vegetables and for orchards. The shrinking land base due to the growth in population has started imposing limits on the wealth of this society. In the immediate vicinity of some villages, overcropping has resulted in encroachment by grass on dry lands. Cultivation is not usually practised in areas where the growth of elephant grass is heavy. To ride over this situation, large scale cultivation of cash crops like banana and pineapple has been introduced in some areas. Acquisition of wet fields at the foothills is also on the increase. The return from cultivation is not all that poor, but the surplus produced does not last, as it is spent within the same year on rituals and feasts. There have beenb instances of people taking loans from the Meitei of the neighbouring villages at the beginning of the agricultural season. Loan repayment uses up much of their economic resources. Some minor trading has been developed and contact with plainsmen has stimulated growth of trade at the family level. Trade in such cases is mainly based on subsistence goods. Vegetables, fruits and baskets are carried to the markets in the plains. They have a reputation for basket-marketing and weaving makes a definite contribution towards their subsistence. More recently, selling timber to businessmen from the plains has become a lucrative occupation. In such cases, however, village organisation in involved.

The village used to be a land-owning, territorially organised unit. It used to control hunting, food supply, and warfare. This was done through the village council led by the headman, or *khullakpa*. But the *khullakpa* was not the real head. It was the *khulpu* who by virtue of his superior ritual powers was the leader of the village. Gradually, however, i.e., alongwith his clan Chananga, was relegated to a secondary position. The composition of the council headed by *khunbu*, or *khulou*, is not clearly known. There was the *sakoullu*, the head of defence, but very little is known about any of the other members of the council. One can still imagine a situation when clan leaders and persons who had a high status had some say in political matters. It appears that a full-fledged council headed by the *khullakpa* was a later development. In any case, it can at least be said that the indigenous political system of th Maring was based on the principle of seniority , a social structural priciple which determines obligations, rights and status of individuals. Formal leadership and authority were inseparable from the Maring social structure. Even fights between Maring villages could imply an absence of clanship ties. There was practically no tribal authority which could completely overrule clan authority in matters connected with the management of community affairs. Obviously, clans had political functions.

Village councils today have lost much of their importance in the face of emerging trends and values. Of course, in some cases traditional leaders function with new roles, e.g., *khullakpa* is also the chairman of the village authority introduced by the government. In village councils the *khullakpa* is assisted by a number of councillors. These councillors are not the same in every village. For instance, in the village council of Khoibi, besides the *khullakapa* there are the *khundu*, *meitei lambu* and *sallung chonglor* reperesenting different clans of the village. At Khunbi there is a *chingsanglakpa*, where as a *mantri* is inccluded in the Machi village council. Today, it is the village authority fromed by the government which has grown considerably importance. This body carries out village development work, colects house tax, settles boundary and land sisputes, and is directly responsible to the government.

A large section of this community has embraced Christianity. As a result many of their traditional practices have been discarded. Many of them do not wear their hair in the traditional style. Nor do they drink ricebeer which was once an essential part of ritual. In fact statu-giving rituals are no longer encourgated.. Reference to the supreme being. Pui Tang, is made only in connection with their origin. On the other hand, the codes which bind Chiristians together are not all relevant as far as the customary tribal practices are concerned. The resultant conflict between Christians and followers of the traditional faith sometimes assumes serious proportion. The village of Machi, for example, is clearly divided into two section. Christian (*khunou*) and non Christain (*khaunjao*). Both the sections are deeply influenced by the local natural enviroment. This is expressed through trees, animals and birds which play an important part in their myths floktales and secular songs. Ritual rights connected wiht territory are still recognised. Hornbills and *mithun* have great ceremonial value even among the Christian section. Sacrifice and feast, essential ingredients of their ritual life, are still followed with vigour evne by the Christian section. Because of these rituals, tradition is allowed to continue more or less uninterrupted. The spread of Christianity ushered in a new phase of solidarity among its followers and continued to function as a powerful integrative force.

Their artistic talent is apparent in the way they design ceremonial dresses and head dresses. Tattooing is however, unknown. The art of body decoration is confined to the use of ornaments made from various materials. During *upak hongba* an almost forgotten ceremony connected with Thelbung or Lammal worship, figures representing elephants, tigers and some cosmic bodies used to be made by carving them on wooden poles. These wooden poles could be considered as totem poles, although how they actually represent the clans is not very clearly known. Their artistics skills also find expression in basket-marking. They know a wide variety of songs and dances covering almost all aspects of social life.

There are stories (with morals), associated with some of the songs. The songs have a religious, even magical content. Western tunes are very much in evidence in some of the more modern songs. Tribal identity, which is still a powerful force in modern statheood, has a ritual background. Social content and group behaviour are also reflected in rituals. Today one can never expect to find the society of the Maring purely in its traditional from. The traditional village council has lost much of its importance as a result of emerging values and trends. Tribal policy is now determinded solely by the government. Inter-tribal and intra-tribal disputes, quarrels between the tribal leaders, the imposition and realisation of taxes, the undertaking of new public works are all within the jurisdiction of the state administration. The *khullakpa* and other village elders act more or less as government servants under the district commissioner and his subordinates. The loss of importance of traditional leadership has its repercussion on the soocial organisational patterns.

Traditional experience and traditional rights are clearly at a discount. As a corollary to this developement, some voluntary associations at the tribal level have grown in importance. The Maring Naga Racial Association, with its head-office at Machi, has been formed with a view to intergrate the Maring into a well-knit tribe. Mr. Rongman, so far the only Maring MLA of Manipur, took the initiative in this venture. He was also instrumental in providing incentives to the *uparub* assembly, an association of older persons. The Maring Naga Student's Union has been functioning since 1970. It has in its ranks a number of student represntatives including girls. The church also interests itself with the economic development of the people. Of the Christian organisations, the Maring Naga Baptist Association is very active. The association for Roman Catholics is still at an incipient stage. Some Maring, particularly those living in the western group of villages, have been in contact with the Meitei cultivators in th foothills for a long-time. They now possess small plots of wet land in th foothills and in some cases are involved in share cropping with the plains Meitei. Of late, some new Maring villages have sprung up along the lower slopes close to the Indo-Burma road. The desire to own wet land and to have places that could serve as marketing centres has contributed to the fromation of these villages. At present, they have to cover long distances to reach Kakching, Wangjing, Pallel, Thoublal, Heirck and Tengnoupal for trading. It was reported that villages on the eastern side, close to the international border, had relations with some of the Shan settlements in the Kabaw valley. These relations included trade with people across the border. One would naturally expect that state government jurisdiction, a gradual awareness of modern education, contact with mission aries and outside economic instituations have altered the life of the Maring in a big way. But they cannot be said to have crossed the subsistence lever as yet. The benefits of wage labour have reached only a small section of the people.

Educational opportunities are on the increase. Every village is provided with one lower primary school. These are the villages of Tuisimi, Chekthong, Langkhangching, Thamjai, Khangching. Kharou Khunou, Khaibu. Langol, Lamlong Khullen, Withuou Khullen, Kharam Chingsang and Leihi are each provided with a junior basic school. A high school functions at Machi. There is tremendous enthusiasm among youngsters towards education, but they are handicapped because of the insufficient facilities availble in their villages. Moreover, people are critical about the way the existing schools are functioning. In some cases the villagers themselves have taken the initiative in managing the affairs of the schools. It is expected that the process of change will be accelerated with better educational opportunities.

However, education alone cannot produce the desired result unless it is accompanied by increased economic opportunities. At present, economic opportunities other than traditional one are neglible in this area. This is also reflected in the small, marginal impact of development programmes initiated by the government. Welfare activities and agricultural development programmes of the government, though acceptable to the Maring, have not made much headway because of infrastructural constraints. Without improvement in communication systems, the cultivation of cash crops such as pineapple, lemon and banana cannot be taken up on a large scale. The need for shifting cultivation is being felt because there is no suitable substitute available. Until 1984-85 government grants were made available to about 160 individuals under the following integrated rural development planning schemes : (1) lemon plantations (2) ginger growing, (3) cane and bamboo work, (4) banana plantations, (5) pineapple plantations (6) pig-farming. (7) fishery, (8) supply of buffalo, (9) wool and knitting and (10) business.

From a long-time perspective, all these schemes may not appear to be of practical benefit to the people. But at last four schemes deserve a special mention. These are, banana plantations, piggery, supply of buffalo, cane and bamboo work. Banana cultivation is becoming increasingly popular; pigs and buffaloes are in great demand and there has already been established a base for cane and bamboo work. Special attention could be given to these fields. What is needed is a comprehensive development plan.

Those villages which are situated near the valley have better access to development resources. Waithou Khunou, Sandangsenba, Lamkhai and Nungourak, which are electrified, belong to this catetgory. There are at least ten known cases where family planning methods adopted by the government have been accepted but generally the prople are rather apprehensive about such measures. Awareness in this field is limited to only a very small group who are educated and exposed to urban values. Since 1961 there has been an improvement in medical care for women and girls. This has resulted in a better female sex ratio. Medical facilities at the village level, however, are yet to be made available to the people. Mobile units for spraying DDT visit rather, infrequently. Despite personal consciousness about healtheare and hygiene having risen and the people becoming more aware of the efficacy of modern medicine, faith in indigenous healing methods still remains strong.

II

Ecological Setting and Demographic Pattern of Anjan-A Tribal Village

The Chotanagpur Plateau with its elevation ranging from 1000 to 3000 ft. above the sea level froms the North-eastern part of the great plateau of Peninsular India. The two large plateaus, namely, the plateau of Ranchi and the plateau of Hazaribagh from the central part of this Chotanagpur plateau, and are separated by the basin of the Damodar. Ranchi plateau with its average altitude of 2000 ft. above the sea leave is one of the most distinct physical units of Bihar. The country to the south west covering Gumla and Simdega sub-divisions (which fall in the Sankh basin) is partly different from the rest of the pene plains on account of a markedly dissected surface and a slightly lower level (1500-2000 ft). The village of Anjan, with its picturesque landscape is situated in this very part of Chotanagpur.

Gumla, the thana, block and sub-divisional Headquarters and the nearest (through railless) town is about 13 miles south-east from the village whereas Ranchi, the district and divisional Headquarters, is about 78 miles to the east. On ones way to Anjan from Ranchi one has to travel on the Ranchi-Gumla highway stopping at Toto (a bus stop on the highway); from Toto the village is connected with a four-mile kutcha road. The nearest railway station Lohardaga, the terminus of the narrow-guage railway, is also at a distance of 30 miles from the village. No wonder that only a few persons of the village can claim to have seen the train. The bullock-cart is the only conveyance available at Toto and that too during dry season only. During the rainy season even the bullock cart cannot reach Anjan because for problem for the passerby.

The communication from Toto to Anjan is extremely difficult and a such the village is practically cut off from the rest of the world. Indeed Nature has tried to keep Anjan in isolation by fencing it with hills in three direction and the khatwa river in the fourth. One may manage to reach this village either on foot or by cycle from Toto during the dry months of the year ; but during the rainy season it is really quite a task for the villagers themselves to cross the strong currents of Khatwa river and reach their homeland.

Greater Anjan

The village of Anjan with its 190 households of 1225 people has a very compact settlement. The settelment is situated on a single elevated piece of land which presents a typical view of a densly populated mixed village of Chotanagpur. In addition to this compact settlement there are a few independent settlement too, which are the component parts of single maza. But it is important to note that each of these settlements, namely, Kashi tola, Chirodihm Upper Anjan, Semardih and Harnkhar has its independent institutions like sarna, Akhara act. which facilitates the day to day transactions in the village. The author has therefore excluded these small villages from Anjan, because of the fact that they have nothing in common except the name as recorded in the Mauzabandi records. Probably this mauzabandi had some functions in the remote past when it offered some sort of unity. Hallett has rightly observed "For census purposes the mauza, or settlement of village, was taken as the unit, and the mauza often compises a very large area and consists of numerous scattered tolas which contain only two or three houses a piece[1]"

For Census department village has the same meaning as a revenue mauza which is evident from a few following lines "The term 'village' has the same meaning in census as a revenue mauza". The code of census Procedure, 1961 defined it as follows : "A mauza means a parcel of land which as a rule is partly built over but mostly cultivated and waste with a definite position and area, the boundaries of which were defined either at the time of cadastral survey or at the time of revenue survey. It may contain no house at all or, on the other hand, several hamlets each bearing a different name"[2]

But social-scientists cannot conceive about a village which contains no house at all. An anthropologist is interested in the study of a populated village having definite traits and features which have been defined and described by various anthropologist. Since the village was never studies by a social scientist, this old scheme continued to exist for pretty long time. It is interesting to note that the village map of Anjan which was published in the year 1930 has also divided the old mauza of Anjan into eight parts. The eight sheets of this map cover all the different settlements mentioned above, but curiously enough there is no link between one settlement and another.

The village of Anjan has been shown in the sheet No. 7 whereas other settlements, namely, Semartola and Harnakhar have been shown in the sheet No. 5 and 1 respectively. Sheet No. 3 represents Malik ka Rakhaut (a reserve for the land-lord). Similarly sheet No. 2 represents Raiyat ka Rakhaut (a reserve for the Raiyats).

It is gathered that even in the year 1930 (when the village map was drawn) the people of different settlements regarded their own settlement as an independent unit having all the institutions required for normal life. This becomes all the more convencing if we study the village map carefully. Sheet No. 7 which represents the main village of Anjan shows that it was independent and self-sufficient in its institutions in the year 1930 because we fined references to different institution on the different plot nos. in the foot notes of the map. According to this scheme Anjan proper has its khut-sarna on the plot nos. 2467 and 2505. Sarhul-sarna on the plot no. 3371 Akhara on the plot no. 2933, Mahadeo-Asthan on the plot nos. 2383 and the cremation ground on the plot no. 3106. Similarly, Simartola, which is more than 3, miles far from Anjan proper, but a part of the same mauza, has been its independent Akhara on the survey plot no.1361, Devi Mandap on the plot no. 1852 and cremation ground on the plot nos. 1800 and 1842 respectively. Thus, it can be said that now-a-days Simartola with its population of 353 persons and independent Pahan, Akhara, Sarna, Devi Mandap, and cremation ground is an independent tribal village like Anjan and discuss the nature and location of all the settlements within this mauza will amount to mere repetition. This is why the author has excluded these settlements, namely Simartola, Chirodih, Harnakhar and Kashitola which are the component parts of Anjan mauza. He has limited his studies to Anjan proper because it appears to be the oldest settlement and because the boundary as well as the settlement scheme of the village are compact and vivid. Moreover, it has an ideal population of 1225 persons of 14 different tribes and castes and has all the institutions necessary for the independent and smooth functioning of the village all this has distinct advantages when such a study is undertaken.

Boundary of the Village

Nature has very cautiously bounded the village on all the four sides. From a distance it looks like a rare village which has the advantages of natural fortifications no all the sides. On the north the villages is bounded by Khatwa river which run closely and Dumarla and Kulhi villages are situated at a distance. On the west is the long continuos chain of Netarhat ranges which take a turn to the south ; hence the south is also partly covered by the hill ranges. Village Hurhuria is situated of the North-Eastern corner of Anjan and on the east the river Khatwa serves a natural boundary line.

Physical Features :

The district of Ranchi lies between 220,20' and 230 44' North Latitude and 840 57' E Longitude. It is bounded on the north by the district of Hazaribagh and Palamu, on the est by the district of Singhbhum, and on the west by the Palamu district of Chotanagpur. Ranchi has an area of 7,104 sq. miles and is one of the largest districts of the State of Bihar.

These physical features including the picturesque landscape itself are characteristic of the Chotanagpur plateau in general and that of the plateau of Ranchi in particular. The village is surrounded with forests and hills and the Khatwa river adds to the natural beauty. At the first a Sanskrit scholar might be remainded of Kailidas's Alkapuri, as the natural beauty of this village would remind him of some descriptions given by the famous poet. The shape of the village is not regular, partly because of the fact that every year the swift currents of Khatwa riger erode the banks : but even this erosion can hardly be regular. Wherever the banks have hard rocks the bed is narrow but deep, but when the bank has soft soil the bed becomes wide and shallow. Hills and forests are also partly responsible for the irregular shape of the village in as much as they surround the village on more than two sides.

The Khatwa river which originates from the local hills is important not only scenic beauty but much economic benefit as well. Let it be mentioned that it is the only source from which the villagers manage to produce green vegetables round the year, both for consumption and exchange. Further the lower levels of the river bed, Shallow and wide, contain green vegetables plants and creepers all the year round and for the strangers these are a substitute for an ever green park in a tribal village. This river is useful for bathing and washing of dirty clothes and the animal kingdom totally depends upon the khatwa for the supply of drinking water.

Springs

One can see a few surface springs there in the village. The villagers call it Daris or Chuals. The Daris have regular and natural supply of water and the people have a belief you may take out all the water of a Dari, it will not dry up because the loss of water which has been taken out is soon made up by an automatic and natural scheme. In the village of Anjan people normally do not drink the water of a Dari but irrigate their field with it. The Makhia of the village has installed a pumping set to irrigate his own big plot of bari land from water flowing out Dari.

Hills and Forests

The village of Anjan is surrounded by hills and forests

on three sides. The hill ranges which stretch far and wide at Anjan all meet the Netarhat Ranges, which is normally covered with thick forest. The foot of the hill has thin forest and bushy shrubs are a very common feature of the fringe area, which may be regarded as the animal's paradise.

The Anjani hill, on which stands the beautiful image of Goddess Anjani, is a place of tourists interest and the Anjani Gupha is very close by.

Flora and Fauna

It has been mentioned earlier that the village is surrounded by hills and forests, and as such it is very rich in flora and fauna. Sal, kend, karma, pipal, palas, karanj, amla and guller trees abound in the Anjan forests ; but in addition to these the forest is full of innumerable other small and big plants and creepers.

The fauna of the village can be put under two groups domesticated and wild. The domesticated animals of the village are the same as those of any other poorest of the country ; however, the bear, the wolf, the neel gai, the Sambar, the fox and numerous rabbits are characteristic fauna of the village and its fringe area. The Anjan forest is also full of small and big reptiles and snakes of different sizes, some poisonous and other harmless.

Minerals

The district of Ranchi in general is believed to be very rich in the mineral resources and the village of Anjan is not an exception. Of course, very little is known about the mineral wealth of the village, but even in ancient times the Asurs of neighbouring villages used to extract Iron-ore from the local mines, situated in the foot hills and they used to prepare still from the ore by indigenous methods. From steel they manufactured tools and implements for the use of locla call agriculturists. Next to iron-ore the village has rich deposits of lime stone. A large number of persons fetch lime stone from local mines near the village and prepare lime by burning the lime stone. They may sell it in the local weekly market of Toto and Kulhi and may leave a small quantity to be conseened by their family.

It is interesting to note that a team of Geologist from the Geological Survey of India visited the village in the year 1966 and studies the possibilities of minerals for about a week. After that they declared that there was a huge store of lime stone and iron-ore deposits in the hills of Anjan.

Land Use and the Principal Crops

Out of the total area of Ranchi district only 39 per cent is under cultivation, whereas inspite of mass deforestation, 27 per cent is covered with forests. This is the average ratio of forest area and the area under cultivation. In Anjan about 930 acres of land is cultivated annually. Mostly the soil is laterite (redsoil) which is typical of Chotanagpur. However, the river terraces of Khatwa have black cotton soil on which the villagers grow green vegetables.

For agriculture purposes the soil of Chotanagpur plateau is generally poor. It is only in the hollows between the ridges of two uplands that good clayey soil is met with. In many of the lower traces of rice fields there is a good deal of admixture of sand with clay. In many of the upper terraces of low lands (Don) the proportion of sand is very high. The quality of the soil in the uplands (tanner) is still poorer. These uplands consequently require manure every year they are cultivated, and most of these lands have to be left fallow at intervals of a year of two. Except in the jungle areas the soil deficient is due to humidity. The productiveness of the soil in any particular year depends largely on adequate rainfall.

The main crop of the village is rice and the dons of Anjan are fertile for paddy cultivation. The villagers grow Kulthi, Arhar and Barley on the tanner land. Mustard, Til and Surguja are also producted for local consumption. On the other hand vegetables of various kinds are grown and considered to be a money crop because the villagers sell them in the weekly markets of Toto and Kulhi.

Climate

The climate of the whole of Chotanagpur Plateau in general and that of Ranchi and Hazaribagh in particular is salubrious. Ranchi is the only hill station in Bihar which has been a tourist paradise and a health resort. Owing to its elevation the Chotanagpur Plateau has a much cooler climate than that of the adjoining districts. Except for about a month in summer, when the sun hits fiercely and the heat is somewhat tring, the days are partly hot, but the nights are delightfully cool. In fact the variation of temperature between day and night in this region is much greater than in the plains of Bengal and Bihar. Climatically Anjan is very similar to Ranchi. The presence of green ranges of hills and the Khatwa river has a soothing effect on the eyes and is conducive to the health of the people of the village. The village is comparatively neat and clean and open for sufficient ventilation and the Khatwa river provides a natural drainage. The average mean temperature rises from 62.20F in December to 87.80 F in May. The mean minimum in the cold season is 510 and the mean maximum in the month of may is 1000 F. The highest recorded temperature in summer is over 1100 F. The annual rainfall varies from 50 to 65 inches. Situated at a distance from the sea and at an altitude of 2000 the village has on the whole a dry climate.

The Temperature Cycle

March to May (summer Season)

This period is said to be the hottest season of the year. The temperature tends to increase and great heat prevails throughout the period. In the month of March, the mean maximum temperature is nearly 900 F and mean minimum tem perature flutuates between 600 F and 650 F. Humidity is comparatively lower. The highest temperature rise is recorded in the month of May which is hottest month of the year and the average temperature is 900 F or more. Rainfall is practically nil during this season.

June to October (Rainy Season)

In the month of June monsoon sets in the temperature comes down with the monsoon showers. An average decrease of about 400 F is noticed in the month of June and this decrease comes upto 120 F. 1 in the month of August.

November to February (Winter Season)

After the rainy season is over, a period of bright and sunny weather pervails, There is a gradual fall of temperature and in the month of November the real winter season begins. During this month the mean minimum temperature fluctuates between 600 F and 550 F. In the following month the temperature falls suddenly by 100 F to 120 F which makes the month the coolest of the year. Again from the month of February the temperature tends to rise gradually.

Rainfall Cycle

March to May

During this period rainfall is negligible. There are frequent storms and afternoon storms initiate occasional rain, which is about 5 per cent of the total rains of the year.

June to October

The Monsoon breaks in the middle of June. The monsoon rainfall is comparatively heavier in the plateau of Ranchi. The main source of rain in this season is the monsoon wind of the Bay of Bengal which turns southwards after being obstructed by the middle of October. At the onset of Monsoon wind a rapid change of June and continues upto the middle of whether takes place. Decrease in tempreature is remarkable. On the other hand humidity increases considerably. About 90 per cnet of the total annual rainfalls during this period. The annual rainfall in the Ranchi district in general and Anjan in particular is between 55 inches to 65 inches and this is an ideal rainfall for paddy cultivation.

November to February

During this period the rainfall is generally negligible. The occasional rain of this period is caused by cyclonic storms which originate from the Arabian sea. It is about 5 per cent of the total annual rainfall of this area, which is certainly meagre, but the rainfall of this period is of great importance for the rabi crops.

II

History of the Village

Anjan is considered to be one of the oldest village of the Arangi Pargana and there are substantial evidences in favour of this belief. The reconstructed history of the village is discussed here on the nature of the historical infromation and from the careful observation of the historical relics of the village it would appear reasonable to discuss the history of the village in three groups :

(i) History of the village in myth and legend

(ii) Secular history of the village

(iii) Immigrational history of the village.

(i) History of the village in myth and legend

This section deals with the account of the village in the oldest days and we have no record in black and white. But there are a few very important myth which reveal the glorious past of Anjan.

Anajn has a mythological background. People believe that Lord Hanuman, the monkey God of the Ramayan was born of anjan in a cave of a hill on the out-skirts of this village, and that is why the village derives its name from Anjaui, the mother of the Lord. The old folk of the village known many strories regarding Anjani Mata and her mighty son, Hanuman. It is said that once upon a time there were 365 Shivalingas and the same number of tanks in the village Anjani mata used to worship one Shivalinga every day after taking her bath in a particular tank. Thus she could worship all the 365 Shivalingas in a year by the process of rotation. Even today one can see eight Shivalinga at a glance in the courtyard of Chakaradhari temple and the village preserves the relics of those Shivalingas which may be 100 or more. Majority of these are in the original state while a few are seen in delapidated condition.

There is an Anjani Gupha (i.e a cave) on the top of Anjani hill. The enntrace to the cave is closed and one cannot get in. The devotees of Anjani Mata can throw the Akshat (sacred rice) and flowers inside the cave through a very small manhole in the door and put the vermilion marks on the upper part of the door. A few sacred flags can also be seen just in front of the door of the cave. A very beautiful image of mother Anjani is stationed just by the side of the roof of the cave. People believe that a secret underground route about 500 yards long leads one from the cave to the Khatwa river. Legend has is that Mother Anjani used to take her bath occasionally in Khatwa river and would come back to her cave through the underground route. Actually there is a very dark tunnel which opens at the Khatwa river and the villagers believe that this goes straight to the Anjani Gupha of course no one has some through this route in living memory as it is very dark and the tunnel could be a den of wild animals.

There is one Dhamdhamia Pahar just by the side of the Anjani Cave, and if one strikes the rock with a heavy object like the head of an exe or spade one can hear the viberaton of sound which shows that inside the big rock there may be hollow space. The people believe that Dhamdhamia Pahar is the treasure of Mother Anjani in which she keeps all her valuables.

There are two different stories about the closure of the door of the cave. (1) According to late Mana Singh, a Kharwar centenarian, the villagers used to have a vision of Mother Anjani occasionally in remote past. But it so happened that one day Anjani Mata was brushing the locks of her hair after a bath and one Late Ajgut Singh, Kharwar, the father of the infromant saw her, and enquired who she was. She ran towards the forest and the followed her. She crossed the forest land and reached the door of cave. As he reached there he found the door of the cave closed with a very big and heavy piece of stone and since then neither the door has opened even once nor Mother Anjani has been seen by any one. (2) the Hindus of the village believe that the Kols also used to worship Mother Anjani. One day it so happened that a Kol sacrificed a goat before the image of Anjani - an act which she did not approve of ; she closed the door of her cave in protst.

The belief that Anjani was the birth place of Lord

Hanuman is supported by a document- a village note which dates back to the 26th February, 1927 reads : "The village is said to have derived its name from Aujani, a mythological character of Mahabharat. It is said that Anjani used to build one temple and excavate one tank daily and dedicate them to the Gods. The village is an old one. There are images of Shiva scattered all over and a very large number of tanks. It is believed that they are the remains of Anjani's time. The villagers both Kols and Sadans mention Anjani an Anjanimata or "Mother Anjani". This village note singed and sealed by the Assistant Settlement officer is dated the 26th Feburary, 1927.

Everyone of the village has a special respect of mother Anjali who is regarded as "Gram Devta" and the villagers are very fond of talking a lot but her glory. They believe her to be a very kind hearted deity and for that reason she is universally referred to as mother. They expect the same reverence for their mother from the outsiders as well, and cannot tolerate any criticism. Late Mana Singh told the author a very useful story about Anjani mata.

Once Shri Suraj Prasad, a Tahsildar of the Maharaja of Chotanagpur, visited Anjan on some important work of the Estate. He was unnecessarily arrogant and would not believe in the powers and existence of Anjani Mata, - feeling which he expressed before many villagers. The villagers took exception to it but could not say much as he was a terror to the villagers. But soon after his boast he did not believe in her powers, he found his diamond ring missing. He was extremely unhappy at the loss of his precious ring. The Pahan knew the secret and he announced that it was a punishment for not showing due respect to Mother Anjani. He further advised Suraj Parsad to go to Anjani cave and apologise to Mother Anjani. Shri Suraj Prasad realised his folly and went to the Anjani cave, on the top of the hill, where he felt the divine smell of incense and Bel-Patra, he was horrified and arranged for ritual worship in a very elaborate and decent manner. As they were coming back after the ceremony Suraj Parsad saw to his astonishment that his precious diamond ring was very cautiously kept on a sal leaf just the side of foot-path. He picked it up at once and thanked Mother Anjani for her kindness. Since then whenever he visited Anjan he made it a point to visit the Anjani cave on the hill top to pay his respects. This incident filled the villagers with awe and even strangers felt that it was imperative to show proper respect for Mother Anjani.

The Chanda Khal : It is a place on the Anjan range which has very important association with Hindu Mythology. People believe that once the Chanda (God Moon) in disguise of Gautam Rishi indulged in the sex act with Ahilya, the wife of Gautam. It is said that Ahilya was a rare beauty. Once the moon-god saw her and overwhelmed with passion he copulated with her in the disguise of her husband but soon after this sinful act, reason Prevailed upon him and he thought that Gautam by virtue of his Yogic power would come to know of the sin. Then he (Moon) would be reduced to ashes as Gautam would pronounce a curse upon him. He saw the danger to his life and wanted to evade it. It is believed that Moon hid himself to evade the curse in this very Chanda-Khal of Anjan, which is a very safe cave and opens at top only; it looks like a very big bucket of water. A person hiding in Chanda-Khal was safe from even a careful searcher. The Chanda-Khal looks like a solid piece of stone but is hollow within like a water bucket.

(ii) *Secular History of the Village*

There is another opinion among the villagers regarding the name 'Anjan'. They say that there was a king in the village whose name has been forgotten but he had a very beautiful queen who was named Anjani. The king loved her very much. She died a premature death and the king decided to name the village Anjan, in the memory of his late wife. There are some evidences to show that Anjan was the home of a king. There are a few relics of big buildings and temples and there are remains of a very wide and deep foundation. The bricks in this foundation are of unusual size (18"x 9"). The foundation stretches to a few miles and at several places big stone tables have also been unearthed. The tablets had some inscriptions which have eroded due to exposure and weathering. One can see the ruins of a few domes of temples and walls even today and the Anjani Garh which is an elevated flat spot is still a relic treasury of those days. Only a few years ago a man got a golden necklace (weighing one seer) from a pit of the garh. A careful and scientific excavation of this garh may reveal something quite unique; but nothing convicing in this regard has been found in black and white and this recent history of the village is also based on verbal reports of a few infromants.

(iii) *Immigrational History of the Village*

Now we come to the living memory of the villagers, that is the phenomena within the past 100 years, which the old men of the village remember very well.

Needless to say, impact of 'Hinduisation' due to immigration of Hindus in the village is a distinctive feature of this period. The village has been experiencing the influx of various caste Hindus for approximately 100 years. This has converted the old tribal village of Anjan into a full fleged Hindu village. The details of immigration are given in Table No. 1.

History of Immigrants

(i) *Brahmin* : It appears that about 100 years ago there was no Brahmin family at Anjan. Shri Bishnudhari Mishra, the Grandfather of Shri Parasuram Mishra, the present Mukhia of the village,was a wrestler of village Bala in Gaya District. Once he visited Palkot Raja in connection with a wrestling programme, of which the Rajwas very fond. The Raja was very much impressed with the perfromances and behaviour of Shri Bishnudhari Mishra and he wanted to keep him as a Sipahi for rent collection. Shri Mishra was given /12/- annas of rent free land there at Anjan which was a village held by the Raja and as such he settled there. He used to keep many big horses and had brought a few more persons as Lathait from Gaya who would help him in the collection of rent. In those days there had been tensions between the Raja and the tribals of the locality for rent collection ; but Shri Bishundhari Mishra with his giant stature and Lathait followers proved to be a terror to the locality who would not spare any one without realising proper rent due with the Raiyats. Thus, Shri Bishnudhari Mishra was the first Brahmin who immigrated from Gaya to Anjan

Table 1.

Table Showing the History of Immigration of Different Communities to Anjan.

Sl. No.	*Approximate Years (in past) of immigration*	*Place of migration*	*Name of the head of the family.*	*Caste/ Tribe*
1.	Uncertain	Unknown	Unknown	Munda
2.	-do-	-do-	-do-	Oroan
3.	-do-	-do-	-do-	Kharwar
4.	-do-	-do-	-do-	Chikbaraik
5.	-do-	-do-	-do-	Lohra
6.	-do-	-do-	-do-	Ghasi
7.	100 years	Bela (Gaya) (Gumla)	Bishundhari Mishra	Brahmin
8.	75 years	Murkunda	Manikanth Pandey	Brahmin
9.	74 years	Nawadih (Lohardaga)	Sitaram Soy	Rajput
10.	70 years	-do-	Basi Thakur	Hajam
11.	60 years	Songra (Binda)	Kisu Matho	Kumhar
12.	60 years	Unknown	Sunu Dhobi	Dhobi
13.	50 years	Sisai (Gumla)	Guja Dhobi	Dhobi
14.	40 years	Totambi (Gumla)	Mangru Mahli	Mahli
15.	40 years	Unknown	Nandu Goala	Ahir
16.	17 years	Toto (Gumla)	Triloki Sah	Bania
17.	15 years	Upper Anjan	Ghasi Mahto	Kumhar
18.	12 years	-do-	Bhagat Mahto	Kumhar

about a 100 years ago. He amassed some property there in the village but died a premature death. His only son Shri Baidyanath Mishra was still a boy when he breathed last.

Shri Baidyanath Mishra a minor and as such he had no alternative than to invite his brother -in-law, Late Manik Nath Pandey from Murkunda in Gumla to settle at Anjan. Accordingly Shri Manik Nath Pandey came over to Anjan and settled there. He got a few acres of land from Shri Baidyanath Mishra for the maintenance of his family and he started looking after his property in return. Thus, Pandey's is a second Brahmin family to settle at Anjan.

Shri Baidyanath Mishra started reading Sanskrit and in course of time became a very good Pandit of the locality. He used to visit Palkot off and on when called for some business of Raja and the villagers had special regard for him. By virtue of his scholarly behaviour he gained many villages in Jajmani and later one had to transfer a few Jajmani villages to his brother-in-law. Shri Manik Nath Pandey however failed to manage such a large number of villages within his Jajmani. After the death of Pandit Baidyanath Mishra his eldest son. Shri Parushram Mishra looks after his property including Jajmani.

Shri Manik Nath Pandey also breathed his last inn the year 1962 and his only son, Shri Laldeo Pandey looks after his father's Jajmani.

(ii) *Rajput*: Shri Jiwan Soy was the first Rajput to settle at Anjan. Originally he was a settler of village Kasmar (Nawadih) in Lkohardaga Thana. He was favourite Barahil (Sipahi) of the Raja of Palkot. The Raja had given him-/16/- annas of land there at Anjan to till and the produce of the land would be his salary. This was a very old scheme and Shri Jiwan Soy was not a stranger to her village. There was one Kapargharia at Anjan who was a very rich but had no issue. When Shri Jiwan Soy came to settle at Anjan the Kapargharia developed a soft corner for him and in return he too had affection and respect for the issueless old man. As a result of this the Kapargharia adopted him as his son towards the end of his life. Thus, Shri Jiwan Soy took over the property of Kapargharia after his death. Jiwan Soy became the richest man of the village. He had two sons, namely Kanchan Soy and Bucha Soy. Shri Jiwan Soy died long ago and his eldest son Kanchan Soy is also dead. Now his only son Shri Kestu Soy looks after the property of his father. He has separated his estate from that of his uncle Shri Bucha Soy, who is alive with four sons. Thus, now there are two nuclear Rajput families in the village.

(iii) *Hazam (Barber)* : There are two families of Barbers at Anjan. The history of their immigration is given below:

It has been stated above that Jiwan Soy who was a Barchil in the court of the Raja of Palkot came to settle at Anjan from Kasmar (Nawadih) and by good luck he became a rich man of the village. At the time when Jiwan Soy settled at Anjan there was no Barber in the village. Jiyan Soy managed to bring a family of Barber from his original village of Nawadih and gave them some land to cultivate. Thus, Basi Thakur was the first Barber who immigrated from Bawadih to Anjan and now the two families of Barbers are none by the grandsons of Basi Thakur and Hari Thakur.

(iv)* Bania *: Triloki Sahu, who is a Roniar Baniya, was originally an inhabitant of Toto (Gumla). He came in contact with Shir Pars huram Mishra and in due course they became good friends. Triloki Sahu wanted to settle at Anjan and Shri Mishra helped him in Purchasing land and constructing a house there. In the year 1951 Triloki Sahu left Toto and settled at Anjan permanently. Now he has a small shop of grocery at Anjan and that is the only source of the subsistence for his family.

(v) *Potter* : There are five families of potters living at Anjan of which two have very gold history in the village, and they consider themselves to be very old settlers of the village. They do not know as to when and how their forefathers had come over to Anjan. The remaining three are comparatively recent immigrants. The details follow in the chronological order :

Nandi Mahto is said to be the first Kumhar (Potter) settler of the village, because even in the Record of Rights there is reference that one Anna of rent free land was given to him as Khaparkheta (land given for the manufacturing of earthen tiles for thatching and repairing the houses of Raja). 70 years old Mahli Mahto, the only grand son fo late Nandi

Mahto, is still the owner of that Khaparkheta. Thus, this family of Potters is a very old one in this village.

Another potter family which has very old history in the village is that of Kajroo Mahto. His father Manager Mahto and grand-father Birjoo Mahto also lived at Anjan. Kajroo's ancestors also may have lived in the same village. The Third family of potters is that of Bhambha Mahto whose history of immigration to Anjan is given below. Kishoo Mahto the grand father of Bhambha Mahto was a resident of village Songra near Binda. Bina Mahto father of Bhamba and son of Kishoo was also living with his father there at Songra. When Bina was still a boy and his mother was living, his father, Kishoo married a second wife at Anjan and settled there. Bina was living at Songra with his mother. Kishoo had a son by his second wife, namely Sitoo Mahto. But Sitoo died issueless after which Bina came over to Anjan from Songra and settled there because he inherited sizeable property.

The fourth and the fifth families of Potters, namely those of Ghasi Mahto and Bhagat Mahto have recently immigrated to Anjan from Upper Anjan. They are now settlers.

(vi) ***Dhobi (Washerman)*** **:** Presently there are two families of wahsermen in the village. They have a very short history in this village. One Sonu Dhobi was the first man of his caste to be settled by the Raja in the village. He was given two annas of land as his wage. He had his Jajmani in a few other villages of this locality. After his death his only son Chaman Dhobi looked after his jajmani but he too died a premature death when his only son Lalmani Baitha was just a child. As his Jajmani was too big for him he invited his maternal uncle Guj Dhobi to settle at Anjan and help him. Thus, Guju Dhobi came and settled at Anjan.

(vii) ***Ahir (Malkman)*****:** There is only one family of Gwalas there at Anjan. The history of their immigration to Anjan is not very old. One Nandu Gwala settled in the village about forty years ago. He is survived by his grand son.

(viii) ***Mahli*** **:** There is only one family of Mahlis at Anjan. It has a very short history in this village. Mangroo Mahli came from Totambi and settled here. His younger brother Manoo Mahli also came here alongwith his brother but he died a premature death without any issue, whereas Gandul Mahli is the only son of Mangroo who lives in the village.

From the persual of the immigrational history of the Hindu castes of Anjan, it become almost clear that they are compartively new settlers in the village, whereas the claims of the tribals of being autochthon appears to be reasonable. It further reveals that the history of the settlement of Brahmin, Rajput, Barber, Potter and washerman is less than a hundred years old.

It is very interesting to note that the history of tribal immigration of any particular tribe is represented by a single Mahil family in the village while almost all of them have been living at Anjan since time immemorial.

Demography of the Village

About a hundred years ago, before the immigration of the Hindu Caste-men in the village, it could be safely regarded as small tribal village of Chotanagpur : but at this stage when Hindu castemen constitue 17.6 per cent of the total population it should be regarded as a mixed village of Chotanagpur inhabited by 14 different tribes and castes .

The author took a field census of the village in May, 1965 in which door-to-door, investigation of all the houses was done. The sociological census was carried out again in October- November 1967 for a comparative study. Numerically the important tribes are Oraons, chik-Braiks and Kharwars who constitute 65.5 per cent 5.3 per cent and 4 per cent respectively of the population of the village.

In caste group, Ghasis, though very low in the caste hierarchy have the second largest numerical strength, constitution 9.8 per cent of the total population of the village. Brahmins, Rajputs and Barbers though numerically negligible, constituting only 1 per cent of the total population separately, may regarded dominant groups economically and politically.

Table No. 2 below shows the details of tribes and castes

with their numerical strength of the census of 1967.

Table 2

Different Ethnic Group and Their Sex ratio

Sl. No.	*Caste/Tribe*	*Census 1967*			
		Male	*Female*	*Total*	*Percentage*
1.	Oroan	400	404	804	65.7
2.	Ghasi	59	57	116	9.8
3.	Chik-Braik	35	30	65	5.3
4.	Lohara	30	32	62	5.0
5.	Kharawar	20	29	49	4.0
6.	Kumhar	24	15	39	3.1
7.	Munda	8	15	23	1.8
8.	Brahmin	6	8	14	1.1
9.	Rajput	6	8	14	1.1
10.	Hajam (Barber)	5	9	14	1.1
11.	Dhobi (W.man)	2	5	7	0.6
12.	Mahli	4	4	8	0.6
13.	Bania	4	2	6	0.5
14.	Ahir	2	2	4	0.3
Total		605	620	1225	100

Sex and Age

From the persual of table No. 2 it is clear that there are 1025 females for every 1000 males in the village. But the study of sex ratio community wise reveals a more fluctuating trend than the village as a whole. Where the Mahlis and Ahirs have 1000 females for every 1000 females for every 1000 males, the Dhobis (washerman) and Mundas have 2500 and 1875 respectively, females for every 1000 males. Contrary to this the Banias have only 500 females for every 1000 of male population.

Sex ratio study in age group shows that whereas

children below five years have 1065 females for eery 1000 males, in the age group of 16-20 years it comes to 1000 females for the same number of males; but in the age group of 56-62 years there are 1857 females for every 1000 males.

The age group composition of the village has the following features 48.97 per cent of persons of the village belong to the age group of 0 to 15 years whereas only 29.29 per cent of persons have returned in the age group of 16-30 years. A further sharper fall because only 21.74 per cent person of the village have returned from this group. Thus to sum up the age composition of the village it can be safely said that the number of elder members of society goes on decreasing with the rise of age.

Maerital Status

The study of Table No 3 reveals that the total number of unmarried persons in the village is higher than that of the married ones. 45.79 per cent of the village population are married whereas 47.68 per cent person are unmarried. Commonly there is not much difference in the sex ratio of married to unmarried. But a few communities, namely, the Brahmin, the Mahli, the Dhobi and the Ahir deserve specific mention here. Whereas among the Brahmins the sex ratio of married to unmarried is 4:8: among the Mahli it goes upto 2:6 and the disparity in this ratio is highest among the Ahirs 0:3. Contrary to this the Dhobis have more married persons than unmarried : the ratio of married to unmarried being 4:2. 4.89 per cent of the total population of the village have returned widow and 1.55 per cent as widower and there is only one Ghasi woman who is an example of divorce in the village.

Functional Composition of the Village

The composition of the literate population of the village has the following features. The general literacy rate of the village comes only to 11.76 per cent of the total population. The Hindus have higher literacy as compared to the tribals, because 19.63 per cent of the Hindu have returned as literate : whereas only 19.09 per cent of the total tribal population have returned literate. Among Hindu Brahmins have the highest literacy of 92.9 per cent. The Kharwars

Table No. 3

Table Showing Age and Sex Composition of Social group

Age gro Up in Years	*Oraon*		*Ghasi*		*Chik Baraik*		*Lohar*		*Kumhar*		*Munda*		*Brahmin*		*Rajput*		*Hazam*		*Mahli*		*Dhobi*		*Baniya*	
	M	F	M	F	M	F	M	F	M	F	M	F	M	F	M	F	M	F	M	F	M	F	M	F
0-5	77	79	20	22	9	7	9	7	2	3	4	3	0	1	0	3	1	2	0	0	1	1	0	1	0	0
6-10	76	77	6	5	4	4	3	5	4	5	5	2	3	4	3	1	1	1	1	0	1	2	0	1	3	1
11-15	45	45	5	3	5	4	1	2	2	3	0	2	1	3	1	0	1	0	1	4	1	0	0	0	0	0
16-20	36	34	7	5	3	2	3	5	1	2	3	2	1	0	0	0	0	1	0	1	0	0	0	1	0	0
21-25	43	42	6	6	2	2	5	3	2	3	2	1	0	1	0	1	0	1	1	1	0	0	1	0	0	0
26-30	47	47	5	4	4	3	2	2	1	2	3	2	0	1	1	1	1	0	0	0	0	1	0	0	0	0
36-40	26	22	4	3	3	3	4	3	4	5	2	1	2	2	0	0	0	0	1	1	0	0	0	1	0	1
41-45	10	10	2	3	2	2	1	0	2	2	0	1	0	1	0	1	0	1	0	0	0	0	0	0	1	0
46-50	7	8	3	3	0	0	0	1	1	2	0	1	0	0	0	0	0	0	0	0	0	0	0	1	0	0
51-55	4	6	0	1	1	0	0	0	0	0	4	0	0	0	0	1	0	0	0	0	0	0	1	0	0	0
56-60	5	7	0	0	0	1	1	1	0	1	0	0	0	1	0	0	0	0	1	2	0	0	0	0	0	0
61	2	3	0	0	0	0	0	0	0	0	1	0	0	1	0	0	1	1	0	0	0	0	0	0	0	0
Total	400	404	59	57	35	30	30	32	20	29	24	15	8	15	6	8	6	8	5	9	4	4	2	5	4	2

having 28.5 per cent of literacy top the literacy list of the

Table 4

Table Showing the Marital Status of the Villagers

Commu-nities	*Married*	*Unma-rried*	*Wodow*	*Widower*	*Divorced*	*Total*
Oraon	378	385	30	11	0	804
Ghasi	52	59	4	0	1	116
Chik-Baraik	26	31	4	4	0	65
Lohra	28	29	4	1	0	62
Kharwar	22	19	7	1	0	49
Kumhar	20	17	1	1	0	39
Munda	8	10	4	1	0	23
Brahmin	4	8	2	0	0	14
Rajput	7	6	1	0	0	14
Hajam	8	5	1	0	0	14
Mahli	2	6	0	0	0	8
Dhobi	4	2	1	0	0	7
Baniya	2	4	0	0	0	6
Ahir	0	3	1	0	0	4
Total	561	584	60	19	1	1225
Percentage	45.79	47.68	4.89	1.55	0.09	100

tribal groups. The distributions of literacy sexwise reveals that only 6.61 per cent of the total female population is literate whereas this goes upto 17 per cent in case of male. The number of total literate persons is 144 in which total male literates 103, i.e; 71.53 per cent of total literate persons. Only 41 literate females have returned from the village ; this is 28.72 per cent of total literate.

So far as the degree of education is concerned 10.42 per cent have returned such as know how to sign their names;

47.27 per cent are educated from 1 to III class. The percentage or persons from IV, VIII to XI and those educated upto college standards is 29.17, 11.11 and 2.8 respectively.

Table 5

Table Showing theLiteracy Rates Among the Various communities

Community	*Total Population*	*No. of literate*	*Percentage*
Oraon	804	65	8
Munda	23	3	13
Chik-Baraik	65	16	24.6
Kharwar	49	14	28.5
Lohra	62	4	6.5
Mahli	8	-	-
Total Tribal Population	1011	102	10.29
Brahmin	14	13	92.9
Rajput	14	4	28.6
Baniya	6	3	50
Kumhar	39	6	15.4
Hajam	14	3	21.4
Ahir	4	-	-
Dhobi	7	2	28.6
Ghasi	116	11	9.6
Total of Hindu Population	214	42	19.63
Grand Total	1225	144	11.76

The Birth Rate

From the perusal of the Total No. 6 showing the birth

rate of the village from 1957 to 1967 it is clear that the highest number of births, i.e., 38 children, has been shown in the years 1959 and the lowest has been represented by 16 births in the year 1964. The trend of birth rate study sex-wise shows that in the year 1959, 19 male and same number of female childern were born. The highest number of male childern were born in the year 1960 and the highest number of female childern was born in 1966.

Table 6

Table Showing Birth Rates

Year	*Total Population*	*No. of births Male*	*Female*	*Total*	*Birth rate per 1000 Population*
1959	1103	19	19	38	34.4
1960	1128	23	12	35	31.0
1961	1145	13	9	22	19.0
1962	1158	11	15	26	22.4
1963	1162	11	12	23	19.6
1964	1171	7	9	16	13.6
1965	1174	13	16	29	24.8
1966	1204	14	18	32	26.5
1967	1225	15	16	31	25.3

Source : These figures have been taken from the register of births and deaths available in the office of Gram Panchayat.

The Death Rate

The death rate study of Anjan from the year 1959 to 1967 given in Table No.8 shows that the highest number of death (24 persons) was reported in the year 1964 and the lowest number of 5 was reported in the year 1967. The highest number of male deaths occured in 1964 and the lowest number was in the year 1967. Similarly, the highest number of female deaths was reported in the year 1960 and lowest in 1961.

Table 7

Table Showing Dealtrate

Year	*Total population*	*No. of death Male*	*Female*	*Total*	*Death rate per 1000*
1959	1103	5	1	6	5.2
1960	1128	4	9	12	11.1
1961	1145	5	-	5	4.9
1962	1158	9	4	13	11.1
1963	1162	7	2	9	8.1
1964	1171	17	7	24	21.5
1965	1174	3	3	6	5.1
1966	1204	5	3	8	5.6
1967	1225	2	3	5	4.0

Sources : These figures have been obtained from the register of Birth and deaths available in the office of Anjan Gram Panchayat.

Table 8

Table Showing the Distribution of Families and Population According to the Social Hierarchy of the 14 Communities of the Village.

Sl. No	*Caste/ Tribe*	*Community*	*Total family*	*Total Population*	*Percentage*
1.	Hindu	Brahmin	2	14	1.1
2.	Hindu	Rajput	2	14	1.1
3.	-do-	Baniya	1	6	0.5
4.	-do-	Hazam	2	14	1.1
5.	-do-	Kumhar	6	39	3.1
6.	-do-	Ahir	1	4	0.3
7	-do-	Ghasi	23	116	9.8
8.	-do-	Dhobi	2	7	0.6
Total			39	214	17.6

Sl. no	*Caste/ Tribe*	*Community*	*Total family*	*Total Population*	*Percentage*
9.	* Marginal Caste	Kharwar	10	49	4.0
10.	-do-	Chik-Baraik	11	65	5.3
11.	-do-	Lohra	12	62	5.0
12	-do-	Mahli	1	8	0.6
Total			34	184	14.9
13.	Tribal	Munda	5	23	1.8
14.	-do-	Oraon	113	804	65.7
Total			118	827	65.5

*The term marginal caste has been used for such tribes as have adopted the Hindu way of life, and one of them, the Kharwars have achived the caste status of the Rajput : whereas the caste status of the Chik-Baraik, the Lohra and the Mahli has not been finally recognised in the village.

The village has been experiencing the forces of two traditions the little (tribal) and the great (Hindu) for about a century. The fromer being the autochthon is rich in number: whereas the latter being immigrant has more developed technology. Thus, the struggle between the little and the great traditions has been that of the number and the technology and the results of the interaction show that it is the technology which has always been welcomed by the number.

The population of Anjan is made up of 14 communities namely, the Brahmin, the Rajput, the Hazam, the Baniya, the Kumhar, the Ahir, the Ghasi, and the Dhobi in caste group and the Oraon, the Munda, the Kharwar, the Chik-Baraik, the Lohra and the Mahli in tribal group.

The traditional varna system is not very helpful in classifying the fourteen communities of the village because of its tribal population. But from the point of view of caste superiority which is symbolically represented by inter-dining, acceptance of food and water (from other castes), sitting arrangement in a group and the manner of greeting, these fourteen communities have been grouped in different vertical and horizontal orders. All the fourteen communities have been kept in four horizontal groups and the comparative superiority of a particular community depends upon the vertical order in a particular group. The details are given in table 9

Table 9

Table showing the hierarchical grouping of the fourteen communities of Anjan.

Twice born Caste	*Functional Caste*	*Marginal Caste*	*Tribal communities*
Brahmin	....	Kharwar	....
Rajput	Hazam, Kumhar		
Baniya	Ahir	Chik -Baraik	Munda, Oraon
....	Ghasi, Dhobi	Lohra	
		Mahli	

A careful study of this table reveals that out of a total number of 191 families only 18 were joint families which was 9.4 per cent of the total number of families. Nuclear family was represented by 173 families which was 90.6 percent of the total. Growth of individualism, deviation from traditional occupation, lack of faith in the elderly persons, migration to Assam or other places and dishonesty of the headman were some of the important causes responsible for the breakdown of the joint family system.

From table 12 it is evident that cultivable land of the village is not equitably distributed among all the communities of the village. As many as 26 m families (i.e. 16.6 per cent of the total number of families) are landless. Among the landless families the Ghasis are the highest in number. As many as 14 Ghasi families (about 60 percent of the total Gahsi population) are landless. Similar, the Mahlis and the Baniya have no land worth the name. On the other hand the Rajputs, the Brahmins, the Mundas and the Kharwars have 19.74,18.71,8.68 and 8.48 acres. Mean land per family and

Table No. 10

Table Showing the Size of the Families

Community	*No.of family*	*No.of joint family*	*1 membered family*	*2 membered family*	*3-5 membered family*	*6-10 membered family*	*11-15 membered family*	*16 & above family*	*Total*
Oraon	97	16	0	2	45	50	12	4	113
Ghasi	22	1	0	2	12	8	1	0	23
Baraik	10	1	1	1	5	3	0	1	11
Lohra	12	0	0	0	6	6	0	0	12
Kharwar	10	0	1	1	4	4	0	0	10
Kumhar	6	0	0	0	1	5	0	0	6
Munda	5	0	0	1	2	2	0	0	5
Brahman	2	0	0	0	0	2	0	0	2
Rajput	2	0	0	0	0	2	0	0	2
Barber	2	0	0	0	0	2	0	0	2

Community	*No. of family*	*No. of joint family*	*1 membered family*	*2 membered family*	*3-5 membered family*	*6-10 membere family*	*11-15 membered family*	*16 & above family*	*Total*
Mahli	1	0	0	0	0	1	0	0	1
Dhobi	2	0	0	0	0	2	0	0	2
Baniya	1	0	0	0	0	1	0	0	1
Ahir	1	0	0	0	0	1	0	0	1
Total	173	18	2	7	78	86	13	5	191
Percentage	90.6	9.4	1.04	3.66	40.84	45.03	6.81	2.62	100

per capita is 4.82 and .76 respectively. It is

Table 11.

Table Showing the Distribution of Land in the Village

Sl. No.	*Communities*	*Land in acres*		
		Total	*Per family*	*Per capita*
1.	Oraon	601.22	5.32	0.75
2.	Ghasi	29.24	1.23	0.25
3.	Chik-Baraik	31.92	2.90	0.49
4.	Lohra	31.06	2.63	0.50
5.	Kharwal	84.81	8.48	1.73
6.	Kumhar	15.11	2.52	0.39
7.	Munda	43.41	8.68	1.89
8.	Brahmin	37.48	18.71	2.67
9.	Rajput	39.48	19.74	2.82
10.	Hazam	13.90	6.95	0 .92
11.	Mahli	....	....	....
12.	Dhobi	4.10	2.05	0.59
13.	Baniya	....	....	....
14.	Ahir	0.0	0.9	0.20
Total		930.96	4.82	0.76

only the Oraon villagers whose per capita land come to 0.75 acres which is very close to the exerage (0.76) for the whole village. Other communities have either very low or very high average of per capita land. The Baniyas and the Mahlis who have recently immigrated to Anjn have no land at all. All other communities of the village have land and their per capita land varies from 0.02 to 2.82 acres.

Production of Grains

After the distribution of land under cultivation have been analysed, the condition of the villagers, in respect of grains produced, deserves attention. The total population of the village is grouped under three classes- first being those who grow surplus grains, second, those who are self sufficient in grains and third, those who have deficit in grains. This scheme of classification is very important because Anjan's economy largely depends upon the production of grains, and they, who grow more than their domestic consumption are considered to be prosperous in the village economy. Again, the economic status of a particular person is very closely related to his social and political status. Thus, those who have surplus of grains have definitely a superiority over those who are in deficit.

The details, showing the number of families, community-wise and divided into surplus, self-sufficient and deficit in grain are given in Table 13 below :

A careful study of table 12 reveals that only 13.09 per cent of the villagers grow surplus grins and 28.80 percent are self sufficient in grains whereas a very large population of 58.11 per cent (i.e. more than half the population) are in deficit.

Table No. 13
Showing Economic Conditions

Sl.	Community	Total number families	Surplus in grains		Self-sufficiency in grains		Deficit in grains	
			No.	Percentage	No.	Percentage	No	Percentage
1.	Oraon	113	17	15.04	33	38.05	53	46.90
2.	Ghasi	23		.....	..	....	23	100.00
3.	Chik-Baraik	11	1	0.09	1	9.09	9	81.82
4.	Lohra	12	..	...	1	8.33	11	91.67
5.	Kharwar	10	2	20.00	2	20.00	6	60.00
6.	Kumhar	6	..	...	2	33.33	4	66.67
7.	Munda	5	..	...	4	80.00	1	20.00
8.	Brahmin	2	2	100.00	..	...	..	...
9.	Rajput	2	2	100	..	...	..	...
10.	Hazam	2	1	50.00	1	50.00	..	...
11.	Mahli	1	..		...	..	...	1 100.00
12.	Dhobi	2	..	...	1	50.00		1 100.00
13.	Baniya	1	..	...	..	...		1 100.00
14.	Ahir	1	..		...	..	...	1 100.00
Total		191	25	...	55	...	111	...
Percentage		100.00	13.09	...	28.80	...	58.11	

III
Tribal Culture in Central India

I. Inroduction-Area, population and Myths of orign

The area

If one takes an aeroplane from Broach or Surat on the west coast of Gujarat and flies straight to the east to get down at Ranchi or Rourkela he would be flying over a line, a belt of about 160 km. to the north and south of which would form Central India covering parts of Gujarat and Maharashtra (this would be western Central India). Madhya Pradesh (the heartland of Central India) and parts of Bihar and Orissa (which would form eastern Central India). Here the Sabarmati, the Mahi, the Tapti, the Narmada, the Chanbal, the Maha, the Godawari, the Son and the Indravati with many of their tributaries traverse their rugged course in hilly terrain full of thick forests, at places almost inaccessible, in which live a major part of the tribal population of our country. Counting from west to east, some of the tribes living here are the Bhils, Dublas, Konkanas, Warlis, Korkus, Gonds, Baigas, Abujhamarhias, Kawars, Birhors and Oraons with dozens of their known and little-known brother-tribes.

Habitat

To get an idea of the habitat where these Central India tribes live, let us take Mandia district, which is one of the districts in Central India where there is a concentration of their population. It forms the south-east portion of the Jodhpur Division of Madhya Pradesh and lies between latitude 23° 22' and 22° 22' North and longitude 80° 1' and 81°

51' East. It has a total area of about 12,800 sq. km. The district form a part of the high and rugged table-land of the Satpura Hills which separates the cotton-growing country of the south from the wheat-growing region of the Malwa plateau in the north and is the watershed of three distinct river-systems. The district is dominated by the range of the Maikal Hills which generally increase in height from west to east. The elevation of the district varies form 445 meters above sea-level to 1,150 meters.

The principal river system here is that of the Narmada; a small tract in the south being drained by the Halen and the extreme north and north-west by the Johilla. The hills, rivers and forests give an unbeatable grandeur and picturesqueeness to the scenery of the district. The climate here is cool and exhilargating, the heat being dry and healthy, and the winter having occasional frosts. The rainy season is unhealthy. The Gond suffer very much from malaria and colds.

Another area in Central India which is almost a-bujh, not known, is Abujhmarh, one of the most unapproachable tribal areas in this region. It falls in Baster district and is inhabited by the Abujhmarhia also known as Hill Marhias. It has an average altitude from 830 to 1.000 meters although in some parts it goes up to 4,000 feet, especially in the centre. It is served by rivers like the Kotri, Naiberat,Gudran Kokmunda and many other small streams all of which drain into the river Indravati, which forms the southern border of the region. There are many clear perennial springs whose fresh water is used for drinking purpoes by the people.

On the northern and eastern slopes there are fine patches of sal and other ever-green trees, while on the hill tops and sloppes, exhausted by shifting cultivation, high grass andstunted trees are to be found Bamboo growas luxuiously in this region.

Here are found the jungle fowl, the snipe and the pea-fowl which the Marhias catch by special trap made for the purpose. Man-eating tigers are a great nuisance in the area. Pigs and bullocks, cowas and goats are domestic animals; fish and rats make items of Abujhmarhia food. In some parts of the region, bears are also found. In some villages their visits are frequent.

Thus, the Central Zone is traversed by different mountain systems from morth to south (the Aravaslli and the Sahyadri) and from west to east (the Vindhya and the Satpura) which cut it up into separate area where inter-communication is possible only along certain routes. The existence of forests and mountains has affected the migrations of people from north to south and has also affected the settlement of agricultural castes which are the backbone of the northern, central and southern zones.

Population

Let is go into the demographic details of the main tribes as found in this region. In Gujarat, according to the 1961 census, the tribal population was over 3.7 million. In 1961, the population of the major tribes was:

Bhils	1,124,282
Dublas	323,644
Dhodias	275,787
Gamits	158,703
Chodhras	143,576
Rathwas	135,730
Dhankas	128,024
Konkanas	110,054
Naikadas	108,029

I would include them in western Central Indian region for purpose of this paper.

Part of Maharashtra would also fall in western Central India and the important tribes here (1961 census) would be the following :-

Bhils	575,022
Malhar Koils.	274,244
Warlis	243,980

Thakurs	159,000
Konkans	212,836

Of the others Gonds (274,244), Korkus (50,279) and Andhs (30,261) should be included as living in the heartland of Central India. The total tribal population of Bihar, according to the 1971 census, is more then 4.9 million and in 1961 it was about 4 million. Out of this I would put the Oraons-647,444; Mundas-525,816; Santal-192,744 etc., in eastern Central India. Similarly, in Orissa, the 1971 census showed the tribal population to be about over 5 million. Numerically the most important of them (1961) figures) were :-

Bathudi	104,542
Bhutada	159,091
Bhuyan	156,878
Bhuminj	116,181
Gond	445,705
Khond	818,847
Kisan	125,668
Kolha	203,515
Oraon	129,061
Parja	159,866
Santal	411,181
Saora	311,614
Sabar	193,613

Many of them also I would put in eastern Central India. In Madhya Pradesh, which is the heartland of Central India, the total tribal population in 1971 was about 8.39 million, the most population as per 1961 census :-

Bhils	1,229,000
Gond	3,160,000
Kanwar	328,000

Kol	301,000
Korku	131,000
Orano	283,000
Saharia	165,000

Myths of Origin

Of the many legends of Central India, regarding the creation of the world, this one from the Gonds of Mandla is interesting :

At the beginning there was nothing but water. On its surface floated a lotus flower on which sat Mahadeo. When he saw nothing but water, he made a crow from the dirt of his body and sent it to find earth. The crow flew and flew till it came to rest on the claw of the great crab, Kakramal Kshattri. When the crow said 'Kao', the crab exclaimed, "At last after many days I have got something to eat." The crow replied, "Uncle, my father has sent me to you." The crab said, "Nephew, why have you come? Tell me quickly." The crow replied, "My father has sent me to get earth to make the world."

Then the two of them went to Singradip. There Nal Raja and Nal Rani had earth. After searching for a long time, the crab and the crow went to Nal Raja and Nal Rani and began calling them aunt and uncle and asked for some earth as a loan. They promised to give it and said. "Take some food and then go your way." Nal Rani prepared poison for the guests. When they had eaten, they became drunk and then unconscious. When they saw them safely asleep, Nal Raja and Nal Rani stole the earth and prepared to run away. But the crab awoke and caught them in its clawas and squeezed the earth out of their mouths and gave it to the crow.

Then the crow took the earth to Mahadeo. Mahadeo made seven leaf-cups of lotus leaves and put a little earth in each. He stirred it up in each cup and called for Makramal Kshattri. He said to her, "Now spin your web over the face of the sea." The spider prepared her web and Mahadeo put the seven cups of earth upon it and fanned them with a lotus leaf. With the breeze of his fanning, the earth was carried over th web and the seven kinds of earth were prepared-the block earth, the red earth, the milk earth, the barren earth, the gravel earth, virgin earth and swampy earth.

When all was ready, Mahadeo said to Bhimsen, "I have made the earth, but I do not know whether it is split or not." Bhimsen was pleased and said. "I will come and look." As he went, his feet sunk into the earth. But he lay down on the ground and rolled about, Thus, making the mountains.

Pardhan, bards of the Gonds, are great story tellers. About the origin of man they say that while the world was forming, setting like curds on the face of the water, the wind blew from the east and the world began to form towards the west. Then the wind changed and it formed to the east.

Then Mahadeo was born. He sowed seven kinds of her seed in seven seed-beds. The first was the sweet herb; the second was the herb that stays hunger; the third was the herb that makes one happy; the fourth was the herb that brings one all the newas; the fifth was the herb that if one eats it and then rubs a little dirt from one's body and makes something, that thing will live; the sixth was a sorrow-giving herb and the seventh herb give children.

After the herbs had been sown, the earth was still quaking and trembling. Mahadeo said to Parvati, "I am going to drive nails into the earth. You can eat all the herbs except the seventh; don't eat that." He took a gold axe with a silver handle and went to Kajliban Pahar. There he cut a sandalwood tree, made nails of the wood and fixed the earth in place.

But Parvati thought and thought. Why did he tell me not to eat the herbs in the seventh seed-bed? At last she could not resist it and cooked and ate. She was pregnant at once. She knew that Mahadeo was in Kajliban driving nails of sandalwood into the earth. She wanted to call him, but could not. She ate the fifth kind of herb, made a tiger from the dirt of her body, and told it. "From today you are king of the jungle. Go to Mahadeo; hide behind the trees and frighten him home."

The tiger went to Mahadeo and he threw some of the shavings of his nails at it. They rurned into wild dogs and drove it away. But Mahadeo went home to see what was the matter. When he saw that Parvati was pregnant he went to Bhagavan and said, "why did you let her become pregnant?" Bhagavan said, "Unless she is pregnant how will we people live in the world?"

In time Parvati gave birth to many boys and girls. She felt ashamed to be bearing so many at once and burried the babies under different trees. The best of the boys she kept; Mahadeo saw him and was pleased. But he said, "What have you done with the others?" So Parvati brought the other out. Mahadeo gave them names and divided them into tribes and clans, and arranged their marriages.

At the time of the Rama-Ravan war, a Gond and Gondin lived together in the thick jungle in the territory of Ravan. Mahadeo cursed those Gonds and said, "Until Rama comes to Lanka and you wash his feet and drink the water, you will have no children."

So when Rama went to Lanka, he met that Gond and Gondin and they washed his feet and drank the water. He gave them this blessing : "You will be Ravanbansi Gond and you will have three sons whose names will be Alko, Talko and Korcho." Then Rama killed all Ravan's followers save the Gond who went over to Rama's side. When Rama returned from Lanka he brought them to the other Gonds who were living in the thick jungle. These were Surjbansi Raj Gond and they had five sons, Parteti, Markam, Maravi, Dhurwa and Bhagadiya. The Ravanbansi and the Surajbansi lived together as brothers.

Ravan had lost his glory and his honour; he turned into Bara Deo. To Parteti he gave a dream. "Bara Deo will be born from both Ravanbansi and Sirajbansi. Make a platform of mud and erect a pillar for him." Parteti told the others his dream and they made a pillar. Then Bara Deo was born.

They all agreed that the youngest brother should have a bana and should worhsip Bara Deo, while the eldest should sit on the throne as Raja. Such was the order of Bara Deo. When the youngest boy, Bhagadiya, danced and played before Bara Deo, Parteti gave him. many presents-cattle, gold and silver. He said to him. From todyay you will be our *Pathari*. We will give you *Sikdam* and when any of us die you will have your share."

II. Material Culture and Economy

Material culture

The tribal's aesthetic sense can be appreciated from his selection of village sites and house construction. The plan of a tribal village gives the impression of energy, equality and community loyalty. The Gond like the Baiga have an eye for a good site. They set their villages in places convenient for *Bewar* but it is hard to believe that aesthetic considerations ae ignored. Bohi is a charming village with a waterfall near it and with a view of undulating hills dense with forest. There are other beautiful Baiga villages like Rupnidarar visited by every wind with vistas of great beauty just visible between its surrounding trees and Amadob in the quiet forest glades.

Outside the Oraon *basti* is a beautiful grove of trees called sarna, sacred to the principal village-deity called Sarna Burhia. Ancient custom forbids anyone to cut trees or branches of trees standing on the sarna groves. No *Bhuinhar* of the village may take or use of the wood of sarna trees. Other symbiotic tribes also have the village sarna, which is really artistic, soul-soothing and cool, where one would like to sit for hours and read or meditate. And if you want to see how aesthetic calculations count in the selection of a site you have to see the ashram of Gahra guru near Gai Guda, Rai*garh*, where he has created a magical place near a small waterfall with caves to live in and rest, forest trees growing one upon the other and fruit trees now young but happy in growing there.

In house construction nothing more spacious and beautiful than a kawar house has been witnessed in Madhya Pradesh. The thick, tidy mud walls, the relief ornamentation thereon, the long *parchhi* and the utilitarian rooms so uniformally made; are breathtakingly beautiful.

The fences around the tribal houses and the fields near them also very artistic. The Marhia weave a fence from branches of tress. It are stands erect in the form of a slanting, wavy but strong warf and weft giving a most pleasig impression to the eye and the mind. The Oraon *Pachri* is a mud wall about a metre high running at exact right angles around the house and the farm and is covered with country tiles to protect it from the rain. It looks very nice. Straightness, smoothness and geometrical arrangement of the tiles on it evoke the admiration of anyone who sees it.

Among the least known tribes of Madhya Pradesh are the Binjwars whom I studied in the Bilaspur district. They have an excellent sense of decorating their mud walls with designs and drawings in relief of elephants, horses with riders, sword-in-hand soliders, flowers, birds, the swastika, trees and creepers. They look exquisite on the clean walls. Decoration with relief designs of their taks and windowas is also found.

On some Binjwar house walls, there are coloured paintings made by the *Adolia* at the time of Diwali for which he gets some paddy. These paintings known as *putri* by the tribe consist of birds, beasts and hunters or of gods and goddesses.

Let us pass on to the artistic personal adornment of the tribes. One of the most artful tribes as far as personal decoration is concerned are th Mundas, who are found in a small number in Madhya Pradesh. Young Munda women are very fond of decorating their person with a large variety of ornaments. Ear-rings made of silver and even of gold and occassinally used. They wear for the arm brass bracelets, *sakom* and *kakana* lac bracelets called *lathi* brass armlets called *tar* and glass armlets called *churla.*

Similarly intricately designed ornaments for the neck and the nose are also there. The poorer Munda women use a peculiar artistic ear ornament made of plam leaf. Wooden combs called nakis and hair pins are used. Necklaces or *hisirs* made variously of coral, of kasi grass, of birni reed and of glass beads are also worn.

The Gond, Korku, and Pardhan women of Chhindwara. Betul, Seoni, Balaghat and Mandla districts use *hamel, bindiya* and karanphool which are lovely silver ornaments.

The Bhilala men and women almost compete with the Mundas in personal decoration. It is an eye filling sight to see well-dressed Bhilala girls in a fair where they look almost like a painter's dream come true of pristine beauty.

In the course of a cultural survey of tribal Madhya Pradesh, about twenty-four types of ladies hair dressing done on various and other occasions were noticed. In a study of the Bhilala of Dhar, ceremonial I found that it takes about four hours to do the hair of a Bhailala woman, it is so minutely and finely done. It was also observed that tribal women know how to perfume their favourite mahua oil with different flowers in different ways.

Most striking of all is their gaily coloured beadwork. The Murias wear bead bands, sometimes three or four of them round the head; keeping the hair in place. Round the neck are two or more broad bead collars and a profusion of necklaces made of coloured beads, tied symmetrically colourwise and designwise. A tribal woman may not have ornaments to put on but she can hardly afford to go without tattoo marks on her person. Tattooing is not merely meant for personal decoration but it has a magico-religious significance and a social bearing also. A study of tattoo marks will clearly show that there are patterns with specific names and meaning, e.g., among the Bhils we find such patterns as *ambe moidi*, i.e., a square and *sitan van* i.e., the garden of Sita.

Tribal dress is also full of colours and variegated designs. The Bhil-Bhilala dress have designs called *juoria attha* and *taharia*, on the body of a sari and *malia ka adya, thuddi, bod danda wala adya, jad, chup kulya, pola adya, kinar* and others on the pallu.

The headgear of the Bison-horn Marhia of Bastar is a rare artistic piece, made of the horns of a bison. The scarcity of bison horn makes it all the horns of a bison. The scarcity of bison horn makes it all the more valuable nd important. The cowrie decorations and peacock feathers artistically tied round it and the shine of the horn make it lovely to look at.

The Korku headgear for marriage is elaborately made from the plam leaf which is ceremonially brought from the tree and the artist names the designs he makes on them as *jhela, machhli, kalsa, solgola, bonhta, ful, bicchiya* and *tikiya.*

Let us pass on to their household articles. The Baiga make a variety of baskets, *e.g., sikoshi* is a aquare basket of board twiled bamboo strips 35 cm. square and 15cm. high. A cover is made to come right over the basket. The result is a double basket very useful for storing clothes.

Jhapi is a beautifully made basket for storing clothes, ornaments and dresses for the dance. It is made of strips of bamboo of various sizes. *Mara* is a shallow open basket, 23 cm. square and 13 cm. deep of bamboo strips. 25 cm. board plaited checkwise and used for baling out water from a stream which has been dammed for fishing. Then there are *mora, dhuti, dauri, dali, kikrahi, tukna, pitla* and others.

The basket which is carried by the Bhil women in the Bhagoria bazaar or which is used at the marriage time to carry the gift for the bride is also very artistic. Some of the bamboo-ware made by the tribal Pandos and the Turis are specimens of beautiful, strudy, technically perfect basketry. A small tribe called the Dhulia specialise in basket making or agricultural purposes. Their handicraft is pleasing aesthetically also.

The tribes also do beautiful wood-carving. As we move across the centre of th Muria country in Bastar we find more and more elaborate carving of wood used as decoration of the *ghotul,* which has stimulated artistic creation not only in the realm of personal decoration but also in wood-carving and wall-painting. The *chelik* desire that their *ghotul* really should be lovely as a bison's horns. In many of the Muria *ghotul* there are excellently carved pillars. They may be seen at Almer, Nayanar, Ramavand, and elsewhere. At Almer, one of the pillars has kiddari birds at top, another has tortoises. On the body of the pillars are carvings of the moon, boys and girls dancing the *Hulki* and elephants. At Nayanar one of the pillars is decorated with tortoises and another has hooded snakes projecting from all four concerns.

Wood-carving is done by the Gonds also. An example of this is provided by the door frames of Gond houses at Lahgadua, Chhindwara district. Each door frame has designs carved upon it, door boards are also sometimes carved profusely but with sobriety. The Baigas also know wood-carving. A few specimens of these may be seen in the museum of the tribal Research Institute at Chhindwara. Korku wood carving is at its best in their memorial *gatha* for a dead, on which are ceremonially carved the figures of a man, sometime on a horse back. On the top corners are the sun and the moon and in the top centre shown a symbolic spider and Binnayak (their god of well-being).

A survey of the tribal art of wood-carving will not be complete if the Marhia memorial pillar is not mentioned. It is a solid tall wooden slab, about 2.5 meters high and about .6 meter wide and .6 mete deep, on all sides of which scenes from daily life are depicted. The top of the pillar is well curved, with floral designs, and has a carved bird placed on it.

The art of making musical instruments is very well developed by some of the professional music-making tribes like the Pardhans and the Lanjhas. The stringed instrument with which the Pardhan does singing at the door of his Gond clients is known as bana which to him is the very birth-place and seat of Bara Deo, who appeared among men only when the *bana* was made. It is a simple instrument but when it is fully decorated with bells, peacock feathers and balls of coloured wood it looks very pretty.

A more fascinating fiddle is the one used by the Lanjhas, who are bards to the great kanwar tribe. They call it *benbaja* or *kathway.* It is slenderer and finer and instead of the bow a small plucking instrument is used to play on its strings. The instrument is so lovely that I rushed for it for many hot dusty km. from one Lanjha village to another of Rai*garh* district but even today I am a disappointed art collector and anthropologist. I have not yet been able to get one for my institute; but its mere sight has given me an imperishable pleasure.

Another field where we find most elaborate and

artistically rich material is the metal images and idols of the tribal deities, the most revered of whom is the Budhi Mata goddess of Bastar, who is represented by an elephant having a palanquin on its back in which is seated a small idol of the goddess. The Marhia Muria have Ghoda Deo on a horse back, Nag Deo or the serpent god and Firangi Deo or the god riding a horse with a gun in his hand. This and other metal images or idols found in Bastar are manufactured by an indigenous was process, which is used for hollow casting, in which the Bharewa specialise.

Economy

With the help of the material equipment some of which has been described above, the Central Indian tribes eke out their livelihood by undertaking many activities. Agriculture is their most important economic occupation. Agriculture may be settled or it may be shifting. How the latter works among the tribes of the region can be seen from Abujhmarh.

All the elders of a village allocate forest sites for cultivation to each family. There is no guarantee that a man will have the same plot as that allotted to him when *Kaghai* was previously cultivated. Usually, however, he is given the same plot.

Once the plots are allotted and cultivated, they are the private property of the cultivator.

The felling is done mostly by men. He is merely assisted by women and children. It is a very arduous task. Heavy timber is sometimes reserved for the purpose of fencing; other wood is left to dry through the heat of April and May. These two months being leisure months for the Marhias, most of the ceremonies and marriages are preformed during this period. There are a series of dancing parties arranged from village to village.

Towards the end of May when the wood is sufficiently dry. the *ksyeq Gaita* fixes the day for firing. All the villages gather together. *Kasyeq Gaita* takes the initiative by firing first dried bush weed. Then the whole congregation joins. This operation takes about two to three days normally depending on the size of the plot. In some cases when the wood is not sufficiently dried it may even take a week.

Between firing and sowing there is a very little time left when the Hill Marhia has to exert his maximum. Fences have to be put up and field houses have to be constructed for constant safty and watch. They are so strong that even a wild buffalo finds it difficult to break through.

Sowing is commenced immediately after the first monsoon showers which are usually in the month of Na (May-June). The Kasyeq Gaita performs the ceremony with usual offerings of eggs and chickens to the village Mother. At first early ripening varities of hill millets are swon. The shwoing is done by broad casting. Til is also sown to mark individual holding. Later on the varieties are sown. From the information gathered the following crops are most commonly grown : Kasra ikka, Arku, Gendku (Millets), Pupul, Udud (Pulses), Nai (Peas), Jirra Nudgu (Til) and Kakad zonna (Jwar) which is grown almost in negligible quantity. Immediately after sowing and heavy showers of rain, there is a rapid growth of vegetation of all kinds. There is a plentiful crop of shoots form the stumps of the trees already felled. There is a thick growth of grass as well. Weeding becomes a necessity. There are some lazy cultivators who do not carry out any weeding but its necessity is being appreciated in all the villages. But even their best efforts appear to be indequate, as the growth of grass and other weeds is very excessive and rapid.

The ripening fields present a very picturesque site. The thick forest growth with tall tress on the slope of the hill and *penda* clearing with field houses, men and women working hard is a rare sight of idyllic beauty. *Penda* cultivation is a riotous growth of variety of crops. Various grains and pulses are sown all over the field. There are no separate fields for different crops. Cucumver and bean creepers over poles add much to the beauty.

Because of unsystematic sowing, reaping is an arduous task. It has to be an electroc and slow performance. The cut crops are stacked on the wooden platforms, *paki*, constructed on the fields. Threshing floor plastered with mud is also made ready before the reaping. In the centre of this, a bamboo railing on posts is erected. With this support, threshing is done by men by dancing and prancing. Bullocks are not used in hills expect in Khalpati areas. After threshing the grain is winnowed by men only. It is the usual way, the man standing on a raised platform and pouring the grain from a baske. If there is no wind, winnowing is done by fanning by baskets. In harvesting help of others is always needed. Both the operations are mostly done by joint efforts of the families of the villages, but each cultivator is required to pay in some way or the other to those who come to help. By way of wages, all men who work have to be fed and given wine or *sulphi* (sago plam juice). This has to be done daily. Sometimes wages are paid by giving 2 or 3 pailes of grain daily.

The winnowed grain is then carried to granaries, which are either situated in the living house itself on the field or any other convenient place in the jungle on way to the village. There is no fear of any theft. The grain is stored in a huge basket-like construction whose inside is plastered with mud and which is sealed from the top. The grain can Thus, be preserved even for a period of two years. The grain is never a joint prperty of the village. It belongs to the individual.

III. Socoal Structure and Political Organisation

Social Structure

Let us have a glimpse of the social structure of the Central Indian tribes.

As for the social structure of th Bhil tribe they are organised into a number of large patrilineal groups known as *atak, odakh, got* or *kul.* An *atak* is a clan consisting of a number of lineages, each bearing the same name and claiming descent from the same mythical ancestor and hence assuming kinship with each other. This kinship group includes all those wonen who marry into the lineages of the clan. The clan is an exogamous group. The priciple of exogamy is sought to be extended among these Bhils to all such persons who are the personal affines of the clans or members of such clans as have given their dauthers in marriage to this clan in the past. But since a strict enforcement of this principle would reduce the field of choice to a very great extent, exogamous restrictions are applicable only within a span of five or six generations. Actually, however, the Bhils do not remember their affines generally beyond two or three generations.

The lineages seem to have a tendency to concentrate in particular tracts of land. Most of them claim to have migrated from some part to the country which they claim as their original home. The Pargis say they came from Ajawa in Rajasthan. Everywhere there is seen a process of segmentation continually at work in an atak. Whenever the size of the lineage concentrated over a particular area becomes too large or whenever a particular segment cannot pull on well with the rest of the group, it would move to another area and settle down in its new hunting grounds. Occasionally a group might be driven away by another, sometimes the times may be bad and a segment moves out to areas of hope. Thus, today lineages bearing the name of the same *atak* are found scattered in many places. The villages Thus, would be known, as in the Ratlam district, as a camp, *chhavai* of a particular *atak* segment.

As a norm, the Bhil village would consist of a single dominant lineage and a few others belonging to affinal lineages. The headman would be the person who lead the segment from it original home to this camp or his male descendent (generally the senior-most). The other families who settle in this village have to seek the permission of the village headman.

The Bhil headman is known as *todvi* in Ratlam, and *vasawo* in Khandesh and Rajpipla. He holds on enviable position in the village. His advice is sought by other villagers, Bhils and others, in the time of need. He can by his prestige silence dissidents, discipline a drunkard or control a stubborn husband. He can settle quarrels between two villagers and ask debts to be paid off or postponed. In festivals he holds the key position, e.g. when Holi comes, it vesits his house first and it is his previlege to light the holi bonfire.

The *Punjaro* is an expert medicine man, well-versed in

the indigenous pharmacopia. The *madvi* or the badvo is the priest of th village. The pardhan in Rajpipla is an official in bigger villages who can proxy the headman and can attend to certain minor matters. The *Kotwar* attends to the touring officers and conveys governmental orders to the people. The Bholi in Ratlam is a lowe caste person who plays on a special drum on a Bhil death. He is also a genealogist. So is a Bhat for some Bhils who have crossed over from Rajasthan. The *Gori* is the cattle-grazer of the Bhils.

The basic residental group is the family, consisting of a man and his wife, their children, wives of their sons, their grandchildren and so on. The sons separate after marriage from their parents. The father is the dominant figure and exercises a great deal of control over the behaviour or his sons and their familes, even when separated from him. He can even disinherit his children as has been done by the headman of Chhawni Bhabor in the Raltam district with his eldest son.

Gond Social Structure

Gonds organise themselves on the basics firstly of *garh* which literally means 'fortress', 'citadal' or 'hill' in Hindi, But it also signifies a territorial unit. Some of the Gond *garhs* obviously derive their names from the forts and citadals which in mediaeval times were manned by the Gond chiefs and their retainers; or from old village sites or hills which gave their names to the sorrounding area to form a territorial unit, *garh.* The Gond families and clans living in a certain *garh* assumed the name of this territorial unit as their *garh* name which was retained even after the original habitat was abandoned for settling elsewhere. The old *garh* was remembered when they had to lay the soul of a departed clan member to rest; which invariably had to be done in the original ancestral home village. It may so happens that the original *garh* name may be replaced by another where the Gonds settled after leaving the first one. Bhu Singh Rajnegi enumerates 21 such *garhs*. These originally must have been exogamous; but *garh* exogamy is not strictly enforced now a days. They lay more emphasis on another organisational principle, viz., that of *gotia*.

A Gond *gotia* or *kur* comprises a group of persons who belive that they are descendents in the male line of common ancestor. While a man never changes his *gotia* a woman gets a new *gotia* through her husband; children take the *gotia* of the father. The Gond practise *gotia*-exogamy; a person marrying in his/her own clan gets outcast. In eastern Mandla, Fuchs listed 47 clans, some of which are: Ayam, Dhurwa, Koram, Kumhra, Markam, Marram, Maurawi, Neti, parteti, Pussm, Sarrati, Tekam, Uika and Workera. Some of these clan names are common to the whole Gond group. Most of them are in the Gondi language. Some clans bear the names of animals, others of plants and trees.

All the Gonds clans of eastern Mandla are organised in groups of 18 clans but 18 is not an exact number. Members of each group of these clans (phratry) call each other *saga bhai* (blood) brothers and marriage within the same phratry is forbidden.

Among the Gond another important principle of social organisation is what is sometimes called *deval* or clan-god worship wherein the emphasis is not on the names and nature of clan-gods but on their number. The Gond accordingly do not care by what names they should address their clan-gods as long as they know how many there are to be worshipped. This is not found in any other caste or tribe. In the Gond villages near Mandla the following gods are worshipped-Bada Deo, Dulha Deo, ratwali, Dehriwale, Poiter-Poi, Dewala and Deshiwala. Gond clans which worship seven gods worship all these seven (some informants give others names for these seven gods).

Some of these Adivasis have a very interesting and a peculiar institution : the dormitory for the adolescents. These are called *ghotuls* by the Murias of the Bastar district. A *ghotul* means a hut where the bachelor boys and the maidens of the village sleep together at night. In the Murias, the boys and the girls of the age-range 6 to 16 years do not sleep in their own homes. They are required to sleep in the ghotul of the village. The boys are called *cheliks* and the girls motioris. Every evening, the motiaris will clean the *ghotul* and they welcome the *cheliks*. Then commences their folk dance programme which continues till late at night,

Then they sleep-every *chelik* having one *motiari* as his partner. In the *ghotul* they have to be much disciplined in their behaviour. One who fails to do his duty is punished. Laziness is ridiculed. If any of the villagers is in need of manual labour the *ghotul* members have to make *Sharma-dana.*

Kinship

For the general pattern of kinship here, Iravati Karve says : "The Central Zone includes Central India i.e. Rajasthan, Madhya Pradesh Orissa, Gujarat and Maharashtra. In this zone people speak languages predominatly Sanskritic, though it also includes many tribes speaking Drvidian and Mundari languages. The kinship organisation in the Central Zone, through modelled on the northern pattern, showas some very significant differences which can best be described as being due to cultural contact with the other two zones, especially the Southern Zone of the Dravidian language area."

The Political Organisation

It was not recognised so far by many that the tribals in India have different kinds of political organisations. But a detailed ethnographic study of the tribes from the political point of view and a sociological study of Bhil crimes has led me to conclude that the tribes to have different political organisations ranging from anarchy to democracy through monarchy. I am describing the political organisations of the Oraons and Bhils, two Central Indian tribes, below :-

The Oraons : A Democracy

When the Oraon villages felt the necessity of working together for protection from natural and supernatural foes, arose the *Parha* organisation modelled on the old Oraon hunting groups though formed not upon the principle of association of kindred but upon the basis of local contiguity. The *Parha,* as it now exist, is a confederacy of a number of neighbouring villages with central organisation known as the *Parha Panch.* In the *Parha* organisation we find the ancient spirit of the clan-group clothed in a new body suited to the new environment and changed conditions of life.

Although in the outer form of the organisations- in the names of its different functionaries and the nature of their formal functions we see the influence of the Aryan Hindu monarchical system, in its inner soul-in its ruling idea-its aims and objects and the methods of pursuing such objects, we recognise characteristic institutions of the Dravidian Oraon who is essentially a democrat and an animist.

Each Oraon *Parha,* as we have said, consist of a number of villages. One of the villages is called the *Raja* (king) village another the *Dewan* (Prime Minister) village, a third the *Panrey* (Clerk of the Crown) village, a fourth the *Kotwar* (Bailiff) village, and so on. Such of the villages as have got no such denominations are known as *praja* (subject) villages. The *Raja* village is the head village of the *Parha;* some headman of this village presides at meetings of the *Parha Panch.* The *Pahan* of this village or, in his absence, the *Mahato* may act as the *Kartana,* and in his absence any elderly *Bhuinhar* of the village may be chosen to officiate as the *Kartana* at a social or socio-religious ceremony of the *Parha.* In some *Parhas* however, there is a separate *Kartana* villge, and the Pahan or, in his absence, the *Mahato* or other elderly *Bhuinhar* of such village officiates as *Kartana* at a social or socio-religious gathering. The *Mahato* or other headman of the *Kotwar* village officiates as the *Kotwar* of the *Pahra* . An iron spear with a long bamboo handle is ordinarily carried by him to a *Parha*-meeting as his insignia of office. Nowadays, sometimes only a thick bamboo-staff is used instead of spear. With the exception of the *Parha-Kotwar* the other functionaries of a *Parha* have no particular insignia of office at the present day. It may be noticed here that some of the Oraon emblems of office appear to be considered as possessing a special virtue of te nature of mana. Thus,, the *Parha-Kotwar,* as we have seen while distributing the game bagged during a hunt, gives a stroke of his bamboo stick to each hunter as the latter takes up his share of the game, and thereby would appear to mysteriously impart mana to the hunter; and the straw whip (korra) used by the *Dhangar-Kotwar* to maintain discipline amongst the young bachelors during the dances, and the whip made of sabai grass used by the spirit-doctor to maintain discipline among his disciplines and also to induce spirit-possession, would appear to have been, in their estimation, rods of occult power. In fact the whip of subai grass used by the Oraon magician and spirit-doctor is still regarded with awe and is regularly marked with vermilion as a sacred object.

Although every functionary of the *Parha* no longer possesses a distinctive badge of office, every village of the *Parha* has its own distinctive flag and other badges which may not be used by any other villages unless ceremonially presented by the village whose exclusive privilege it is to use them.

The *Parha* system which grouped men of several clans together. evidently marked a further advance on the former socio-political hunting clan-groups or the later village-communities. It was a larger whole with a greater complexity of structure. The establishment and maintenance of law and order, and the settlement of disputes between one village and another, naturally came to be added to the list of the recognised functions of the *Parha* council.

Each village would co-operate in the pursuit of common objects of the federation. These common objects were, broadly speaking, the procion of the allied villages from human and non-human foes, from natural and supernatural dangers that beset them on all sides, and generally, securing 'luck' for themselves. Each village was allotted a special function such as that of the *Raja*, the *Dewan*, the *Kotwar*, etc., in the common work of the *Parha*. The different villages of the *Parha* still hunt together, fight together, and on stated occasions meet together in dancing trysts, social feasts, and deliberative and judicial committees. But under present conditions, there is little room for the existence of militant or even of law-giving federations, and practically the only matters in which the authority of the *Parha* is still supreme are those relating to social and magico-religious taboos. The 'luck' of the *Parha* is the main thing which the *Parha* council has always had to look after, and at the present day, it is practically their only legitimate concern. It is the breach of certain social and magico-religious taboos that are believed to affect the 'luck' of the *Parha* and even of the tribe. Of such taboos the most important are those against sexual union between Oraons of the same clan or of prohibited degrees of relationship, and taking cooked food at the hands of a non-Oraon. Again, it is the proper observance of the *Jatra-dances* and of the great annual hunts that ensus the 'luck' of the villages comprising the *Parhas* concerned. Besides cases of infringement of certain taboos, disputes regarding boundaries between two villaes and such other mattes as the village *Panchayats* cannot decide or in which their decisions are not accepted, are laid before the *Parha Panch* for deliberation and verdict. The *Kotwar* of the *Parha* has to *excute* the decrees of the *Parha panch.*

Stronger even than the bond between the different villages of a *Parha* is its link with a Dudh-Bhaya village. Whereas any village of *Parha* may no wdays sever its connection with the *Parha* and go over to another *Parha,* the old bond between a *Parha* and its Dudh-bhaya village is inalienable. A *Dudh-Bhaya* (lit, milk-brother) or foster brother. Almost every Oraon *Parha* has one, and sometimes two, *Dudh-Bhaya* villages. As Presh *Dudh-Bhaya*alliances are no longer formed, the rites and ceremonies by which the bond used to the created are no longer remembered. In fact, some of the Oraons whom we questioned about it apper to regard it as a natural and notanartificial bond. They would have us believe that, in every case, some ancestor of the Bhuinhars of a *Dudh-Bhaya* were related to each other as cross-cousins, and that the mother of such ancestor of *Dudh-Bhaya* village having died soon after she had given birth to him, he was nursed by the mother of his cross-cousin. This explanation is obviously a modern speculation based on the etymological signification of the term *Dudh-Bhaya.* But even if the relationship was in reality (as we believe) an artificial one at its inception, it is now regarded not only as a 'milk relationship' but even as a 'blood relationship', By such alliance, the village comes to be regarded as 'of one blood' with all the villages of the *Parha,* and is bound to take their part in all quarrels and fights (as formerly they did in all blood-feuds) with other villages and *Parhas.* So intimate is the bond of union between a particular *Parha* and its *Dudh-Bhaya* village that although material relations may be, and often are formed between Bhuinar families (not belonging to the same clan) of different villages of the same Parha, such relations are not permissible between a *Bhuinhar* family of the *Dudh-Bhaya* village and a *Bhuinhar* family of any of the villages of the *Parha* of which it is a *Dudh-Bhaya,* although they may belong to clans other than its own.

The Bhils: A Pre-state People

Provisionally I will put the Bhils as being a community having no organised state in the sense that, at times, though they did have a centralised authority like a prince on top at the capital for the area, the tribal people were not consciously organised to form a body politic. The usual mechanism to rule over the people was to portion out land to *thikanedars* under certain conditions. These *thikanedars* would collect land revenue from the people and leave them at that. That is, the organised rule did not reach up to the people, the main agencies of ruling over them was the king and his *thikanedar*, and Thus, the *Bhil* community was not made a part of the body politic. As a result of this the Bhils maintained their own traditional rules and mostly followd the pattern of law prevalent in a community based on kinship.

That the people were not a part of the state is amply proved by the inquiries of Mr. Willongbby that the Bhils were kept quiet by the establishment all over their district of strong military posts. Misbehaviour on the part of the Bhils was always severely punished. If a whole village was at fault it was generally attacked and burnt to the ground and its people of both sexes and every age put to the sword.

It is because of this kind of political organisation (or lack of it) that the Bhils rose against the Government in their areas. The following will sum up their main revolts :

(1) They rose against the Marathas in the 18th century. They were given severe punishment by the Marathas for this.

(2) They revolted against the Britishers in 1800. Captain Briggs in 1828 attempted to subdue them. Till 1828 there were so many Bhil revolts that in that year the Collector of West Khandesh said, “Only after twenty years there is a

continuous peace of six months in this land of the Bhils."

(3) In 1846, Kuvar Jivo Vasawo did not like the interference of the foreigners in his own affairs and he rose against the Government.

(4) In 1857, Bhagoji Naik in Ahmadnagar and Kajar Singh in Satpuda fought against the Government and looted the Government treasury passing from Indore to Bombay and helped Tatya Tope, the famous leader of the 1857 War of Independence. They could not be subdued for two more years. After they were subjugated the subsequent history was one of peace.

(5) The Rajpipla Bhils also showed a history of disorder for a long-time. The British Government had to interfere in the affairs of Rajpipla in 1820 and one reason for this was the urgent need to change the disorderly Bhils into peaceful and industrious subjects.

I do not want to go into details of the history of Alirjapur, Barwani, Chhota Udepur and Mathwad because they follow more or less the same pattern as described above. The Bhils in many of these areas are still at the community level of culture and instead of going to the courts of law for a wrong done to them, manage it themselves and also follow probably as a corollary of the above, the practice of blood-feud. I am working on the crime problem among the Bhils of Alirajpur and one of the reasons why there is this peculiar pattern of crime as found in Alirajpur is to be found in the political history of the area.

Leadership and Panchayats

Let me in passing give an idea of how these two political institutions work among our tribes.

Leaders in Abujhmarh, for example, are so mostly by virtue of the institutional arrangement in their society. Persons who are heads of certain institutions are also the leaders of the tribe-leadership is hereditary. The most influential and powerful man is the *Pargana Manjhi.* Nothing can take place inside his *marh* without his knowledge and none can move in the area and extract any information, cooperation or help from the Marhias without his permission.

The visitors have to contact the *Manjhi* before they enter any village. As a representative of the people, he goes round his *marh* periodically and keeps himself informed of the affairs and conditions of the villages and their inhabitants. Whenever some instructions from the Tahsildar or Collector are to be conveyed to the villagers, the *Manjhi* goes from village to village carrying the message. His role is mostly political and organisational.

He is the arbitrator of disputes within his *pargana* and is approached by the *patels* when they find the settlement of disputes difficult. His authority is based as much upon the goodwill of the Abujhmarhias as upon the power which he traditionally holds by right of birth.

The *Patel* is the leader of a village. Though his authority and influence are subject to that of the *Pargana Manjhi*, he commands great respect from and influence in his villages. His jobs are multifarious.He has to see that each family in the village gets sufficient land for penda cultivation and earns its livelihood. He has to take into consideration the size of and also the number of able-bodied persons in the family. During the critical times, persons approach him for help. In all matters of importance he consults the village council.

The Gaita is the religious leader of a village. He is responsible for worshipping the village deities. He has also to perform the duties of a sorcerer and medicine-man. In the hierarchy of power and prestige, he is next only to the *Patel.* He also gets patients from other villages. He is expected to provide food and shelter to them.

The *Perma* in a Marhia village is the worshipper of the village deity, *mata.* He makes periodical offerings by way of sacrifice to the deity and prays for protecting the village against calamities and epidemics.

Every village also has a Panchayat. literally the Council of Five. All adult men are members of this body. (women are not alowed to become its members). Whenever the Abujhmarhias want to shift their village from one site to another, the council would assemble and decide as to when, and where they should settle. At the new site distribution of land for house construction and *penda* for each family is again decided by the Council.

When any order is received in the village through the *Manjhi*, the *Patel* convenes a meeting of the Council and a decision of collecting the head-tax of Rs. 1.25 from the village only in the Council. Marriages are invariably settled and the amount of bride-price determined in, marital irregularities or disloyalties reported to, and all matters of religious rites, of periodical offerings to deities and of initiation ceremonies decided by this body.

Besides these socio-religious functions, the Marhia Council dispenses justice to aggrieved parties belonging to the village. A complainant approaches the *Patel* first. He summons the Council members, who as they already know the facts of the case, do not usually want the narration of the complaint before them. Outsiders are invited to this meeting if they are known to be somehow involved or can give evidence in the matter. The Marhias distinguish between civil and criminal offences in practice though not theory. Civil offences are those which violate the authority, possessions or prestige of a person. The other offences like hurt, injury or theft are criminal. Both the parties are heard and decision arrived at on the merit of the case. Punishments may vary from small fines for a drink through a feast for the whole village to wholesale turning out of the wrong-doer from the village.

Cases which cannot be decided by the Council are reported to the *Manjhi* for decision. If his decision is not acceptable to anyone of the parties the *Manjhi* approaches the *Panch Mukhia* who is supposed to be a most informed and wise man because of his wider contacts. He is the final appellate authority and no one dares question his decision.

IV. Faiths and Beliefs

Let us take the beliefs of these tribes about the critical periods of life. The Bhils believe that ancestors again take birth in their own family. In order to know which ancestor is born with the birth of a child they take a small vessel full of water with a grain of rice in it. Then they would go on dropping grain after grain in the water taking the name of each dead man in the family. That ancestor is believed to have been reborn with whose name the rice-grain touches the bottom placed rice-grain. Among the Sonars of Vindhya Pradesh, the names of ancestors are given to the children because they are thought to have taken a rebirth.

In a difficult delivery among the Mandla Adivasis a hole in the house roof is made. A virgin girl brings water from the river and this is passed from hand to hand along a line of men and Thus, up to the roof. The expectant woman stands beneath and three mouthfuls are poured into her open mouth. Sometimes the magician waves a winnowing basket the expectant mother and says, "Come out girl, you will soon be clearing rice, you will soon be grinding millet and fetching water."

One of the most general and vital faith beliefs of the Adivasis is in their clan totem which is an animal, either edible or harmless or dangerous and feared, more rarely it may be a plant or a force of nature like rain or water which stands in a particular relation to the whole as its tutelary spirit and proctctor; it sends oracles and though otherwise dangerous the totem knows and spares its children. The members of the totem are under a sacred obligation not to kill or destroy their totem, to abstain from eating its meat or from any other enjoyment of it. It is hereditary either through the maternal or the paternal line. The members of the same totem are not allowed to enter into sexual relations with each other. This is known as *totemic exogamy*. All these restrictions on totem members *vis-a-vis* the totem are known as totoo.

In Adivasi marriages, the role of belief can be seen almost at every stage. I will give only a few examples. They believe that it its a sin to marry in one's won clan as explained earlier. After a wedding is over among the Bhils, the bride is taken to the grain bins at her husband's house and asked if they are empty or full. If she says they are full, it is believed that she brings fortune and fullness. If she says they are empty she is supposed to bring with her misery and misfortune.

In adult life one encounters many moments which are believed in by almost all Adivasis. If a Bhilala going on a businesss trip meets a monkey he believes that his work will not be successful. Again if some one sneezes or he knocks at something he feels that he will fail in his work. A large number of brids and beasts are also ominous, Certain things foretell the arrival of a guest and some forebode death in the house. Similarly dreams are also believed in. The tribals feel that they can meet their dead relatives in dreams when they tell the dreamer what he or she, the dead person, wants. a tiger seen in the dream means the birth of a he-calf to the cow in the house, a buffalo signifies an encounter with a witch sometime or other; a serpent signifies only a rope in actule life; if a marriage party is seen in one's dream it forebodes some death in one's family but a river with turbid water seen in a dream signifies only suffering from cold.

Among the Halbas if a person has been killed by a tiger the people go out and if any remains of the body are found, these are burnt on the spot. The priest is then invoked to bring back the spirit of the deceased. This essential precaution is taken by him by suspending a copper ring on a long thread above a vessel of water. He then burns butter and sugar on the fire muttering incantations while the people sing songs and call on the spirit of the dead to return. The thread swings to and fro and at length the copper ring falls into the pot and this is taken as a sign that the spirit has come and entered the vessel. The mouth of the vessel is immediately covered and it is buried or ket in some secure place. The people believe that unless the dead man's spirit is secured it will accompany the tiger and lure solitary travellers to deruction. This is done by calling out and offering them tobacco to smoke and when they proceed in the direction of the voice the tiger springs out and kills them. And they think that a tiger directed in this manner growas fiercer and fiercer with every person whom it kills.

The Adivasis have many beliefs regarding their economic life. The Baigas were established in the practice of *bewar* or shifting cultivation by Bhagwan himself who, when he called all the tribes of the world together to make a king, at first chose the Baiga. But Nanga Baiga begged that the Gond, his brother, might be king in his place. Bhagwan was pleased at this request and as a mark of his favour took Nanga Baiga by the hand and placed him on his throne by his side. He granted his prayer to make the Gond king but he gave the Baiga an even greater blessing. He said, "You will make your living from the earth. You will dig roots and eat them. You will cut wood and carry it on your shoulders. Your wife will pick leaves and sell them. You must not tear the breast of your Mother, the earth, with the plough like the Gond and other Hindus. You will cut down trees and burn them and sow seeds in the ashes. But you will never become rich for if you did, you would foresake the earth and then there would be no one to guard it and keep its nail in place." Then Bhagwan showed the Naga Baiga how to cut *bewar* and sow seeds in the ashes of burnt trees. This legend is told and believed throughout the length and breadth of the Baiga country.

In the Bihu Shikar of the Oraons persons of the other neighbouring villages besides those from one's own meet one summer day carrying flags, pipes, drums and dholaks and hunting implements. Thus, they go for hunting to the jungle. Before they start, a black fowl is sacrificed to the goddess in every house and the blood is sprinkled on all those who go on hunting. It is believed that by this no danger would fall on them and they would get enough game. They return from the jungle in not less than a week. The persons who are left in the villages have to observe complete chastity, lets danger should fall on those who are out on hunt. When the hunters are expected back in the villages, they are received with caremonies.

The Adivasis also have great faith in magic. The Baiga regard themselves as the most powerful magicians in the world. They are regarded with awe and veneration by other tribes and communities. Even the Brahmins who live in their neighbourhood consult them in every crisis, for the fertility of a barren wife, the success of an intrigue, the ripening of the harvest and the recovery of stolen goods.

The Baiga's charms are believed to help the growth of crops, the potency of the bridegroom, the frustration of witches and the protection of the village against bears and tigers. The highest grade of the Baiga magician is the *Dewar*, who is competent to perform agricultural and other rites, he can close the village boundaries against the man-eating tiger; he can stop earthqurkes by driving a nail in a tree. An ordinary *Gunic* confines his activities mainly to the war against diseases.

Some of the diseases of men, women and children and also of cattle are traced by Bhils to *dakans*, evil-spirited women, who are belived to practise black magic, which they use for vengeance on any body against whom they have a grudge. The *dakan* takes the form of a cat or a serpent or turns into a pig or a calf and in any one of those forms she goes to the house of her victim and eats him or her away or inflicts illness on that person. She can also eat bullocks, buffaloes, etc, not to mention milk, curd and food.

Many of the Adivasis believe in a supreme deity like the Bara Deo of the Gonds or the Bhagwan of the Bhils. They also believe in some of their god heroes like Lingo Pen of the Gonds or Raja Panth of the Bhils or Bhimsen or Laxman Jati of the Pardhans. The Supreme deity is believed to have his family, each member of which is a major god or goddess. In fact, some of them weave the whole cosmos around a single god-family.

Regarding their belief about the sun and the moon and other heavenly bodies, I will mention only the Bhuiyas, who believe that fire and lighting are the children of the sun and the stars, the children of the moon. One day the moon invited the sun to dinner and gave him very nice food. The sun asked what it was. The moon said, she had cooked her own children and on this the sun went home and cooked all his children and ate them and this is the reason why there are no stars during the day. But his eldest sun fire went and hid in a tree and his daughter the lightning went hither and thither so that the sun could not catch her. And when the night came again and the stars came out, the sun saw how the moon had deceived him and, therefore, cursed her saying that she should die for fifteen days in every month. This is the reason for the waxing and waning of the moon. Ever since this event, fire has remained hidden in a rengal tree and when the Bhuiyas want him they rub two pieces of its wood together and it comes out.

Beliefs and faiths have been explained in many ways by scholars. The tribes have this remarkable conception of nature, that is they think that the world is populated by a multitude of spiritual beings which are malevolent or benevolent to them. They attribute nature's causation to these spirits and demons; they consider all animals, plants, inanimate objects animated by them and also believe that human beings have also souls which can leave their habitation and enter into other beings. Death, imagery, shadowas and reflections must have brought about this. Probably this arises from the need to explain the day to day phenomena which otherwise the Adivasis cannot understand.

Thus, beliefs provide them a ready-made solution to many pressing problems not only outside social life but also in society. They can meet the crises of life with confidence; they can also use beliefs in a technical way and help their daily works. Beliefs give them an explanation of their social institutions and this provides them with security. It also reduces tension which would otherwise easily come in a life which is so hazardous.

But beliefs also keep them bound to the old and the existing. They do not allow any innovations and Thus, socio-economic development is obstructed by many beliefs. The Baiga, for instance, who believes that it is sinful to take to plough cultivation will hesitate to improve his methods of agriculture and this ultimately would be to his disadvanage. We have, therefore, to understand the functional and the other roles of beliefs in order to bring in improvement in Adivasis economic and social life.

Of the many tribal festivals in Central India, it may be

mentioned that the Kolams celebrate this festival before and after the rainy season when the village priest, *Bhagat,* draws a line before the boundary of the village with the help of a spear. Hens, eggs, pieces of turmeric, vermilion etc., are buried at a spot near where the line is drawn. The deity represented by three stones is worshipped. Then they dance for the whole night. No one is allowed to enter the village with any footwear on for five days and fines are imposed on those who break this rule. No one, including the guests, is allowed to leave the village on this day. On the following day a goat is sacrificed and its meat is then distributed amongst the villagers and a feast is held.

There is a festival known as Bara Deo which is observed by the Raj Gonds. The hair of a wild cow are pressed in a solver socket to make a fan which is then wrapped in a red cloth and kept in a new earthern pot tied to a branch of the mahua tree. In this pot the Bara Deo is believed to reside. On the festival day, the sacred pot is taken down by the son-in-law of the village priest. It is put in a basket and carried to the village in a procession to the accompaniment of music; from where after a while it is taken to a water front and given a bath. A sacrifice is offered to it there. After all this is over, the pot is put back on the tree. The ceremony is repeated in the month of Bhadrapad.

The tribals of Central India have their own peculiar recreations consisting of different types of colorful dances, melodious songs and witty riddles. Among the Korkus the bride's party puts literary 'obstacles' to the groom's party by setting some riddles to them for solution. Unless and until the riddle is solved the marriage cannot take place. Here are some examples :

1. I am milking the staff after sending away all the crows. Tell me what I am doing.
2. I show the way to thousands and look at a thousand faces. What am I?

We take leave of these highly cultured people, about whose many other aspects of culture we could not see, much with a prayer which is sung among the Korkus of th Mahadeo Hills :

May my eyes be full of lustre,

May my memory be sharp,

May my preceptor be kind unto me,

May I not forget what I have learnt,

May I not forget my art.

IV
The World of Buxas

The Buxas are still living in their past, notwithstanding the fact that hte world around them is changing at a terrific speed. With the present full of tension and turmoil and the figure holding out only uncertainties, they not only love to think and talk of their past in terms of their royal ancestry, their magical and spiritual powers and attainments and their lordship over the Tarai but daggedly cling to it.

In this chapter, we propose to describe briefly the origin, religious beliefs, material culture and level of education of the Buxas because this would help us later in finding out the causes of the socio-economic disintegration and resultant problems with which they are beset to-day and which we propose to deal with in subsequent chapters.

Origin

The Buxas and their neighbours, the Tharus, are kinderd races, Both of them claim royal blood from the female side. According to a Tharu legend, the King of Tarai was defeated by an invader in the remote past. Then the women of royal Place took refuge in the jungle alongwith the *chamars* and *sais* of the place. From them sprang the two indigenous races of Tharus and Buxas, the fromer being descended from chamars and the later from the *saises*.

The Buxas of Baspur claim desent from Raja Jagatdeo[2], a great warrior of Rajasthan. who was a worshipper of Druge (Druga) and who offered his head to her. The Buxas claim to have brought Durga (now known as Kashipur Devi) to Tarai, The narial (palm nut) offered to the deities is symbolic of his head.

Some Buxas say that Jagatdeo had two sons, Chittaur and Nandhaur or Anandhar. While Tharus are the descendants of the fromer, the Buxas have descended from the latter. There are yet others who maintain that Nandhaur (or Anandhaur) was a brother, and not the son of Raja Jagatdeo and his descendants too are Buxas with the difference that such Buxas do not plough the land but only scatter seed on the ground, they also shun meat and fish.

According to Henry Eliot some of them, claim to be Panwar Rajputs and assert that their chief, Udyajit, was driven from home because of a quarrel that he had with his brother Jagatdeo, the Raja of Dharanagar. Then Udyajit had came to dwell with a few dependants at Banbasa on the Sarda. Udyajit had not been there long, before his aid was solicited by the Raja of Kumaon whose territories required defence against some of the neighbouring powers. Success attended the efforts of the Panwar and the gratitude of the Raja induced him to offer his defenders an asylum in his territories.

Crooke also mentions that many Buxas say that they came 'from the Dakkhin, other from Delhi, but they were expelled from the Dakkhin by the Marathas.'

It is, however, now an established fact that the Buxas like the Tharus come from a Mongolod stock and have nothing in common with the plains men of Uttar Pradesh or Rajasthan.

There are conflicting stories regarding the Buxa migration to the Tarai. According to some, Raja Jagatdeo and other Rajput nobles fled to Tarai, then a dense forest, full of elephants, gaints and devils, to seek refugee after a heroic but losing battle with the Mughals. Others assert that they fled from Delhi to escape Mughal presecution which included giving away their daughters to the conquerors. According to Buxas of Channan, Raja jagatdeo colonised the Tarai which was considered unfit for human habitation.

Whatever be the truth, it is an established historical fact that the Buxas and find mention in *Ain-i-Akbari* and the name *Bhuksar* was given to the parganas of Rudrapur and Kilpuri.

Almost all Buxas admit that when they migrated into the Tarai, everyone was not a descendant of Jagatdeo or a Rajput. There were many camp followers belonging to different castes. According to some, they belonged to seven castes namely Thakur (Kshetriyas) *Jat, Teli, Julaha, Bania, Nai* and *Chamar.*

Realising that in their new rugged and inhospitable habitat they could survive only by dispensing with caste and class barriers, they held a nocturnal session at Banbasa and decided to merge all caste and sub-castes into one and draw a veil of secrecy over their past. And to make the decision obligatory and irrevocable, They swore over noon-lota. Since then the Buxas have been casteless.

However, on the basis of their claim of Rajput ancestry from the female side, the Buxas are divided into four classes, namely Rajbansi, Suryabansi, Chandrabansi and Dujbansi. Earlier, the Census returns classified Buxas as Jadubansi, Punwar Partuja, Rajbansi and. However, these classifications seem to be merely notional and do not affect the castlesseness of the Buxas.

The Nehre Buxas of Dehra Dun say that they came into the District from beyond the Ganges at the invitation of Raja Sukhdeo Shah of Tehri who used them as gudes through the jungles on his shooting expeditions. They claim to be Kusabansi Rajput.

As for the etymon of the name *Buxa* or *Bhoxa,* according to some Buxas of Baspur, it was given to them by outsiders, who did not differentiate them from the original inhabitants who were called *bhaksi* 'devourers' notorious for consumption of elephant and horse flesh.

The Buxas of Bijnor have come out with the suggestion that when their ancestors came to Tarai, they had grown long beards, resumbling the unkeampt growth of mountain goats called the *bok* and hence *Bokas, Boxa* or *Buxa.*

Some fo the Bijnor Buxas link their name to the English word 'bogus' contemptuously used by the British for them. The Dehra Dun Buxas maintain that the term is derived from *Buqra* a root that used to be eaten by Buxa settlers of the Tarai.

The author does not consider any of the above explanation of the etymon of the term 'Boxa' as fully convincing. It is quite possible that the word Buxa is corrupted from of the presian word *eksa* which means 'uniform'. Such a name might have been given by the Maghals, who were strick by the fact that as unlike most of other Indian communities, this tribe had no caste or sub-caste differences among its members.

Let us now examine the genesis of the term *Mehra* or *Mahre.* According to Crooke, the meaning of the term is not certain. The sme title is applied to Kahars when it means a confidential person who entres the inner compartments (sanskrit *Mahila* means a 'women').

The author is not quite convinced that the word *Mahre* or *Mehra* has Sanskrit origin. The correct term used for *Kahrs* is *Mahra* whereas for Buxas, it is *Mahre* or *Mehre.* The resemblance of name as applied to the two different communities (kahars and Buxas) appears to be only incidential.

The word *Mahre* is a corruption of the Persian word *Mahram* meaning a 'knowledgeale person'. This view finds support from the Buxa assertion that they were used by Raja of Their Garhwal as guides during *shikar.* It is quite possible that because of their intimate knowledge of the forest, the Buxas in Dehra Dun were locally named as *Mahram* which later became *Mahre.* According to some Buxas of Dehra Dun, they were called by a British officer who being lost in the forest, was escorted back to camp and safety by a Buxa grasier.

Appearance

Describing Buxas of Bijnor, Stewert[13] says, that they are of about stature not differing much from the general peasantry of the area. Their eyes are small, the opening of eyelids being narrow, linear and horisontal (the inner angle not inclining downwards, so far as observed); the face is very broady across the checkones and their nose is depressed thus increaasing the genral fitnesses of the face. The jaw is prognathous and the lower lip thick and the moustache and beard very scanty. The features of the women are similar to those fo the men.

The above description also holds good for the Buxas of Nainital district. The women area, however much more shapely and beautiful than their men. The complexion of both men and women is wheatish or dark wheatish. The colour of their hair is usually black.

Language

The people of the Tarai speak Western Hindi, the principal dialect used being Hindustani mixed with Braj and Kumayuni. Tharus and Buxas of the Tarai are frequently said to have a distinct dialect of their own but apparently this is not the case as they generally use ordinary Hindustani with some admixture of Kumauni.

The above is a fairly correct description of the dialect spoken by the Buxas. The only point I wish to add here is that their language has a much large proportion of Persian and Urdu words than dialects of neighbouring Hindus, obviously as a result of their age-old contacts with the Muslims who established their support with the Buxas not only as rulers in the past, but also through the *sufis* and *fakirs*.

Religious Beliefs

The Buxas are one of the most Hinduised tribes of India. They themselves claim to be Hindus and to prove t hat they are authentic Hindus, they point out that they originally belonged to various Hindu castes and sub-castes-from Kshetriyas to Sudras, who decided to merge into one class under special circumstances in the hoary past.

Despite a clear and distinct impact of Hinduism on their beliefs. The Buxas continue to have a deep faith in the essential ingredients of tribal religion animism and spiritism. But, then these too are not absent from popular Hindu beliefs. The Buxas are very liberal and broadbased in their attitude towards other religions too. Many Buxas hold Muslim saints in great reverence and worship Muslim *pirs*.

The Buxas have also been greatly influenced, like the Tharus, by Guru Nanak, the founder of sikhism and in fact there is a distinct sect owing allegience to 'Guru Nanak Shah'.

Hindu Gods

The Buxas worship and revere most of the Hindu gods popular among the Hindus of Tarai. The important among them are Shiva, his spocese, Parvati, Ganesh, Lakshmi and Mahadeva. Rama, his wife, Sita and his brother. Lakshmana, the pivots of Hinduism in the North are household words among the Buxas. Their extreme attachment to Rama is also clear from the fact that their most popular greeting is "*Ram Ram*".

Krishna is only next or Rama in commanding reverance and affection of the Buxas. He and his *gopis* are extremely popular among women and youth. There are a large number of Buxa songs based on Krishna and his love. Although not worshiped ceremoniously on any occasion, of all goods. Krishna is nearest to the Buxa heart.

Local Deities

There are a large number of local *devis* and devtas who command grant respect from Hindus and Buxas alike. The Buxas claim that they were tribal deities, later adopted by the Hindus.

The Devi, also called as Sunderi Devi or Basundari Devi is most important among them all. She is a married deity and according to the Buxas, her original abode was at Dharanagar in Rajasthan from where the Buxas claim to have originally migrated. When they moved into the Saraj, they brought the Devi also along with them. Her adherents are known as *Deviware* and constitute one of the two sects into which the Buxas are divided.

Buxa Deities

There are some deities, which can be said to be typical Buxa deities, which are not worshipped, by Hindus.

Bhumsen

In every Buxa village, in front of the *Padhan*'s house,

there is a mud platfrom measuring 5'x3' approximately. This is the abode or *sthan* of Bhumsen, the Master of Land and the Protector of the Village. Usually the deity is ceremoniously worshipped once a year.

Bhumia

While Bhumsen is the village deity, Bhumia is the family deity. Its *sthan* is in every home. Bhumia is worshipped ceremoniously once a year by the family after the harvesting season when there is a sufficient foodgrain stored in the grain bins. It is an occasion of enjoyment and feasting to which other families are also invited. Since different families fix different dates, the festivity lasts for months at a stretch.

Teesmar Khan, Budharaja and Purab Baro are other deities worshipped by the Buxas.

Guru Nanak Dev's

While the sikhs consider Guru Nanak as a great religious preacher without any claim to divinity, to the Buxas, 'Guru Nanak Shah' is a deity worshipped by a section of them and Tharus on suitable occasions. The Buxas do not link Guru Nanak with Sikhism and are quite ignorant of its tanets. As such it is safe to conclude that there is absolutely no impact of Sikhism on the Buxas notwithstanding their devotion to Guru Nanak Dev.

The worshippers of Guru Nanak are called *Guruware*. They together with *Deviware* constitute the two sects of Buxa society. The popularity of the Guru among the Buxas is however rapidly decreasing. The main reason appears to be the advent of the Sikhs in a big way in Tarai as land-owners.

At present, the devotees of the Guru condider it prudent to worship the *Devi*, they also do not like to style themselves ad *Guruware.*

Muslim Impact

Having examined that influence exercised by Guru Nanak over the Buxas, let us see how far Muslim thinkers and saints have made an impact on the Buxas.

It is an established fact that the Buxas have been in the contact of Muslims for more than 400 years. As a matter of fact, the fromer themselves link their association with the latter even before they came to the Tarai. There are Buxas of *Muswani gotra* in Dehra Dun District, who unlike other Buxas, shun port.

Legend has it that the *Muswanis* were originally *Muswans* or Mussalmans, working for Rajput *ranis*, who migrated to the Tarai in the hoary past and ultimately decided to merge in the composite community sprung after the merger of various castes ad creeds to which the rains and their humble guards belonged·

The Buxa Seyanas of Pauri invoke the Prophet of Islam, Hasrat Mohammad and his daughter, Bibi Fatma in their *mantaras* to cure diseases and to drive away evil spirits. Crooke mentions two muslim saints, Sarwar Lakhi and Kalu Sayyid among the deities worshipped by the Buxas.

Social Organisation and Leadership

Buxas mostly live in exclusive hamelts of their own. Fromerly, non-tribals did not live even in the vicinity of Buxa habitations. However, now a few non-tribal hutments, can be seen on the outskirts or in the close neighbourhood of Buxa villages. However, in no case, the non-tribales have so far been allowed to construct houses in the midst of any Buxa habitation. In this way, a Buxa habitation still possesses its own entity, identity and presonality.

The Buxas have a well-knit and strong village organisation. As a matter of fact, in their social organisation, the village unit is most important and it is more important than the family unit or inter-village *biradari* unit. They expect to solve most of their problems at the village level.

The Padhan

The affairs of a Buxa village are presided over by a strong functionary called the *Padhan*. The *Padhan* by virtue of his traditional position and authority as well as the prestige of his office, maintains cohesion, solidarity and discipline in the village.

The institution of *Padhan* was created by the *Kham* administration for the purposes of liaison. The *Kham* Superintendent used to settle an area for Buxa cultivation and habitation with the *Padhan* who was expected to distribute them to his men, collect rent from them and deposit with *Kham* authorities.

As the Buxas did shifting cultivation, it was difficult for the administration to keep trace of them or enter their names in revenue records. So it was considered expedient to deal with the head of the group. The *Padhan*, in course of time became the main channel of communication between the Buxas of a village and the Government departments as well as the main spokesman of his people.

Now that the *Kham* Administration has been abolished and statutory *Goan Sabhas* with *Pradhans* as their heads, set up, the Padhan no longer enjoys an official status. However, he still remains the head of his people in a village or hamlet and wields great influence among them. He still provides the most effective medium of communication and contact with the Buxas. The importance of the office of *Padhan* among the Buxas can be realised from the fact that most of Buxa *Pradhans* of statutory *Gaon Sabhas* were from amongst the *Padhans*.

The office of the *Padhan* is, more or less, hereditary. Even during the *Kham* days, the administration usually accepted the eldest son as successor unless he was not fit for the job. There is however, evidence that in some villages a consensus is arrived at before declaring the eldest son or another son if the eldest son is not of sound mind or is considered incapable of shouldering responsibilities, as *Padhan*.

For instance, when Kripal Singh, *Padhan* of *Kpra* Kripali died in 1974, his elders son was chosen *Padhan* only after ascertaining the viewas of eldest at a meeting. It appears that the new generation of Buxas is no longer in a mood to accept hereditary appointments and may press for election in the not too distance future.

It is pertient to cite here the case of village

Dhimerhkera whose *padhan* died four years ago but his eldest son has not been so for accepted as *Padhan* on the ground that he is financially weak and does not process qualities of leadership. There is no plan to chose another man of his family or any other person as *Padhan*. There is danger that this important office may lapse in Dhimerkhera. If this happens, it will be a bad precedent indeed.

Now let us examine the functions and role of the *Padhan*. He is, in fact the friend, guide and philosopher of all the Buxas of his neighbourhood in socio-religious and *Biradari* matters. He is expected to lead on social occasions like festivals, marriages and get-togethers. He is first to host a feast to Holi revellers or guests who are expected to be enterained by different families or the hamlet.

All religious functions and programmes are organised by him. The abode of Bhimsen, the village Deity is in front of his house. Most of collective worship is perfromed at his place. When there are epidemics, the *Padhan* is expected to take steps to rid the village of the disease with the help of *Bharrara*.

Family and inter-family disputes are referred to him. He settles them alone or with the help of a few village elders. As he is able to settle most of the disputes in the village itself, very few cases are referred to the *Takhat*, the inter-village elders council. Even when, the *Takhat* has taken cognisance of a matter, the *Padhan* being a number of the *Takhat* plays an important role in the final settlement.

However, I must remove the impression that the *Padhan* enjoys an unchallenging authority irrespective of his qualities of leadership or personal conduct. It is certainly not so. The new generation is not tolerating incompetent men. There are many Buxas who are members of *Gaon Panchayat*and *Nyaya Panchayat*. They are gradually emerging as new leaders. In villages whose *Padhans*are not oradhans, such Buxa *Pradhans* are incresingly becoming channels of communication with non-tribals and the government machinery. To sum up, where the *Padhan* is not moving with the times, he is losing his influence and grip gradually.

However, the process is slow and not easily perceptive to the eye.

Inter-village Organisation

Although, the *Padhan* is in a position to settle most of minor disputes and inter-family quarrels of his village with or without the help of village elders, there is no traditional organisation or *Panchayat*at village level. There is, however, a well knit inter-village social set-up, a grand *Panchayat*, called *Takhat* to lay down norms for social conduct and behaviour, to ensure observance of age-traditions to prescribe guidelines, in socio-religious and economic matters and most important of all; to settle disputes and punish the guilty, if necessary. The types of disputes by the *Takhat* are as followas :

1. Land and crop disputes,
2. Forcible occupation of public or private premises and demarcation disputes,
3. Disputes relating to waterways and irrigation,
4. Quarrels,
5. Petty thefts and cattle lifting,
6. Sex offences,
7. Marriage disputes.

The inter-village *Panchayat*or the *Takhat* is headed by a chief who, too, is designated as *Takhat.* He is assisted by a number of functionaries as detailed below :

1. *Munsif* : He given advice to the *Takhat* and assists him in disposal of cases.
2. *Darogha* : He is the chief Executive Officer of the *Takhat.* He summons the parties to a sitting and ensures compliance of decisions of the *Takhat.* There may be more than one *Darogha* in a *Panchayat.*
3. *Sipahis* : They are messengers appointed by the *Darogha* to convey messages to bring parties to sittings and perfrom other odd jobs as directed by the *Darogha Munsif* or *Takhat.*

In certain *Takhats*, there are, regional functionaries known as mates who exercise jurisdiction over villages assigned to them by the *Takhat.* They exercise the powers of *Takhat* in their jurisdiction to decide disputes which can be settled at their levels without convening a sitting of the grand *Panchayat.*

A formal *Panchayat* convened to settle a dispute consists of all the *Padhans*of the area besides a number of important Buxas nominated by the *Takhat.* The full bench, however, does not meet usually for settlement of disputes. The *Takhat* using his discretion invites the *Padhans* and other important Buxas directly or indirectly concerned with or interested in the matter under dispute, to the sitting and disposes of the dispute with their help.The full *Panchayat* is convened when a dispute is of an extremely serious nature likely to have wide repercussions or when matters of social conduct or general policy are involved.

The offices of the *Takhat* are more or less hereditary. The eldest son usually succeeds his father. He may also be called upon to assist his father or step in his shoes during the latter's life time, if he has grown old, infirm or incapaciated. if the oldest son is not considered competent, another son is appointed. It is, therefore, usual to obtain general consensus before fromal succession takes place.

While, as stated above, the *Munsif* generally assists the *Takhat* by giving him his advice, in a few cases, separate *Munsafis* (*Munsifdoms*) have been created with the *Munisf* exercising the powers of *Takhat* under over-all charge of the *Takhat.* For example, Udaipur is a *Munsafi* under Chandanpur *Takhat* with Taumi Singh as the presiding *Munsif.*

In the Buxar of Nainital, there are three *Takhat*s functioning, hving distinct and separate areas under their control.

The Headquarters of the *Panchayat*in Eastern Buxar is at Godarpur. But, the *Takhat*; Chandan Singh lives at Kopa Kripali.

Chandanpur is the headquaters of the *Takhat* in Central

Buxar which has 52 villages lying between Kosi and Ghagaoc rivers under its jurisdiction. Chandan Singh is the chief of this *Panchayat.*

Bhoore Singh heads the third *Takhat* located at Birpur in North Buxar. This is smallest of the three *Panchayat*having sway over about twenty villages only.

The *Panchayat*living still North-west of the Western *Takhat* come neither under the jurisdiction of this *Takhat* nor have they any *Takhat* of their own. Theri disputes are settled by their *Padhans*who are assisted by an official assisted by an official called *Kotwal* who combines in him the functions of *Munsif*, *Darogha* and *Sipahi*, all in one. The *Kotwal* also supervises marriage arrangements, feeds biradari and perfroms other odd jobs in social gatherings under the orders of the Padhan.

Mode of Punishment

Before I describe a few cases handled by the *Takhat*, let us examine the mode of punishment and sentence awarded by Buxa *Panchayats*. The most universal and dreaded from of punishments, in serious offences is making a person an out caste for a definite or indefinie period. Returning to the fold, must be accompanied with a feast to the *biradari* and payment of peanality or fine if so decided by te *Takhat.* Sometimes fine, too are leived. The intention behind the sentence of fine, however, is to compensate the agrieved party or to meet expenses on community feasts. The expenses of a sitting are usually incurred by the complainant, who would get a part of the fine imposed on the accused, if he is able to prove his case. Sometimes coropral punishments of the following types are imposed.

1. Beating with shoes,
2. Donkey-ride,
3. Blackening the face,
4. Parading in public,
5. Combination of two or more of the above.

Cases

Let me now cite a land dispute handled by the Central

Takhat. Several years ago, Bale of Bhagle left his home and hearth and became untraceable. The *Padhan* who was also related to Bale, gave the eight acres of land belonging to Bale ro one Man Singh. When the *Padhan* died, his sons being interested in the land, wanted to undo the settlement. So a dispute arose. A *Takhat* was held a Bhagle, which was attanded by representatives from five to six villages. As a result of deliberations, Kanahai Singh, nephew of Bale, was found to be the rightful claimant. Man Singh had to surrender the land, host a dinner of *dalbhat* to the *biradari* and bear expenses of the sitting.

By far the largest number of cases tackled by the *Takhat* relate to offences like rape. kidnapping and abduction besides marrige disputes.

An unmarried young man of Bannakhera Sani developed intimacy with a married girl of the village and she ultimately became pregnant. The Chief of the Central *Takhat* under whose jurisdiction the dispute fell, is reported to have taken bribe and tried to hush up the matter. However, it was agitated by othe olders and a *Panchayat*, attended by olders from about 15 villages, was held. The *Takhat* was made to return the bribe money he had taken and apologise publicly. The young bribe money he had taken and apologise publicly. The young man was found guilty and beaten with shoes. He was temporarily made an outcaste, but after a purfication ceremony by a *pandit* in the *Panchayat*itself, he was permitted to serve water to the *biradari* and taken back in to the fold. The girl was restored to her husband. She too was temporarily ostracised and taken back in the *birdari* after purification. As a matter of fact, she prepared *rotis* and fed the biradari. No stigma was attached to illegitimate child, who treated as son of her husband.

For purification the brahmin is called. He *sprinkles* Ganga, jal (Ganges water) and takes a fee of Rs. 5.

Let us see now the Eastern *Takhat* has handled a similar case. The young daughter of one Maria developed intimacy and eloped with a young man of her village. When the father went to bring her back, she refused to return. A *Panchayat* was summoned at the request of th aggrieved father, but the *Takhat* absented himself and no decision could be taken. The offenders were not even ostracised. In fact the people of the two concerned villages have not even stopped from interdining with the erring couple who are living together. I was told that this was an unusual attitude adopted by the *Takhat* and the community. Usually the girl is returned to the husband or father and the paramour is fined.

The Eastern *Takhat* failed to handle properly a similar case with the result, the agrieved parents of the girl knocked the doors of the police and the Court. About five years back, a few Buxa girls and boys went for-fishing. On the way back, one of the boys caught hold of the eldest girl and had intercourse with her in the bush. Other boys and girls regurned home and leaked the infromation. The girl's parents and a few others rushed to the spot. While the boy ran away, the girl was caught and brought home. A *Panchayat* was called next morning and the boy was given a beating. were, however, not satisfied with the *Panchayat's* handling of the case, so they lodged a report with the police. The boy was later prosecuted and sentenced to pay a fine of one hundred rupees.

The ineffectiveness of the Eastern *Takhat* is also reflected from the fact that although the *Padhan* of Barbadpur is "keeping" his *mausi* (mother's sister) in flagrant violation of rules of exogamy, his cse has not been decided although the *Panchayat*has been held twice.

While ordinary marriage disputes are usually steeled at inter-family or Padhan's level, sometimes these are referred to the *Takhat*. In the Kartik of 1972, the *Takhat* of Central*Panchayat*referred a marriage dispute to his Munsif for settlement after marriage one of the couple complains of mal adjustment etc, or apporaches the *Takhat* for separation, the party taking initiative would be fined Rs. 100.

Some funds for legal aid in the event of Consolidation of Holdings were also collected. These funds were pooled with money already collected in othe areas. It was decided that the funds would be deposited in the account of the Buxa

Parishad.

The Panchayat's directive to curb women's freedom has been resented by women and even male opinion is divided. As such, there are many women who defied the decision and continue visiting the weekly market. The *Panchayat*has not been able to take any coercive measures to implement its resolutions.

Volume of Caste-Work

The instances cited above have shown the type of disputes and manner of handling of disputes by the Panchayats. Let us now examine the quantum of case work handled by *biradari* Panchayats.

An analysis of the figuers clearly showas that the Buxa Panchayats are not getting a large number of cases and usually sex offences and marriage disputes are reffered to them. Land disputes and criminal offences are no longer taken, in any appreciable number, to these Panchayats. If we study the perfromance of the three *Takhat*s *inter se*, we find that Eastern *Takhat* is most active while the North-western *Takhat* is virtually inefective.

Statutory Bodies

In Buxar as in other areas, the State Government has set-up *Gaon Sabhas, Gaon Panchayats* (Executive Committees of the *Gaon Sabha*) and *Naya Panchayats* (judicial Concils) under the U.P. *Panchayat*Raj Act.

The study showas that not a single case was referred to the Naya Panchayats by the 36 selected families. On the other hand, it has been noticed that the Buxas are taking increasing number of cases to police as well as revenue, civil and criminal Courts, when only 15 years back, a Buxa dreaded the very thought of going to a police station or a law court.

The reasons are not far to seek. His own *Panchayat* organisation is in a disarray and has failed to re-adjust itself in the changing circumastances. The Naya Panchayats are tools of non-triblas, where the Buxas do not expect to get justice. The Buxa representatives on the Naya Panchayats, have almost no say. Even a Buxa *Sarpanch* (head of the ujudicial council) had to resign in disgust, finding that he was not able to get any co-operation from his Panches. The result is that the statuory bodies while-definitely damaging and weakining the traditional system of justice, have totally failed to replace them.

The Buxa Parishad

The Buxa Parishad or Bhoxa Parishad is an organisation, of Buxas which is trying to work anong the Buxas on a socio-political plane. It is necessary to mention this institution as it is the only body organised on modern lines. With a Buxa President and a Brahmin secretary it enjoys considerable non-tribal support and has come political overtones.

Set up seven or eight year back, the orginal idea to establish the organisation appears to have been conceived by non-bribals. In any case, it remained a handiwork of the Brahmin Secretary for a long time. The Parishad had no fixed membership but sub-scritpions are collected from time to time and are supposed to be kept in the custody of the Treasurer, a Buxa. in acutal practice, it is the Secretary who controls the purse. The President when interviewed, showed complete ignorance, of the manner in which the accounts were maintained or funds spent. He, however, bitterly complained that the Secretary was misusing the Parishad's funds. He had, it was alleged, misappropriated the rental of Buxa Dharmashala at Ghadapur collected by him.He was ousted latter but has managed to stage a comeback recently.

This being the only organisation covering the whole of Buxar, the Buxas still hve great expectations from it, So far, it has proved to be a complete flop, and continues to be an exotic institution implanted among the Buxas in which the role of Buxa leadership is only subsidaiary.

Changing Life of Buxas of Tarai

Whatever be the pace, every tribal community in India is undergoing change. At many place, the development measures of the Government have greatly improved the tribal economy and environment. Several tribal groups have been greatly influenced by refromist movements, which have affected their basic values. In other areas, industrialisation has been responsible for a complete socio-economic change in the life primitive inhabitants of the area.

Similarly in the Tarai area fo U.P., the main habitat of the Buxas, changes have taken place at a terrific speed since 1947. it will be non exaggeration to say that the were taken almost completely by surprise and overwhelmed with the changes which were mainly due to external factors and forces. The contact with outsiders, which was sudden and all embracing, has caused great socio-economic dislocations leading to new discomforts in their cultural matrix.

This book will fail to fulfil its main objective if it does not spell out the main factors of change, both exogenous and internal and assess the situation arising out of juxtaposition and impingement of Buxa and non-tribal cultures and values and clash of economy interests. as a matter of fact, a study of Buxa society is a study of swift of and sweeping changes, economic conflicts and discontent, as well as distrubing dislocations and re-arrangements in social organisation.

Let us first recapitulate briefly the situation in Buxar, before and after Independence.

Before 1947, the Buxas lived almost an excluded life. The administration and adopted an attitude of indifference and non-intervention towards them. the *Kham* Superintendent, who was considered the "King" of the *Tarai* by the Buxas ruled over the territory through a number of *Peshkars*. Promin Buxas were appointed *Padhans*by the administration, which scrupulously avoided to deal with the Buxas individually.

It was the *Padhan*, who was allotted land and was required to pay land revenue to the authorities. Allotment of land to individual Buxas and charging rent alongwith his hag (usually 10 per cent of land rent which used to be Rs. 2 per acre) was exclusively the *Padhan's* business. Land was freely abandoned and exchanged without infroming the *Kham* Supertendent.

It is, thus, clear that the individual Buxa did not come in contact with the revenue officials. it was the Padhan, who constituted the main source of contact between the *Kham* Administration and the Buxas.

The Buxas were and still are one of the most law-abiding communities in India. Hence, policeman too rarely visited their areas. According to Bihari, if a policeman visited a village, the Buxas would run helter skelter and hide themselves.

The contact with the forest officials, was, however, closer. The Buxas got their requirements of fuel or timber free of cost and hunted freely. They used to give a nasarana of 4 pucca seers (about) 5 kg) of foodgrain to the forest officials at the time of each harvest through the Padhan. Even when the forest officials had any complaints against individual Buxas, they invariably referred the matter to the Padhan for disposal or redress.

It was the money-lender and the Barhaman, who were in direct and intimate contact of Buxas. Most of the Buxas borrowed from money-lenders, who were either Muslim *Banjaras* from neighbouring districts of Rampur and Moradabad or Hindu Banias of neighbouring towns. When the money-lenders caused harrassment, the *Kham* Superintendent and *Peshars* used to rebuke them and exempt the Buxas from payment of interest and fix easy instalments of repayment. The Brahmans arranged marriages and helped in perfromance of rituals.

Ordinary Buxas hardly moved out of their-village. Once in a while, they moved to join a marriage party, or to bring back wives and daughters or to offer condolences on bereavement in a relation's family. The *Padhan* had, however, sometimes to go to Baspur, Gadarpur, Kashipur or Ramnagar on business, like obtaining a licence or just to pay courtesy calls on local officals or to pay respect to a visiting high official.

It is, thus clear that the individual Buxa had little contact with the rest of the world. The *Padhan* was their main source of infromation and contact. The Brahman and the *Banjara* were the two outsiders with whom they came in intimate touch and gathered information of the outside world and discussed their intimate social and economic problems.

Life in Buxar was easy-going, slow-moving, peaceful and simple. The Buxas lived their own life enjoying considerable freedom in choosing their place of residence or land for cultivation. they left their wordly worries in the hands of *Padhans*, spiritual matters in the care of the *Pandit* and daily chore in the hands of their women and lived happy care-free life.

Although many freedom fighters had taken refuge in the Tarai, Buxas themselves remained completely cut out from the political movement to oust the British, because of their isolation. They, therefore, did not understand the full significance or feet the impact of Independence.

According to Daulat Singh, a well-to-do Buxa, who was also a Pradhan "We were all very happy that India had become free. We were called to the tahsil (Baspur) to take part in the celebrations. I returned to the village and hoisted Gandhiji's (National) Flag in the village."

Soon after the Independence Day, the Buxa learnt from the officials of the harrowing tales of plight of Hindus and Sikhs in the Pakistan and the Government's plans to settle some of them in the Tarai. "We received the refugees with open arms", stated Daulat Singh, "We gave them foodgrains to eat and the land to settle."

The genuine refugees were soon followed by Rai-Sikhs, who were tough guys who started forcibly occupying Buxa and government land. Round about 1954, the rosgari (business minded) Punjabis and Sikhs started pouring in. They began purchasing and selling land on a large scale, mostly through dubious means and illegal transaction.

The area was fast developed. Forests were cleared. More land was reclaimed. Metalled roads were constructed within minimum possible time. Malaria was eradicated. A sugar mill was put up as early as 1958. A Development Block was started, which helped the outsiders to modernise their agriculture and to get inputs at a reasonable price at their doors. Later, the Govind Ballabh Pant University came into existance at Pantnagar near Rudrapur and made a significant constribution in revolutionising agriculture in the Tarai. Cane was developed as a cash-crop bringing prosperity to the area.

Schools and colleges were set up at a rapid speed, spreading literacy and education of the people above the state's average. Prosperous Punjabi and Sikh farmers started sending their childern for education to Public Schools and Convents situated in places like Nainital, Dehradun, Shimla and Chandigarh.

Prosperity brought new comforts and symbols of prosperity like-tractors, cars, refrigerators, radios and now even T.V. as well as goods food and good drinks. No wonder, today, the Tarai is one of the most developed parts of U.P. thanks to the initiative and dynamism of Sikh and Punjabi settlers who are not boasting when they claim parity with rich Canadian farmers.

The Buxas, who had little contact with the rest of the World suddenly found themselves open to lots of people, refugees, land-grabbers, adventures entrepreneurs, politicians, many new government officers serving departments unheard of in pre-1947 days with conflicting interests and varied cultures, diffrents valuse and attitueds. No wonder the Buxas soon found themselves aghast, confused and bewildered knowing not what to do in a situation unprecedented in their history.

Soon began the period of problems arising out of forced sudden, swift and unwanted contasts. "Our land was grabbed. Our produce, cattle and flow were stolen. Our women's honour was no longer safe. Things have not improved. In fact, thefts have increased many fold". Thus, bemoaned Daulat Singh. "The government servants were better before Independence. The outsider spolied and corrupted them. Now they are against us as they want to please the Sikhs and Punjabis."

The land revenue authorities failed to keep pace with the developments with the result that soon the records were in a mess. The recorded tenant was a Buxa, and the occupant was someone else. In a belated bid to correct entries and to accept the reality of the situation, a policy of regularisation of trespass was adopted. This led to more transpass and more regularisation and the process still continues.

In 1968 the Samindari Abolition Act as estended to the Tarai, terminating government ownership of the land. This has been more advantageous to the trespassers than to Buxa tenants.

"Now Sardars have become adivasis on our land. The Punjabis have gained by abolition of Samindari. What was iriegular, has the backing of law now", thus commented Daulat Singh.

The land-grab movement was also accompanied by unscrupulous money-lending. Unlike the traditional money lenders and Banjaras, new people entered the business of money-lending and taking possession of Buxa land and crops through outright cheating and deceit.

The General and *Panchayat* Elections brought hectic political activity. The Buxas in general and *Padhans* in particular were wooed, as their votes materially affected elections. We have analysed in an earlier chapter, the forces and compulsions, which came into play in the Election. Electioneering and elections have an intoxicating effect on the people and Buxas are no expection. Their interest in the Elections has been gradually growing. The interest of Buxas in the *Panchayat*Elections has, however, been much more intimate and lasting as may Buxas have been fighting these elections, winning and losing. In the process, a great deal of political consciousness has grown among them. But all said and done, the contribution of the Buxas to the politics of Tarai or even Buxas in negligible.

In June, 1968, the Buxas were declared a "Scheduled Tribe" and since then a number of measures for their development have been taken. In the beginning, they were not aware of the facilities now offered to them. Even when they knew about them, they wre afraid to avil of them. But now gradually welfare measures have started showing results especially in the fields of education and economic development.

To sum up, there have been tremendous changes in the look of Buxar and outlook of Buxas, which have not only greatly affected their way of life but have swept the Buxas off their feet and seriously jeopardised their socio-economic structure and cultural matrix without providing any satisfactory replacements, substitues or solutions. The major factors of change as discussed above are summarised below :-

1. Independence of India in 1947.
2. Influx of refugees followed by land-hungry adventures.
3. Colonisation and development of the Tarai.
4. Declaration of Buxas as a Scheduled Tribe in 1967 and launching of Development Programmes especially meant for them.
5. Enforcement of Zamindari Abolition and Land Refroms Act.
6. General and *Panchayat* Elections.

Impact of Factor of Change on Outside

The story of the Tarai after Independence is the story of success of the Punjabi ad Sikh settlers. It would be quite apt to say that istead of being influenced by the changes, they are responsible for bringing about most of the changes in the Tarai. Development of means of communications, eradication of malaria, economic development programmes and agricultural development schemes of the Govind Bhallabh Pant University, Pantnagar, greatly helped them to modernise and industrialise farming. They took to cane cultivation, which greatly improved their economy.

With their amassed wealth, they were able to attain social status and politicals power and wildconsiderable influence over the local officials. They became a force to reckon with during elections and were approached by contesting candidates and political parties. The result was that many acts of commission and omission of these elements were either ignored or condoned by the administration. Even when the position of trespass on Buxas or government. Land was examined from time to time by the Committees or officials or when ***Kham*** was abolished, the Sikhs and Punjabis managed to retain their illegal possession which, more often then not was legalised on the bargain. The only law which had affected them adversely is the ceiling law which requires them to surrender land above a prescribed limit. They are, however, trying to get the law amended in their favour. It is, therefore, clear that the major changes have greatly helped the Sikhs and Punjabis to attain their present prosperity, political power and social status.

The Bengali refugees, who were also settled in some portions of the Tarai, were however not so successful. Many ex-army men and agricultural gradutes and political sufferers who were given land in the Tarai, too prospered Muslims and Paharis, however, have not been able to improve their lot to any appreciable extent. In fact the fromer's economic condition seems to have deteriorated. The *desis* are able to eke out a living but are no match to the Punjabis and Sikhs either in dynamism, progressive cultivation or the unscrupulous land-grabbing. In short, as a result of lop-sided development of the Tarai, the Sikhs and Punjabis have emerged as the most powerful communities in the Tarai.

Their Changing Life

Now that we have briefly examined major factors responsible for changes after Independence, let us find out how they are shaping the life and values of the Buxas.

The Buxas, have now completely given up shifting cultivation. Gone are the days when land was aplenty and Buxas had freedom to occupy or abandon any land they liked. Now land is scarce and most of Buxas are not in a position to acquire more land. In fact, they are under perpetual fear of losing whatever land is left with them.

Although tribal agriculture is still backward-and even

primitive-the Buxas now fully understand the advnatages of improved techniques, use of fertilisers and high yielding seeds. They are also keen to grow cane. However, due to indifference of local government agencies and uncertainties of pssession, they have not been able to catch up with the settlers.

The freedom to hunt and to collect fuel and timber from the forest has been substantially curbed. The forest area itself has shrunk in Buxar. The Forest Department is imposing fresh bans and restrictions resulting in growing hardship to the Buxas.

The incidence of indebtedness has assumed serious dimensions. While in the old days the money-lenders were content with higher rate of interest or payment in kind, the present-day money-lenders have an eye on Buxa land. They are much more unscrupulous and the rate of interest charged by them is exhorbitant. The State Government has, however, taken a number of measures to regulate unscrupulous money-lending including the fromation of cooperative credit and other types of societies. But the cooperative framework is still weak and has yet to make its presence felt.

The Buxa villages and homes have maintained their traditional look. However in many villages, one or two *pucca* houses, usually grotesque in look, have been constructed and in place of traditional wells, hand-pumps have become popular and can be seen in almost every village. Due to incidence of theft, there is hardly any buffaloe in Buxa villages. Due to scarcity or inadequacy of grasing ground, the population of other animals too has decresed.

Thanks to the state govt. a large number of Buxa villages have been electrified and therefore, we are a cheerful look at night. However, electrification of Buxa homes is still a far-off dream. The houses are still lighted with earthen lamps and hurricane lanterns. Petromax lanterns are owned by some of the well-to-do Buxas and they are used on special occasions and marriages.

During pre-Independence days, licences mainly for

mussle loading guns were issued to the Buxas. Only a few licences for SBBL or DBBL guns were issued to important *Padhans*. Now many more Buxas possess those guns and also revolvers. Daulat Singh, for instance has a DBBL gun. However securing licence has become a difficult job.

"Fromerly a tip of Rs. 10 to Rs. 20 was enough. Now the appetite has increased. My son has applied for a rifle. I have already sent 50 kgs. of rice to the official concerned, but so far, no action has been taken. The official now wants to see me. But I am avoiding, because I know he wants more money. I don't blame him for after all, the cost of living has gone high." Thus said a well-to-do Buxa.

However, it must be emphasized that in the context of the large number of legal and illegal arms in the Tarai, especially with the settlers, the weapons of the Buxas are not of much use to them and do not inspire any confidence in them. They are too limid to use them even in self defence unlike the land-grabbers who make full use of their *bandook*.

There has been no change worth mentioning in the occupational pattern of Buxas and there has been no perceptible occupational mobility among them. However, many Buxas were rendered landless-a thing unheard of berore 1947. But, even these Buxas are subsisting one borrowed land or as agricultural labourers. The Buxas considered it below their dignity to work under someone else.

It was with great difficulty that I was able to presuade a few of them to work in the Sugar Factory at Baspur in 1972-73. Since then, there has been a swift change in their thinking. When I visited Baspur again in December, 1975, the Buxas complained that they were not getting enough jobs in the factory.

Pressure on land is compelling them to change their attitude and take up subsidiary means of livelihood. This is, however, the beginning of the trend which is not yet pronounced.

There is a distinct change in the dress of women. More and more women are taking to saris. Only old women are using *lanhga* and *angia*. The younger women are also bidding goodbye to the old hair-style and are adopting the prevalent practice of typing the hair in a knot at the back. It is, however, significant to point out that no Buxar has been found dressed in Punjabi clothes of *Shalwar, Pyjamas* and *urhni.*

As compared to women, the change in the male attire is not marked. *Kurta* or shirt and *dhoti* or pyjamas with a Gandhi cap, still from the main male dress, Younger men are, however, also using trousers and bush-shirt since 1960 onwards.

The use of shoes is markedly on the increase. Now about 50 per cent of women use footwear. Fromerly men put on open shoes. Now all types of shoes are worn. Boys mostly use laced shoes.

The desire to posses ornaments had remained as intense as ever. It is difficult to say whether under present-day strains on their economy, the Buxans posses less number of ornaments, although Buxas assert that unlike old days the weight of gold ornaments is not even one tola. As a matter of fact, a girl is entitled to have certain ornaments on certain occasions which she must have even if the family has to incur a debt. Preferences are, however, fast changing. Use of khaila, Basuchak, khandua and gold Nath, has been almost completely discarded. It was stated that since there were cases of snatching of gold nose-rings by Rai-Sikhs, it is not considered safe for women to wear *Nath, Bunde, Chainpatti* and *necklaces* are latest crase.

Let us now examine food habits. With restriction on bunting, Brahmanic and refromist influences, use of meat is declining although very slowly. However, by and large, Buxas eat meat off and on and on special occasions. The use of vegetable curries is on the increase because now more vegetable are grown and are also available in the weekly market. There is a marked decline in the use of milk for reasons given elsewhere. The use of tea is common. It is said that very few people drank tea before 1955.

According to Bihari and Daulat Singh, the use of liquor

is on the increase although it is difficult to accept their view. Drinking has all along been popular among the Buxas. There is a common belief that drinking helps one to maintain good health and to proctect from diseases like malaria and stomach ailments so common in the Tarai.

It is said that liquor sale counters were functioning in almost every village and a bottle used to cost only four annas (25 nays psise) in the past. There was, however, no ilicit distillation of liquor. Now the Rai-Sikhs indulge in illicit distillation and many Buxas purchase liquor from them. Although the price of liquor has considerably increased, it has not affected the drinking habit of Buxas.

Smoking is definitely on the increase. Although *hookahs* are still in use, they have yielded their place of pride to *bidis*, which are extremely popular among men, women and childern. Many youngemen also smoke cigarettes. The use of other narcotics like *bhang* and *ganj*, too, appear to be increasing.

As for recreation, the traditional male dancing instrumental music and swang as well as traditional sports continue to be main froms of recreation and entertainment. Similarly visit to weekly markets and fairs are a source of recreation although the Buxans are visiting the markets in lesser numbers now.

In recent years, Ram Lila functions which are being organised on incresingly larger scale year after year, have been attracting Buxa men, women and childern, who throng to these functions in a spirit of devotion and also for enjoyment.

There are cinema houses at Kashipur and Gadrapur but none at Baspur. However for most of winter and summer, there is a travelling cinema. Many Buxas, especially the younger men, are fond of Hindi films.

Although many Buxas do not possess radios and transistors, these are no longer strange or extraodinary things to them. Some of the well-to-do Buxas own radio sets and transistors and the whole village locks to their houses to hear music, specially film songs which have become quite popular in recent years. However the radio is not yet a medium of mass communication as far as the Buxas are concerned.

During the last 28 years or so, there has been tremendous increase in the knowledge of Buxas about technical processes and improved appliances. They now know quite a good deal about use of chemical fertilisers, pesticides and insecticides and improved implements like thereshers, tractors and winnowers. Many can operate pumping sets and make minor repairs of tractors. Many are having dealings with the sugar factories at Baspur and Kashipur. The numerous cane-crushers have become aware of the chemical and mechanical processes involved in the manufacture of sugar. With energisation of the area, the Buxas have become aware of electricity and its use and they no longer consider it a supernatural phenomenon. In this way, there is no doubt, the Buxas have been gaining new ideas and acquiring technical knowledge is only rudimentary and is far far less than that of non-Buxas.

Let us now direct our attention to examine the evidence of change in the social organisation of the Buxas. The family still remains a strong unit and the pivot of the social order. In view of scarcity of land, impossibility of shifting cultivation and threats from outsiders to Buxa land, movable property and honour of their women, the family as fast becoming a more coherent and unified unit.

In the past, sons after attaining majority used to migrate to other villages to possess and cultivate fresh land. Now, either they live jointly with their parents or set up their home near the parental dwelling or in a part of it. Thus, unlike other communities, there is absolutely no evidence of breaking up of the joint family into nuclear families. Preference for the joint family system is going to stay for many years to come in the Buxar in view of the peculiar and adverse circumstances in which the Buxas find theselves today.

Although the women still enjoy the status of near equality with their menfolk and condiserable freedom in their personal life, there is an unmistakable evidence of Buxa men trying to dominate them on the ground of safeguarding their honour from aggressive outsiders. The young men have been active in putting a ban on women going to weekly markets and fairs. These men have been considerably influnced by the social set-up of the neighbouring communities where women have only a subordinate role and status. The non-tribals have also a tendency to ridicule the Buxas for being hen-pecked.

Coupled with this, the recent reformist activities of sadhus, reformers or puritanic Buxas like Bihari, aimed at the Buxas leading an austere and drab lif without freedom in sex matters. This has resulted in a movement to curb women's freedom and to bring their status down to the level of their non-tribal counterparts. The women have, however, not accepted their men's right to put bans on them. Their visits to fairs and markets still continues. The man have not been able to have their way so far. However, if the present trend continues, the women may lose their place of pride in the family and also their livliness, cheerfulness and gaiety which are charactristics of the Buxa women today.

While in the matter of curbing the freedom of women, the younger generation has taken a rigid or reactionary attitude, there is evidence of liberalisation in their attitudes in *biradari* matters. There is a strong section, for instance, advocating the return of the *Domares* into the fold. They were able to get a fromal resolution passed although due to resistence put forth by the diehards, it has not been limplemented so far.

There is little evidence of any change in kinship terminologies or even rules of exogamy or endogamy. There are, however, more violations of these now than in the past, the reason being that the hold of traditional organisations and functionaries in charge of community matters is slackening. The Gaon *Panchayats* and *Nyaya Panchayats* have eroded and encroached upon the functions of *Padhans*and *Takhats* who are losing their grip, the fromer gradually and the latter rapidly. Most of the *Takhats* are not able to take unbiased decisions and enforce these decisions once taken. No wonder the *Takhat* now meets at long intervals and there are many who would not comply with its decisions or even might go to court of law to defy and challange the decision.

However, the Buxas are not satisfied at all with the functioning of Criminal or Judicial system because they do not usually get redress there against their powerful non-tribal adversaries, besides the heavy expenditure involved in litigation. The present position is that while their own judicial system is in a process of decay, the statutory judicial system falls short of their needs and expectations. This has created a vacuum, which is an uneasy situation.

In religious matters, they have all along adopted a liberal attitude, accepting and absorbing useful aspects of other religions. In matters of superstitions, the supernatural world, while their beliefs persist, there are many who no longer take things for granted and like to question and discuss these matters openly. And the community does not show any intolerance. Belief in superstitions and omens is definitely on the decline. The Buxas have, on the whole adopted a pragmatic attitude in these matters.

The impact of Hinduism, is gowing at a rapid speed. This is mainly due to Brahmanic influence and activities of refromists and Hindu Sadhus now coming in large numbers to the Buxar.

While the Sikhs have gained victory on land, they have lost their battle on the spiritual front. The Buxa sub-division owing allegiance to Guru Nanak is fast losing its ground mainly due to adverse impression crated in the mind of Buxas about Sikhs and their way of life.. Even the Guru worhsippers are fast adopting Hindu rituals.

There is also an evidence that adoption of Hindu ways is considered only a matter of social upgradation and prestige.

It should, however, be mentioned that the Buxa society still remains non-hierarchical and no one is high or low because of his original sub-caste. But the possibility that the importance which many Buxas have started attaching to their original superior *gotras*, may lead to the introduction of caste system among them, cannot be ruled out.

After Independence, the Buxas have been forced to live among various types of people settled there and we have already discussed inter-enthic relationships in an earlier chapter. Here, I wish to point out that while the Buxas, because of their peaceful disposition and sloof nature want to maintain good neighbourly relations on the basis of "live and let live", most of the others especially the Sikhs and Punjabis hardly care to naintain good relations with Buxas, who are treated contemptuously.

This is gradually producing a slow reaction among the Buxas too. While they have been mainly defensive and in most cases silent spectators of their ruin, in a few recent instances, they have tried to hit back. While the Buxas cannot be blamed for this, the present state of tension is not at all conducive to orderly living and a peaceful climate. The Buxas seem to pull along well with other communities although the latter, too do not hesitate to take undue advantage of the simplicity of the Buxas.

While the Community Development Programme made little impact on the Buxas, special schemes launched by the State Government after their being made a "Scheduled Tribe" in 1967, have proved benificial to their economic and educational development. Among the voluntary agencies, the *Bhoxa parishad* has not so far made any worthwhile contribution, but the Servants of India Society with its network of *balbaries*, has been able to make its presence felt among the Buxas and has considerably influenced the thinking of members of the younger generation, which is fast becoming conscious of its rights and functions as citisens of this country.

Even during the three years from 1970 to 1973, when I carried out most of the investigations for this book, I found enough evidence of the change of outlook among Buxas during the period of investigation itself, especially in the spheres of education, employment in the sugar factory, inter-dining with other communities and their desire to resist threats to their property.

It is said that contact of the tribals with people of the so called higher "civilisation" is a mixed blessing. No Buxa is, however, going to accept this statement. He sees no good aspects in his contact with non-tribals. He is sore and unhappy and lives in the past. He feels that all developmental measures in the Tarai were meant to assist the outsiders at his cost. There is undoubtedly credulity gap between the Buxa and the administration.

Today, we have a strange phenomenon and the unusul spectacle of tribal backwardness in a highly developed area. In chalking out plans for settlement of refugees and others in the Tarai and development of the Tarai, the interests and requirements of the original inhabitants-Buxas, Muslims, Desis and Paharis-were ignored or not taken into account. The Administration just did not care to examine or anticipate the likely effect on the Buxas of measures they were taking. In their seal to assist one set of people, they completely neglected the other set which was adversely affected by governmental action and action of the other group. It is pathetic indeed although not new in tribal areas, that area development activities should causes havoc to the original inhabitants. What is more tragic about the Tarai is that it was not realised till the problem became acute and chronic. If the Buxas find their present living insecure, dull, and drab and their future bleak and uncertain, they can be hardly blamed.

Inspite of the Buxas' outright and unreserved condemnation of developmental measures, if one reasons with them, they accept and admit the good points of changes that have occurred in the Tarai during the last 28 years or so which we have already touched upon. There is, however, no gainsaying the fact that development of the Tarai has done much more harm than good to the Buxas.

Summing-up

Now that we have examined different facts and facets of Buxa life and the impact of changes resulting in myriads of problems for them, it would be worthwhile to sum them up for the attention of the State Government, public servants, social workers and voluntary agencies connected with the welfare of the Buxa people.

1. Forcible occupation and large scale trespass on the Buxa land.
2. Theft of their cattle, poultry and other movable property.
3. General harassment at the hands of settlers and a general sense of insecurity.
4. Mounting incidence of indebtedness.
5. Problems of fuel and timber from the forests.
6. Use of "*sandook* and *bandook*" (money-power and violence) in the elections.
7. Decay of their social organisation and modern institutions not being upto the Buxa expectation.
8. General lack of interest among the government departments to extend and spread their programmes among the Buxas and their villages leading to economic and environmental imbalances.
9. Backwardness of the Buxas in a rapidly developing area is due to the following reasons :
   (a) Lack of education.
   (b) Antiquated agriculture.
   (c) Inadequate arrangement of credit from authorised channels.
   (d) Problem of marketing of their produce.
   (e) Lack of occupational mobility.
   (f) Under-employment.
10. Problems of culture change and imposition of ideas on the Buxas by refromers, *sadhus*, do-gooders and even government officials and the danger of their assimilation at the cost of their basic values.
11. Unplanned activities of voluntary agencies and social workers.

It is not our intention to offer solutions of these problems here. As a matter of fact, all the problems mentioned above have been discussed in some depth and solutions have been suggested at appropriate places in this book. However, now that we are looking into totality of things, I would like to make a few general observations and recommendations.

Although the problem of trespass in the Tarai has been studied by government officials and the Tarai Lands Committee, the problem of land alienation and trespass on Buxa land has not been the focal point of examination by any Committee. It is suggested that a high-powered committee may be set up to go into all aspects of land alienation. As an immediate step, it is suggested that a special officer should be posted in the Tarai directly under the Board of Revenue with sufficient powers and authority to keep a watch and safeguard the land and property interests of the Buxas.

The Government has already taken measures to ban the transfer of land from tribals to non-tribals and to regulate money-lending. These have to be backed by strong executive action. As a matter of fact, most of the problems of Buxas could be satisfactorily solved if the executive and police could throw their weight in favour of the Buxas and in their right cause. It is absolutely necessary and for this no law is to be enacted that the Buxas should be granteed a peaceful life, free from worries of threat to their person and property. The settlers should be sternly dealt with if they take the law into their own hands.

To remove imbalances in the Tarai, the material development of Buxas at a rapid speed is needed. It is, therefore, suggested that the Government of India, considering the special needs of the area, should immediately sanction and set up an Intensive Development Project in the Buxar providing for a package deal for the Buxas. The present unplanned activities of various departments should be passed on to the Project.

The Buxas have every right to develop their culture ans socio-religious institutions according to their traditions and collective wisdom. With changing times and cultural contact, they are fast engaging themselves into the mainstream of national culture but many people and institutions are now trying to impose their own ideas and values on them. Such refromist activities are causing dislocation and upsetting the Buxa socio-economic order. It is, therefore, desirable that only such organisation and people should be involved in the welfare programme of the Buxas, who possess the correct attitude towards the tribal people and have genuine sympathy and understanding for their way of life. The State and well-wishers of the Buxas would be well adversed to remember the following words of the late Dr. Verrier Swin:

"These are many people greatly admired by society, who have devoted their entire lives to robbing the tribal folk of what little they have. They turn them into vegetarians and give nothing in its place. By introducing prohibition among them, they rob them of a much needed tonic. By suggesting their simple natural way of does as indecent, they lay on them a new economic burden. They cast a shadow on the sweet delights of young love. To steal colour, beauty and freedom from poor people is just as bad as to exploit them in more obvious ways."

V
Habitat and Economy of Netarhat

Netarhat is situated 96 miles west of Ranchi on an elevated plateau about 3750 ft. high above sea-level. Administratively it falls within the districts of Palamau but it has better links from Ranchi. This is the smallest hill town and a health resort on the junction of Ranchi and Palamau distircts in the state of Bihar. It has a temperature which is about 50 F less than at Ranchi round the year. The settlement including the wooden chalet of the then Governor, the dak bunglowas, the rest house, the Public school and orchards lies on a 'Pat' or plateau of about 7 sq. miles in area.

Netarhat is a place of peculiar charm which has casted its spell over many lovers of nature, tourists and visitors from all over the world. The stillness of the forest and the cool and refreshing breeze at dawn and panormic view of hill-ranges all round and below are lovely. There are beautiful pathes of pines and cypresses trees planted by the Forest Department of the Government of Bihar.

The entire main plateau is owned by the Government of Bihar. Netarhat Public School complex, agricultural farm, other government offices, several dak bungalows and rest houses are located on the main plateau. Beyond these there are a few tribal villages on the down-ward slope of the plateau. Netarhat has a wonderful climate one can enjoy the breeze and it does not become moist even in July and August. The rain fall is good, but it does not exceed 60" per year. Previously it used to be malarious but now it has been freed from the Malaria. About a century back, there was a military camp here which had to be closed for want of sufficient good water. people believe that it was sir Edward Gait the then Lt. Governor of Bihar and Orissa and then Governor of Bihar who took great interest in the development of Netarhat and he spent his summer time there.

Why is Netarhat so called

There are various opinion about the naming of Netarhat. Different infromants tell us different meaning of the place. Some of the popular ones are given below :

(1) In the local dielact Netar means religion and Hat means market. Therefore the word meaning of the term is the market of religion.

(2) Another opinion is that it was originally 'Nature-Heart' meaning thereby that the sinic beauty of this place is so unique and charming that it becomes the heart of the nature.

(3) According to another version there were early settlers scattered on this plateau before the Britishers occupied this place. That time there used to be a creeper called Mahulain by the natives. It was very rich in its foliage and greenny and covered this hilly spot. The early settlers used to say that there were 'later' spread everywhere in this place. Suddenly the administrative fores of that time set their foot on this 'later' infested area. The administrative buildings were built in plenty and people from out side began to pour in into this locality and in on time this place was seen teeming with people as if it were a market place which is locally called as 'hat'. Thus, people would talk among themselves. Hello, there has cropped up a huge crowd of people like in a market Hat- in the 'later' area. Slowly this place was being called as Later-Hat and the Britishers mispronounced this as 'Netarhat'.

The Field and Field-work

It has been mentioned earlier that there is no private house on the proper plateau of Netarhat but on the down of it there are two tribal villages in the North-west about 3 and 4 kms. respectively. They are Paeripat and Mohanapat. These were the two villages from which the core-materials for this paper were collected during the summer of 1979 and thereafter. Since the economy of these villages forest oriented. I had to go to deep forest to observe personally the economic activites of the people of these two villages. Hence, the field-work is not limited to these two villages in which they live but to the deep forest where they go for hunting, collection of root and fruits, grazing their cattle and bring the buring fuel and also to markets where they exchange their forest products with the articles of the daily requirement.

Village Paseripat

There is folk-tale regarding the origin of this village which goes like this once there lived an Oraon couple in the village of Kairo near Lohardaga in the district of Ranchi.This couple moved out of Kairo for reasons known to them and settled at Kawadair. This couple could not stay in that village for a long and thereafter migrated to Chhechhari a plain disc of land which was also deserted by them. This couple seems to have been on a constant search for life. Hence, this time they climbed up and finally settled down at Jamtoli on the plateau of Netarhat. This couple had a son named Mangra who succeeded his father after his death.

In course of time Mangra grew as an industrious man. He cleaned the forests of Tahar in the South fo Netarhat and owned a very big piece of land near the present site of the village and hence once again shifted from Jamtoli to Paseripat. This name has a tradition behind it. once Mangra found a stone in the Ghati sarna (sal Grove) in the north east of village Jamtoli. That stone looked just like a Paseri-stone (stone weighing five seer) But in fact it was not a Paseri-stone rather a stone used for Sarna worship. Out of ignorance he carried that stone house on his back. He had a dream at night in which he was told that he was not to carry the stone far from the Sarna. As a result of this unbecoming deed he developed an extra growth of flesh on his back. This extra growth of flesh was exactly like the shape and size of that very Paseri stone. Since this event he was called Paseri-Mangra and his new settlement, Paseri Mangra Toli which later on took the present name Paseri Pat.

There is a stream in the north of Paseripat which the natives call Dhonrhi Jharia which is dry after rainy season. There is also a forest -Thus,-Patra named after a very old little well from where both the villagers of Paseripat and Mahnapat drank water. The village of Mohna Pat is situated in the north of Paseripat.

In the south there is Bhursakhainr forest and there is a perennial lovely rivulet flowing here/in the forest in which the villagers bath and animal quench their thurst. In the east there are Balo Tongari and mangakona forests and betarhat Dam. In the west there are Taria and Pichaipat forests.

Mohna Pat

This village derives is name after certain Mohna Kisan. The natives say that there lived a man named Mohna of Kisan tribe in the village of Chhipadohar about 70 km. north of Netarhat. He was the Baiga (village priest) of that village. The village was held by a king who had hobby of hunting and enjoy the game. Mohna had to do this by virtue of his magical spell and religious powers which no body else was capable of doing. Mohna fulfilled this wishful thinking for a number of years successfully. At last one day he started thinking seriously that so long he was alive, he was able to carry the will of the king. But there would be one day when he would die and the King would demand the same service from his sons who would not satisfy the king, upon which the king might pester them or punish for no fault of them. This thought started vexing Mohna frequently and one day he decided to run away from Chhipadohar, One night he prayed very devoutly for the safety of his children. His prayer was granted by the diety. To the surprise of every member of Mohna. There opened a long tunnel. He drove his cattle first through that tunnel then followed his family members and at the end he himself sat out for the unknown destiny. His cattle came out to the village of Parhatoli and stopped there. Then Mohna and his other members of family also arrived at. Thus they were saved from the expected wrath of the King. They shif from Parhatoli to Mohna pat later onn. Thus, the village gets name after the first settler na (Mohna Kisan).

In the north, there is a village called Naina 5 Km. from Mohna pat. Another village is Pandra 8 Km. from there. There are Ambakona and upper Ghaghry reserved forests. In the south there is Dhanuikona forest. There is a road leading to Sun-set point. In the east, there is Tatakona forest and then the village of Jamtoli and Saranatoli. In the West there are plantation of forest department.

Habitat

In Paseripat, there are 25 houses. Out of these 22 are held by the Oroans and rest are those of Kisan. The road leading to Sun-set point from Netarhat passes through this village dividing it into two unique parts. There are 6 houses on the left side and 19 houses on the right side of the road. These houses are not crowded at one place rather they spread widely over an area about 500 meters long and 200 meters wide. The Oraons of the village speak 'Kurukh' whereas the Kisan speak Sadri and both the terms and believe in the 'Sarna' religion.

The entire village of Mohnapat is held by 17 families of Kisan. They are settled in three clusters of houses over a radius of about 200 metres. All of them speak 'Sadri' and believe in the 'Sarna' religion.

Thus, the present study is based on the empirical facts collected from among 42 families of the Oroans and Kisans having a total population of 185 and 150 respectively the details of which are given in the following tables :

Table 1

Population and Sex Ratio

Sl. No.	*Tribe*	*Year in 1979*				
		Male	*Female*	*Total*	*%*	*Sex Ratio*
1.	Oraon	94	91	185	55.22	968
2.	Kisan	65	85	150	44.78	1308
	Total	159	176	335	100.00	

Table 2

Table Showing the Sex Composition in age Groups

Age group in years	*Oraon M*	*Oraon F*	*Kisan M*	*Kisan F*	*Total M*	*Total F*	*Total of both*	*Percentage*
0-5	17	11	12	18	29	29	58	17.30
6-10	16	11	14	12	30	23	53	15.82
11-15	14	9	3	12	17	21	38	11.34
16-20	8	12	4	7	12	13	31	9.25
21-25	5	13	4	5	9	18	27	8.06
26-30	8	6	9	14	17	20	37	11.04
31-35	4	7	5	3	9	10	19	5.67
36-40	8	8	4	7	12	15	27	8.06
41-45	8	4	2	1	10	5	15	4.48
46-50	0	3	2	1	2	4	6	1.79
51-55	2	3	0	2	2	5	7	2.98
56-60	2	1	5	2	7	3	10	2.08
61 & above	2	3	1	1	3	4	7	2.09
Total	94	91	65	85	159	176	335	99.98

Table 3

Table Showing Quantity and Quality of Average Land Per Family in Acres

Sl. No.	*Villages*	*Don*	*Chawra*	*Bari*	*Tanr*	*Katat*	*Total*
1.	Paseripat	1.67	1.64	1.50	2.79	2.35	9.95
2.	Mohnapat	0.81	0.67	1.32	1.58	0.73	5.12

Note : Don : Deep fields with possible water sources.

Chawra : Upper fields with no water sources.

Bari : Land near or around the house.

Tanr : Plain flat up lands.

Katat : Forest land after clearance.

Economy of Netarhat

It is vivid from the perusal of the ecological setting of the two villages that these are located on a high altitude. The terrains are not plain. They are generally rocky and fromed of various terracees of on slope of irregular order. The soil of this area may generally be regarded as laterite and rocky of compact hydrated oxides of aluminium and iron. The fromation of rock in general is very hard and is devoid of organic maters and other fertilising agents and has very low capacity to retain moisture. It is only towards the dam side that there are a few good paddy fields of considerable area which have clays and capacity to retain moisture is also high.

Traditional Occupation

Traditionally the Oraons and the Kisans are cultivators. It is largely through the cultivation that they get their loaves and fishes and keeps them busy round the year. The males are kept busy with the hard job of filing the fileds, raising and repairing the embankment to arrest water. The female folk help them in transplantation, weeding harvesting and other duties. Since the Don land per family in the villages of Paseripat and Mohnapat is only 1.67 and 0.81 acres respectively the people are forced to fall back on some non-traditional accupation which is not less important for these villagers.

Agricultural Calendar

	Months	*Agricultural Activity*
1.	Magh (Jan-Feb)	They plough their fields and the terms of Dhangars are renewed.
2.	Phagun (Feb-March)	The Work of leveling of the earth is done.
3.	Chait (March-April)	Leveling of earth and breeking the clouds and ploughing.
4.	Baisakh (April-May)	Ploughing, manuring and sowing.
5.	Jeth (May-June)	Sowing of Gora Dhan and Godli.

6. Asarh (June-July)	Watching the field and transplantation done.
7. Sawan (July-August)	Sowing of urid, transplantation of paddy and weeding the paddy fields.
8. Bhado (August-Sept)	Harvesting Gondli and sowing of 'Kurthy'
9. Ashin (Sept-Oct)	Gora Dhan and Urid are harvested.
10. Kartik (Oct-Nov)	Paddy in Upper fields harvested.
11. Aghan (Nov-Dec)	Paddy in Don fields harvested.
12 Pus (Dec-Jan)	Threshing of paddy and storing.

It is clear from the observation of the agricultural calendar that the farmers are kept busy round the year in this or that work, but the fact remains that since the Don land held per family in the villages of Paseripat and Mohnapat is meagre to the tune of 1.67 and 0.81 acres respectively and other lands are not so fertile, the natives are forced to fall back on some non-traditional occupations for their livelihood.

Table 4

Working Lands

Village	*Total Population*	*Male*	*Female*	*Working hands*	*Male*	*Female*
1. Paseripat	200	101	99	122	67	55
2. Mohnapat	135	58	77	83	39	44

Thus, it is clear from the observation of table No. 4 that working hands at Paseripat and Mohnapat were respectively 122 and 83 but persual of Table No. 5 given below may reveal many things.

Table 5

Table showing main occupaiton of individuals

Villages	*Agric -ulture*	*Gard -ening*	*Char -coal*	*Total*	*Services Inside*	*Outside*
Paseripat	11	3	1	12	6	6
Mohnapat	19	1	1	6	6	-
Total :	30	4	2	18	12	6

This is clear from the observation from Table 5 that out of a total working force of 205 only 54 persons could reply about their main occupations out of which only 30 persons which is less than 15% had agriculture as their main occupation. Next largest group was those of service holders of 18 persons out of this only 6 persons served outside Betarhat and 12 inside it, mostly in the school and agriculture farm.

Similarly their subsidiary occupation were many and they named many of them at a time. It was only after enquiring from them, the amount or the product that they used to get out of that one can find out their principal subsidiary occupation. The principal types of their subsidiary occupation are given below in Table 6.

Table 6

Table showing main occupation of individuals

Villages	*Wood cutting and gathering*	*Chawk Digging*	*Charcoal making*	*Hunding and gathering*
Paseripat	13	6	5	All
Mohnapat	16	10	7	All
Total :	29	16	12	All

Wood Cutting and Gathering

Thus, it is vivid from the persual of Table 6 that wood cutting is the most common subsidiary occupation of the natives of Netarhat. As has been mentioned elsewhere that these are the pat villages surrounded by forest they bring fire-wood for home consumption and also to sell them in the weekly markets. Some times they succeed in bringing timbers either by stealing or with the convienance of the petty officials of the forest department. They sell these too in the weekly markets.

The natives have to wait for several favourable conditions only when they can bring either firewood or timber-wood should be dry, the forest guards should not be there and other co-villagers are of the same mind to go to the same forest. If there is a gap they may not bring the fire-wood in such circumstances they are bond to dig some tubers, roots, and collect fruit or honey. These forests have edible roots and tubers of innumerable type of few of which are described below :

(1) Karil : The natives call it Sadhna in their local term. This is the 'Kopal' or tender root of baby bamboo which is still budding. This growas near the bamboo groves in the forest soon after the rainfall. The natives break them very often with hands or may cut it with the small exe. The upper portion of this is removed with the help of a knife and then it is cut into smal pieces which may be consumed after boiling. This has two types (i) Pahari Karil and (ii) Ropa Karil. Generally the natives consume the Pahari Karil.

(2) Pitharu Kanda : It is also known as Girus in the local term which is found just after the rainy season. It is the root of a creeper. An old creeper of three years may have about 3 feet long Kanda, may weigh 4 to 5 Kg. The natives dig this out, remove the upper portion with knife and them consume this. They say that this tastes like sweet potato.

Besides these there were seven other Kandas which were cultivated in the forest near some spring or rivulet by the natives. The details of a few of which are given below :

(1) **Semral Kanda :** This is one of the most popular Kanda grown by the tribals or Netarhat. A small branch of the Kanda is planted during the rainy season and by the winter the Kanda weighing 1 to 4 kg. may be ready for consumption. The upper portion of Kanda is thick which has to be removed before boiling after which it can be

consumed.

(2) **Sakhin or Kisgo :** This is another very common Kanda cultivated in Netarhat. First of all a long and narrow ditch about 3 feet deep is dug which they fill with dry grasses and other leaves to act as manure in due course.Then they keep the knot of Sakhin which will work as seed. When twigs come out of the knot, they cover the ditch with soil soon after the first rain. The cultivation of Kisgo needs good water for irrigation. It takes about one year for the root to mature after which it is dug for consumption.

(3) **Gethi Kanda :** It is a very common Kanda. Its leaf resembles to that of Pipal. It is grown during rainy season. It looks like a big potato in size but it tastes bitter. There is normally only one Kanda in the root of creeper which has to be dug and its cover is removed. Its bitterness is the main problem. The natives in a bid to ward off its bitterness remove their cover first, cut the root into small pieces keep them in basket, carry them to river and keep the basket in the flowing water of river for one day. It is believed that the flowing water carries away the bitterness of the Gethi Kanda gradually after which it can be consumed when boiled properly.

(4) **Banu Kanda :** It is also found soon after the rainy season. One has to dig only a few inches of the green found leaf can get one kanda of the size of big potato on each joint of the plant. This could be dug very easily even with the help of a pointed stick. This can be consumed raw after removing its thick cover. Its taste is sweet. Besides these other common Kandas which the natives consume are semal Kanda, Lakma Kanda, Pahar Kundri Kanda, Ram Kanda and the like.

Natarhat forests are very rich in the wild friuts and the most common of them which are edible for the natives one : Amba (Mango), Jamun, Bel, Kend, Piyar, Dumar, Dhui, Jack fruit, Kusum, Karojda, Pithor, Bar, Pipal, Chenberi, Dhotho, Benal, Karela, Aura, Nim, Dori, Char, Mouna, Durkho, Ber, Sihon, Ketal, Imli, Papaya, Velba etc.

As fruits so there are varities of edible flowers some of

which are Kedali, Harin Godi, Kachnar, Burju, Gihur, Koynar, Kaita etc. The common leaves which are edible and are found in the forests are Katai, Futkal, Konayar, Imli, Pipal, Derangi, Sarala, and Lao etc. Beside these several types of wild oil seeds are also found in the forests and Muzjani, Bendom Karannj, Mahua and Kusum are very very commonly collected by the tribals.

In addition to the edible products enumerated above, the local forest yields valuable materials like Katha, Silk, Honey lac, gum, sabai grass and several other creepers from which rope is made, and innumerable types of herbal medicines which the natives collect and sell them in the weekly markets.

Thus, to sum up this can be safely mentioned that wood cutting and gathering is perhaps the most popular subsidiary occupation of the Kisan and the Oraon of paseripat and Mohnapat which sustains maximum population.

Chawka digging : Under this scheme the villagers are engaged to dig out soil and deposit it to make a small platfrom on which a tree seedling is planted by the forest department. This circular ditch protects the plants from the ravage of animal. This making of platfrom is locally termed as digging chawka. One can see innumerable such platfroms on either side of road and on the various pats of Natarhat, on some of which young plants are growing and on other seedlings are yet to be transplanted. The villagers are engaged in the job of chawka digging on the labour contract basis and the payments are made according to the number of chawka one has dug. These days this scheme has attracted good number of labours from the neighbouring villages and they may do this job when they are free. As many as 16 persons of the two villages indicated this to be the is main subsidiary occupation.

Charcoal Industry

Production of charcoal on a very large scale is done at different places in the forest. Dhondari Amba which is about 5 k.m. in the west of Paseripat had a big organised industry in which about 20 persons were from of Paseripat and Mohnapat. There was one Sardar Sujit Singh who was a forest contractor and had purchased 90 acres of forest near Dhonadri Amba. He was the owner of that charcoal industry. One Kamal Oraon of Paseripat was the Munshi (record keeper) there who had engaged other co-villagers in that trade. There were eight ovens operating during my field work and each oven had a capacity of 25 bags of charcoal weighing 22 to 24 K. G. per bag. The labours most of whom were on contract got Rs. 1=25 per bag as wage and those on daily wage got Rs. 4to5 according to the nature of job and experience. October to June was the season for this and charcoal was sent to Lathar and Daltongunj in truck load. One truck carried 175 bags of Charcoal. Thus, loading also engaged a few labours on contract.

Hunting and gathering : This was rather so common subsidiary occupation that all the inframants opted for this. Thus, rarely there was any person who never collected an forest product and did not hunt a game. Hunting was very common cultural trait. There were occassions on the eve of Sarhul and Jani-Shikar when there would be organised group hunting which was locally termed as 'Hanka-Shikar'. Under this there were some persons who would beat drum and make noise with bamboo sticks which would drive the games to a particular point and the hunters would be waiting for the Harka-Party and games there. When the games come within the target they are killed with the help of gun, bow and arrow, axe or Gulel as per demand of situation and the nature of games.

When it was an individual hunt a hunter was more interested in the small games like here, lamha and Siar etc. or binds like Titir, Porki, Pahar-Murgi, Fikro, Kat-Kutti and the like.

Economic Problems

It is vivid from the perusal of the main and subsidiary occupations of the natives of the two villages that their annual produce from agriculture which is their main traditional occupation was hardly sufficient for the whole year for many families. They said that there had been crop failure due to poor monsoon rains since 1958. most of the lands of Paseripat were rocky and uncultivable lands on which cultivation was dine were repeatedly washed away by the heavy rains and it also washed away the manure applied in the field process of erosion was operative on which the poor farmers had no control. The ravages caused by the wild bear and other animals to the standing crops was a constant problem for the villagers. Their subsidiary occupations of various types provided some relief to them. But most of them were uncertain and also seasonal. The problem of drinking water was very serious. The natives were always anxious to collect water from the springs which were away from the villages.

Thus, to sum up about the habitat and economy of Netarhat it can be mentioned that Natarhat is the smallest hill town which has a peculiar magical charm of being a beauty spot and a place of tourist interest. It is surrounded with forest and hills. There are several villages inhabited by the Oraons and the Kisans near Netarhat. These tribals have agriculture as their main traditional occupation. But due to several ecological factors only handful of persons get their livelihood through agricultural. It is blessing for them that there are several subsidiary occupation which offer them opportunity of employments. Forests and the wild products are the main source of livelihood for these people. The inhabitat are economically poor but away from the clutch of money lenders. The standard of living is low and there are economic uncertainties. Hunger has not been solved as problem yet but they do not die of hunger. They are providentially well supported.

Psychologically, they are sure to get some edible root, fruit and game in the forest. Hence once they moved towards forest they never come empty handed and this reliance on the forest is a great strength for them. Ecologically they are so attached to their hilly and pat villages, forest, springs and soothing air breeze, that they rush hurriedly to their homeland even if they go downs, so close a place like Banari weekly market or any other place. Thus, one can find that the natives one so sick of their providentially rich homelands that they are happy in peace free from tension only when they are at Netarhat. There is a common belief among its natives that they can live comfortably only at Netarhat which is better than heaven for them.

VI

Tribal Indebtedness and Indigenous Banking System in a Tribal Village

Tribal indebtedness is such a colossal problem that it captures the attention of anyone and everyone who goes to a tribal village with an eye of observer. In the present paper an attempt has been made to illustrate the suffering of a tribal village-Pugu in Gumla sub-division within the district of Ranchi, whose majority of population was thoroughly exploited by the village money-lenders and Mahajans. The innocent tribals and incurred heavy debts and most of their earnings were utilised in making large scale payments of interest. It will further reveal that financially ruined tribals could give little thought for improving their cultivation and there were many burning examples when the villagers were forced to sell their Cultivable land to pay off the debt. When I sincerely view the wretched lot of the poor tribals of Pugu, I am at once reminded of the famous line form the Agricultural Commission Report "No one desires to see a whole sale resort to insolvency and no one, we trust, desires to witness a continuation of system under which innumerable people are born in debt, live in debt and die in debt, passing on their burden to those who follow."

Pugu, the village in question had a total population of 217 persons living in 29 families of which Oraon alone lived in 24 families and rest of 5 families were inhabited by 3 converted christians and 1 each by the Lohra and Ahir. The total area of cultivable land under the possession of the villagers was only 172 acres as such the per capita land owned by the villagers would come even tro less than half acre. Actually, the area of Don Christians and I each cultivable land under 172 acres as such the come even tro less 1 and, used for paddy cultivation would come roughly to 80 acres. Tanr land was used for maize cultivation whose per acre yield was very low. Practically, there was no irrigation facility, excepting Kachcha well to irrigate the kitchen garden. About 90% of the population was illiterate hence the pressure on land was very heavy. There was only one person in the whole village who had a job of a post-man in the Post and Telegraph department. Except him the entire village was dependent an agriculture. Those who were landless worked as agricultural labour. Growing vegetables and selling milk was the main subsidiary occupation of the villagers. Thus, from the perusal of the economic sketch of the village it is apparent that the villagers had very limited economic resources at their command. As Such, whenever there was some need, they rushed to the village money lender.

Regarding the causes of indebtedness the following may be noted as the most common:

(1) Excessive pressure of population on the land.

(2) Failure of crops due to gambling with monsoon.

(3) Decline of cottage industry.

(4) Tribal extravagancy.

(5) Excessive love for litigation.

The villagers mainly grew paddy, maize, and vegetables. The solitary family of Ahir had a few milching cattle. To sum up the asset side of the villagers it could be safely said that while most of them were below subsistence level and had mostly to purchase and nothing to sell. A very few persons, who had some surplus, sold the articles at a very low price for the following reasons:

(i) Substantial portion of agricultural produce was sold by the tribals in the village Pugu itself at a very low price. They failed to reach their produce even to Gumla market which was hardly three miles from the village for two reasons - (a) A large number of middle men travelled from door to door in the village to buy the produce at a very low price and (b) in many cases the tribals were heavily indebted to the local money-lender cum trader as such they had no alternative but to surrender the bulk of their produce at nominal prices.

(ii) Inadequate transport and communication facilities were second responsible factor for the sales in the village at a low price. It is really shocking to mention that even bullock-cart could not reach Pugu, as there was no road worth the name which might connect the village from rest of the world.

(iii) Thirdly the villagers had no knowledge about the market price of various commodities prevalent outside the village.

(iv) Some of the villagers who had been to Gumla market to sell their produce had a very sad experience of being cheated by the brokers of organised market.

(v) Inadequate warehousing facilities also forced them to sell their produce just after the harvest when prices were usually low.

Tribal Indigenous Banking System

In the foregoing pages it has been mentioned that due to limited economic resources and various limitations in gaining the optimum prices of their produces the villages had to go to the local money-lenders. Hence a few lines about these money-lenders and the system Hunter (1877) for the first time took pains in writing a few lines about the then system of money-lending where he observed "The old landed proprietors of the district had no large savings, and they did not enter into money transactions as lenders. Such transactions were carried on by Mahajans or professional bankers and merchants, a few of whome were also landholders and Capitalists." A persual into the account given by Hunter reveals the that I loans were of two types. Those in which land was given as a security and (2) Those where transactions took the form of a mortgage. Lenden or petty loans to raiyats were generally given in cash in the month of June when the prices were at their highest, and repaid after harvest, in kind , when prices were very low. Interest was charged at the rate of one-third of an Anna for each rupee per mensem, and was also paid in kind. So that for every rupee advanced in June, a raiyat had to pay in December a rupee's worth of grain at the price the ruling, in addition to the worth of two or three Annas on the rupee as interest.

Regarding the exorbitant rate of interest an observation of Hallet (1917) will not be out of place to be mentioned. "The capacity of cultivators to tide over the periods of stress, engendered by a partial failure of crops was small. The aboriginals and the semi-aboriginals could subsist in the midst of conditions which could play havoc with people accustomed to higher standard of life, and maintain themselves, even crops failed, on jungle fruits and vegetables, but even in years they frequently had recourse to loan to meet some extra expenditure, e.g. on marriage, or narrow the seed for their holding at exorbitant rates of interest from the Banias who were found in every aboriginal village. Interest at 75% per annum was the normal, but not the maximum rate of interest charged to the cultivator and it was no easy matter for him to extricate himself. The oppression of the money lenders had reduced same of the cultivators and labours almost at the position of serfs and frequently drove the whole families to migrate to the labouring districts".

Government Measures against the exploitation of the Mahajans and money-lenders:

Pre-Independence Policy

Since the last quarter of the 19th century, the tribal indebtedness was gradually assuming serious proportions. With the onset of the famous depressions, the tribal indebtedness problems was the most alarming. The British Government could foresee that if some preventive measures were taken in time the situation might go out of gear. The Money-lenders Act of 1938 deserves mention in this regard. According to this Act, to my knowledge for the first time Government came to rescue the poor tribls by fixing 9% of single ad 12 % of compound interest. It goes without saying that the cooperative movement which started even before 1872 under the able guaidence of E. Muller was gradually gaining ground and by 1909 it was seen helping the converted Christian population in coming out of the clutch of the Mahajans.

Post-Independence Policy

The attainment of independence of India in 1947 marked a significant change in the responsibility of the state. Now India was a welfare state hence the assumption of responsibility by the state for the provision of minimum standard of economic and social security to all was not hypothetical. The basic obligation of the welfare state was to guarantee fundamental human needs like food, shelter and protection against exploitation also render assistance to individuals in adverse circumstances. Late Pt. Nehru, the first Prime Minister of India had seen the wretched conditions of rural and tribal India. He wanted to uplift the downtrodden. I am tempted to quote a few lines from speech made in the Indian Parliament on 3rd April 1948:

"However, I consider that in the present context of affairs in regard to these unfortunate countrymen of ours, who have not have any opportunities in the past, special attempt should be made, of course, in the educational and economic field even in political field we must see that they have a proper place till they find their own legs to stand upon without external aid."

At the initiative of late Pt. Nehru, the National Government. felt that , prior to agricultural reorganisation and development in a planned manner, it was necessary to undertake a thorough investigation of the problem of rural and tribal credit. Accordingly in 1951-52, the All India Rural Credit Survey was conducted by a committee appointed by the Reserve Bank of India, with Mr.A.D. Gorwala as its chairman and Prof.D.R. Gadgil as a member. The report was submitted in 1954. The highlights of report may be summed up as follows:

(a) The performance in institutional agencies were much below expectations. The government agencies provided 3.3%; the cooperatives 3.1% and the Commercial banks 9% if the total amount of rural credit.

(b) The private individual credit agencies such as money

lenders, traders, relatives and landlords provided about 9.3% the total amount of rural credit. In fact, the money lenders alone supplied about 70% of the total amount of the borrowed funds.

(c) The most starling revelation of the survey was that the major portion of the loans from cooperatives went to the bigger agriculturists.

(d) 32% of the borrowing by the cultivators was for capital expenditure on farm, about 15% for current expenditure on farm, about 47% for family expenditure and the rest for non-farm business expenditure. This means that about half of the borrowed amount were utilised for un-productive family expenditure.

(e) Regarding the security that could be offered by cultivators, it was discovered that about 50% of the families surveyed were willing to offer their immovable property as security; of the rest, about 25% indicated personal security.

(f) The village average of outstanding debt per family varied from Rs. 29 to Rs. 1200. The average borrowing of a cultivating family during 1951-52 was Rs. 210/-.

Magnitude of Indebtedness of Village Pugu

In foregoing few pages a sketch of rural and tribal indebtedness in India has been presented. Here a case-study into the indebtedness of a particular tribal village is attempted which is based on the empirical data collected from the field. By the method of Individual interview, with the head of each family of the village it was calculated that 20 families out families of Pugu were plunged into loan-both in cash and kind. The total amount of money borrowed by the entire village was Rs 2245/- in cash and 59 maunds of paddy in kind. Thus, the average burden of loan per family would come roughly to Rs.77/- in cash and two maunds of paddy in kind. Hence keeping an eye on their poor economic resources and ability to repay the debts, the burden was quite heavy.

Loan Advancing Institutions of Pugu

After the magnitude of indebtedness has been measured, it is high time to examine the sources of credit from which the villagers borrow. A study of existing rate of interest and terms and conditions for borrowing also deserves specific mention. The field data show that there were three main sources of credit from where the villagers used to borrow during need. The details of each institution are given below:-

(1) The Professional village money-lenders and the **Mahajansa :** The professional village money-lenders and Mahajans alone advanced 38% of the total loan requirement of Pugu. These persons namely Rampratap Sahu, Mahadeo Sahu, Harkhu Munsi and Janamiai Sahu all from Gumla used to advance loan at Puqu. Normally a loan could be advanced only to a familiar person, but in some cases loans were not directly known to the in such cases the bailer would get something from the creditor and a little from the debtor also. The rate of interest was highly flexible and varied from 20% to 70% according to status, ability to bargain, tact and urgency of the problem. Chhotia Bhagat of Pugu borrowed money from Mahadeo Sahu of Gumla @ 15K% whereas Birsai Oraon of the same village had to pay @ 30% interest to the creditor.

In addition to an exorbitant rate of interest, the method of calculating the interest was also entirely arbitrary. The poor debtors of Pugu narrated their sad experience of repaying the loan. The theme of the narration was that although looking into the pages of register for the principal amount was a must, at the time of repayment of loan, the calculation of interest was rather funny. The actual chargeable interest had nothing to do with the principal. In most of the cases the interest would surpass and even multiply the principal within a very short period of time. If some one called in question about the genuineness of the account the Mahajans had a set answer that everything was written in the register and anything written was perfectly correct and beyond doubt.

The villagers had various experiences in each transaction and I am tempted to mention one of a many cases recorded in the field. One Birsai Oraon of Pugu borrowed Rs. 300/- from Harkhu Munsi in the 1958. Birsai paid Rs.350/- in 1959. Again in 1960 he paid Rs.135/- in cash and 4 maunds of paddy in kind but even then in the year 1961 Rs. 150/ were recorded due against his name. Thus, it is vivid from the perusal of the case mentioned above that the country is in the grip of debt that shackle agriculture. I am very much in agreement with Dr.M.Arokia Swami, "Those who have eyes to see, let them turn to any village in India and they would find crushing poverty and utter destitution with perhaps, a sprinkling of wealth here and there. Rural indebtedness and rural poverty from a vicious circle because the one leads to the other ad-in-finitum".

(ii) **The Village Co-operative Bank :** The idea of co-operative bank came to Chotanagpur as early as 1872, but due to lack of the proper knowledge of five the pace of progress was rather slow in the beginning. The growing need for credit with ever increasing rate of interest coupled with the cunning attitude of Mahajans compelled the innocent tribals of Pugu to incept a mini-cooperative bank of her own. The historical background of the inception of bank is very interesting ad useful. Actually it was a famine like situation prevailing over the village of Pugu in the year 1948 in which the villagers were left to lament at their miserable lot by the Mahajans, that the Pugu cooperative, bank was barn. It happened so, that there was a total crop failure in 1948 in the locality of Pugu due to draught. The farmers had to face a very hard time. In the beginning they lived on by borrowing from the neighbours, who had some old stock, but keeping an eye on the magnitude of demand it appeared a drop in the ocean. After that there appeared a famine like condition in the village as everyone had run short. The grief stricken and panickly of starvation, people rushed to Ram Pratap Sahu of Sumla, a the then landlord of the village for loan. Seeing a large number of needy persons, Rampratap wanted to exploit the situation. Firstly he refused to pay any loan, but after some persuasion and assurance of the offer of a very high rate of interest, Rampratap agreed to invest a few maunds of paddy interest being 30 pailas per Kath which was 75% of the grain borrowed. In addition to the exorbitant rate of interest, much against their will the tribals were forced for Theppa (Thumb impression) as a proof of the debt, which pinched them very much as well as made them suspicious also. But as necessity knows no bound, they had no alternative than to borrow with heavy heart.

As it is very commonly mentioned, that misfortune never comes alone, was true with the poor people of Pugu. The next harvest was also not good. The poor farmers were crushed with the heavy burdens of debt. They could not pay the arrear debt of Rampratap and had to hear the scolding instead.

It was really a very hard time in the history of Pugu where starvation was hanging like sword of Democles, but thanks to a few village leaders like Gopi Gope, Mahali Gope, Somra Oraon and Jhagroo Draon whose leadership saved the village in the period of crisis. These villagers lenders thought of establishing an institution which might help by advaning loans during the period of scarcity. As has been mentioned that the harvest of 1949 also was not good. They started collecting one Katha of paddy per family for incepting a cooperative bank in the village. They could collect only 5 Kaths due to hard time, but the mass consensus was in favour of the inception of bank. When Rampratap Sahu, the Mahajans of Pugu came to know about the reaction of the people over his scolding and inception of a mini-bank at Pugu, he was shocked at first, but that was not all. He disliked the move of the villagers who might go out of his clutch and needless to mention his prestige was also involved in it. As such he was restless to nip the bank in bud. He instigated Maya Mahto, the village- Mahto, (employed by the landlord for the collection -of rent), to sabotage the plan of inception of the bank by all means. Maya was assured for some prise for the task. He started propagating against the leaders in the village and confessed that the leaders had a plan to grab a huge quantity of paddy. A few persons were influenced by Maya and they did not pay paddy inspite of their commitment. Thus, partially due to bad harvest and propaganda of Maya the leaders could collect only small quantity of paddy in 1919.

The harvest of 1950 was good and the leaders saw a ray of hope. Inspite of best disturbing attempt of Maya the leaders collected 24 Kath of paddy that year. Thus, in the year 1950 the Pugu cooperative bank started functioning with its initial capital of 29 Kaths of paddy, with Soma Oraon as the Munsi (account keeper) and Gopi Gope, Mahali Ram, Jhagroo Oraon and the Phagoo Mahto as its members. The rate of interest was fixed @15 pailas per Kath per annum. This rate of interest continued till 1959 after which it was lowered to 10 pailas per Kath.

Of late till 1957 this bank was dealing only in there was no capital in cash. The same year a few persons who had been to Bhutan and Assam paid the dues in cash. After bank started dealing in cash also. In the year 1961 the capital of the bank increased to 125 Kath of paddy in kind and Rs.500/ in cash. The rate of interest was kept 25% for cash and 30% of kind. The rate of interest was kept quite high for two purposes.

(i) To allure the tribals to save more and invest more in the bank and to increase the capital of the bank thereby.

(ii) To discourage the debtors to take loans for unnecessary expenses like litigation and drink.

The villagers were very happy with the working of the bank and were thankful to the leaders for its inception. They cared a fig about a high rate of interest and told that if they paid more interest the bank would become more rich in less time, moreover whatever they paid was deposited in their account as they were share-holders of the bank. Only after a few years of working, the bank had advanced 58% of the total loan requirement of the villagers in 1961. Today, people of Pugu are very much proud of the fact that no one has to go outside the village in search of loan. Thus, to sum up it could safely mentioned that owing to the felt need of people whenever any institution is born there is every possibility of its nice thriving.

Gumla Graingola

State sponsored graingola was the third source from where the villagers of Pugu borrowed paddy. Although this was comparatively more rich institution, sponsored by the Goverment of Bihar, the villagers of Pugu had taken only 4% of the total loan in the year 1961 where as the little

Pugu cooperative bank had advanced 58% loans the same year. The following is a short casestudy of Gumla Graingola:

The Gumla Graingola was established in the year 1940 by the Revenue department of the Government. of Bihar. The management of the Graingola continued to be under the control of Revenue department till 1946. After the Independence of India in 1947 it was transferred from Revenue to Welfare department . In the beginning it was in a rented house of Sri Ramlal Sahu of Gumla at a monthly rent of Rs.28/- only. In the year 1955 it was shifted in its own building constructed by the Government of Bihar.

The Gumla Graingola was invested in 1940 initially with 327 Kath of paddy as its capital. This increased to 854 Kath in 1950 and by the end of 1960 it further increased 1336 maund of paddy There were 32 villages within the jurisdiction of Gumla Graingola and the village of Pugu was also one of them. Thus, keeping an eye on the vastness of area, the meagre stock of the Gola appeared to be a drop in the Ocean. In addition to the short supply of the capital there were various technical handicaps in procuring the loans. There were very limited purposes when loans could be had. As per Government. directive loans could be advanced only to owners and occupiers of arable lands, for relief of distress or for seed. Again there were limited specified period of time for the release of the loan and also for the repayment. all these rules and time bonds acted as limitations for the tribals who hardly cared for time. Even in procuring the loan there were fixed and formal procedure regarding making application, executing agreement all these had more of paper work for illiterate tribals and this was why that the villagers of Pugu had borrowed only 4% of their total loan requirement from the Grain Gola. The consensus of people regarding the graingola was that it was a white elephant of the Government. of Bihar.

Thus, from the perusal of the working of the three loan advancing institutions -(i) the village moneylender and Mahajans (ii) the indigenous cooperative bank and (iii) the state sponsored graingola it could be safely mentioned that while the village moneylenders and Mahajans charged a very exorbitant rate of interest and practised all the blackmails to exploit the innocent and illiterate tribals, the state sponsored graingola had a chain of formalities in writing hence not congenial for the illterate tribal folk. The most popular was the village cooperative bank. Though small in sise and capacity, people had full faith in its working and competence. To sum up the working of village cooperative bank it could be said that any small institutions of indigenous origin and based on the felt need of local people rate more welcome and also useful than some big Government. sponsored scheme which is always regarded as an eotic institutions served by the aline people in the folk society. Such big schemes have a tinge of imposition and as such fail to get local patronage, instead some foul Play is suspected and as a result fail to deliver any good in want of local cooperation. Though this is the story of a solitary tribal village, it should work as an eye-opener for the planners and social engineers who are always in haste to recommend some schemes to cure the common ills without any knowledge of Cultural setting and of the local felt need. I wish, we had many more village leaders like Mahli, Gopi and Jhagroo and may more village cooperative banks like Pugu. What I feel is that cooperative movement is not a bew thing. Some form of cooperation is as old as human race itself, moreover there is a human drive to cooperate also. Hence, it should be the duty of responsible persons first to educate the people about cooperation than to experiment some big plan to fail. Once they are convinced about the importance of cooperation in human life, they will themselves try to solve their problems on cooperative basis and after the felt need of local people is known to the planner and Government. even the slightest help will enable them to solve the most difficult problems.

VII
The Hindu Jajmani System in a Tribal Village of Chottanagpur

The village Anjan with its picturesque landscape is truly a beautiful village of the Chotanagpur plateau. It falls within Arangi Paragna of Gumla subdivision in Ranchi district. The village, inhabited by 1225 persons of 14 different communities, both the study a Hindu institutions of Jajmani systms in a tribal village.

Caste Determinism

According to Hindu law the birth determines the caste, and every caste has a fixed economic and social status. Thus, a Brahmin child, by virtue of his high caste becomes a Pandit in society. Similarly, a carpenter child adopts his traditional occupation of carpentry; and Thus, in an agrarian society the selection of an occupation is not a problem. References to this effect are found in the writing of Manu when a particular 'varna' was assigned a specific task to perfrom not only for the benefit of the very verna but for others as well. It will not be out of place to quote a few lines of Manu as translated by Maxmuller in the "The Sacred Books of the East, "Vol.XXV," But in order to protect this universe he, the most resplendent one, assigned separate (duties and) occupations to those who sprang from his mouth, arms, thighs and feet. To Brahmins he assigned teaching and studying (the veda) sacrificing for their own benefit and for others giving and accepting for (of alms). The Kshatrya he commanded to protect the people, to bestow gifts, offer sacrifices, to study (the veda and to abstain from attaching himself to sexual pleasure. The Vaisya to tend cattle, to lend money, and to cultivate land. one occupation only the lord prescribed to the sudra, to serve meekly even these (others) three castes".

Thus, from the careful study of Manu, it becomes clear that the traditional occupations of all the Vernas anre determinded by the birth; moreover a Verna is directed to have monopoly in one or more trades allotted to it. Again there is specific mention that each specialist in one or more trades is obliged to serve all other communities of society. Thus, the mutual exchange of services of all the useful functional communities is a permanent featute of the Indian caste-system and this constant interaction of the cfunctional castes on permanent basis might have resulted in bringing home the Jajmani system.

The word 'Jajmani' has been derived from a Saskrit term 'Yajman' which means a man who perfroms a Yajna (sacred rite). The vedic literature is full of the use of term Jajman and here and there we find references to the family priest (Purohit) praying to God for the prosperity of his Jajman (client). From the study of religious scriptures it is clear that the perfromance of a Yagna was faishon of the Vedic day for which the presence of a responsible Pandit was a must. Religion is a matter of belief, Thus, someone developed faith in a particular Pandit and whenever he needed the service of a Pandit he might call in the familier one. Thus, that particular pandit would become a permanent family priest and in course of time his sons and grand-sons may have gained his Jajmani-right over the family. Therefore, the present (Hindu) Jajmani system has its root in the habitual sacred perfromances of the attached family priest for the welfare of the Jajman. After the Brahmins got their Jajmani rights, the other functional castes like the Barber, the Potter, the Goldsmith, the Carpenter and the Dhobi who also helped in the Yajna come in an agreement with the client conerend to help him in such other occupational services as would insure a regular labour supply of the functinal castes. The same pattern of labour supply continued when the society was gradually changed into an agrarian one and a few more castes that were useful for the agricultural operations came into being, with Jajmani rights and duties. Now, when more importance is attached to economy than to religion the Jajmani system itself has acquired implications concerned more with economy than religion. As such the modern anthropologists discuss the Hindu jajmani system in the context of economy.

W. H Wiser deserves congratulations for his book 'The Hindu Jajmani Systems' published in 1936. This is the first work of its kind, in which wisher has fully succeeded in describing Jajmani relations as a system. Under this system each caste-group within a vilage is expected to give certain standardised services to the families of other castes. The family of the family head served by a functional caste is known as his Jajmani, on the other a man who performs servuce for his jajmand, is caled Kamin or Kam Karnewala (one who works).

The characteristic feature of this system is that it runs very smoothly even without transaction in terms of money. Morever, payments have not to be made for every item of service rendered by the Kamin. The payments are made in grains periodical it or yearly or half-yearly basis. Jajmani rights are regarded as a from of property which passes from father or son and it is like the leaded property which is equally apportioned among brothers when they separate from a joint family. Jajmani rights can be transferred and sold by the Kamin and it is in this context that the villagers say "GAON RAJAKA DECHE BAKHO" (The village is owned by the king but the Bakho-a professional dancer and singer sells it).

The most important function of the Jajmani system is to assure a stable and regular supply of labour. If the kamin has the right to seek a regular payment from his Jajmans, he in return is obliged to see that the work allotted to him does not suffer. Both the kamin and his Jajman try to abide by the terms and conditions of the Jajman's agreement and if one of them fails in duty the other may warn against sackness. But now-a-days the kamin is better organised and try to exploit the Jajman because usually there is a dearth of kamins in a particular village and a developed trade unionism protects the kamin from being dismissed by the Jajman. According to professor Dube, "This system is both complex and delicate. It is not easy for ann agriculturist to remove a family attached to this household and secure the services of another. For example, A, a barber is attached to the family of B, an agriculrist. If for any reason B is greatly dissatisfied with the services of A and wants those of another, he cannot abruptly dismisss A. His difficulty will not be in dismissing him, but in finding a substitute. Each of these castes has its own inter-village council. Occupational castes have developed trade unionism, and their code of professional ethics and etiquette too is very rigid.. The dismissed person will be protected by this professional etiqutte. No one else would be willing to act as a substitute, for fear of being penalised by the caste Panchayat". Dube, (1955-pp.60).

Population of Village Anjan

There are 1225 souls in the village and belong to various tribes and castes. Their community -wise figure is presented here in the following table.

Table 1

Sl. No.	*Caste/Tribe*	*Total No. of family*	*Total Population*	*Percentage*
1.	Oraon	113	804	65.7
2.	Ghasi	23	116	9.8
3.	Chik Braik	11	65	5.3
4.	Lohra	12	62	5.0
5.	Kharwar	10	49	4.0
6.	Kumhar (Potter)	6	39	3.1
7.	Munda	5	23	1.8
8.	Brahmin	2	14	1.1
9.	Rajput	2	14	1.1
10.	Barber	2	14	1.1
11.	Dhobi	2	7	0.6
12.	Mali	1	8	0.6
13.	Baniya	1	6	0.5
14.	Ahir	1	4	0.3

THE JAJMANI SYSTEM IN ANJAN

The Jajmani system in Anjan is a bit complex because of the fact that tribals of the village have not been used to this systm from the very beginning. It is true after the immigration of the important functional Hindu castes in the village, the tribals also wanted the extension of their services on the Jajmani basis and it was readily available. But it has been the common experience of all the Hindu kamins that their tribal Jajmans do not have as much faith in this Jajmani system as the Hindus. This lack of faith in the Hindu kamins, has in return compelled to kamins, to give the tribals a different treatment as compared to the Hindu Jajmans of the village. Again the Hindus of the village are independent in the sense that they can pull on well even without the help of the tribal people of the village, because it is the Hindu castes which gave monoply in the skilled trades. A single tribal community of the village, Lohra is important for the Hindus, because it is a Lohra who makes and repairs the plough and plough-share for them. But the Lohras have also changed due to the impact of the Hinduisation. Now they call themselves Hindu Lohras and consider themselves to be Sadans. This is why that the auror has classified Lohra as a marginal group.

A careful observation of the Table 2 reveals that there are only six communities-the Brahmins, the Hasam, the Kumhar, the Ahirm, the Dhobi and the Lohra of the village which can be both kamins and jajmans. But eight communities namely, the Rajput, the Oraon, and Ghasi, the Kharwar, the Chik-Baraik, the Munda, the Oraon, and the Mahli are such as are jajmans only. It further reveals that those who are both kamins and jajmans are usually Hindus, whereas those who are only jajmans are both Hindus and tribals. From the Jajmani point of view the services of the six communities mentioned above, which are both kamins and jajmans are comparatively more important as socio-economic studies than those of the other eight communities of the village, which do not serve any one else but are being served by others. The economic activities of all the 14 communities of the two groups, mentioned above, will be given in two different orders. The details of the services rendered (and rights earned through the services) by all the six communities of Anjan are given below in Table 2.

Table 2

Community	*Nature of service*	*Rights earned through service*
1. Brahmin	Officiating at the functions related to marriage, death in the capacity of family priest.	Rs. 5/- to Rs. 7.50/- for officiating at a marriage of death rites Rs. 2/- to Rs. 5/- in cash and sidha (Raw materials) for Satyanarayan katha.
2. Hasam	Shaving and cutting hair attending to the guests distributing the invitation cards, assisting the pandit.	Annual payment of paddy @ of 1 Kath (40 pailas) per male for shaving and cutting hair. Cash payment
	Hasamin cuts the nails of Baby and mother on the birth of a child.	@ of half paid to the Brahmin priest on the eve of marriage or death rite and Satyanarayan Katha plus free meals or the Sidha as the cases may be.
3. Kumhar	Supplying earthen vessels for daily use and on the eve of marriage and death and manufacturing earthen tiles for the customers.	Cost of the vessel supplied, free meal or sidha on the eve of marriage or death. For manufacturing tiles he charges wages either in cash or kind.
4. Ahir	Grasing casttle of the village.	Annual paddy payment for grasing @ 1kath (40 pailas) per pair of oxen

			and 1khanrai (20 pailas per cow.
5.	Dhobi	Washing the polluted and the dirty clothes on the eve of birth and death in the family of Jajman.	He dose not wash the dirty clothes of daily use. However, his mother washes polluted clothes on birth and death for which she charges seer or rice and Rs. 1.50 p to Rs. on the economic condition of Jajman.
6.	Lohra	Making and repairing agril. tools for the Jajman.	Annual payment of 1 maund of pada per plough for making and repair the plough and sharpening the share.

Brahmin : There are two families of Brahmins having Jajmani ranging over the entire village. They have a monopoly over all the communities of the village and may not allow any outsider to officate at any religious of purificatory rate in the houses of their jajmans. They, however, see to it that when any one of them goes out, there is some one to officiate. Originally all the families of the village were looked after by the grand-father of Shri Parshuram Mishra. But when the late Maniknath Pandey settled at Anjan Permanently, a few families of jajmans were transferred to him. Shri Mishra and Shri Laldeo pandey, son of the late, Manikanth Pandey, being consious, they have divided their Jajmans families. As they continue to have perfect mutual understanding, alternative arrangements are always easy their Jajmans, work never suffers. The Jajmans also are fully aware of it and do not mind so long as they are not in trouble. Priest is called by all the communities of the village in general and by the Satya Narayan Katha, and they must call their family priest for this.

Like the Hindus, the people of marginal castes also call

a Brahnin for all the sacred and purificatory rites. Among the marginal castes the kharwars and the Chik Baraiks cannot observe any important rite without a Brahmin, whereas the Lohars and the Mahlis usually call a Brahmin to conduct the death rites.

The Oraons, among the tribals communities, are very fond of a Brahmin priest. Among the Oraons also, those who have been converted into Hindus by taking the path (Lesson) of the Bhagat Cult are very purificatory in lconsulting a Brahmin preist for all the sacred and purifactiory rites. A few Bhagats keep the record of the time when a baby is born, and they consult the priest for making the horoscope for which they pay Rs. 7/- to Rs. 11/-. The Mundas, who hold a very important post of the village called Phan and deserves respect for the same, seldom call a Brahmin; but they do so when they want to listen to the Satyanarayan Katha.

The family priest calls his client Jajmans but the Jajmans do not call a Brahmin their kamin; instead they use the term Pandit or Purohit for them. They may have learnt these terms from the Hindus of their neighbouring village. The villagers have a special for the Brahmins; as a rule every non-Brahmin must get upon a Brahmins arrival as a token of respectful courtesy. The eldery persons of the village pay saluations to a Brahmin by slightly bowing down and saying pai-lagun, and a Brahmin in response blessed them, which he generally expresses by nodding. The mode of payments to a Brahmin is somewhat special. He always receives he Dakshina in cash and the Sidha in kind. The quantity of Dakshina varies with the economic condition of the Jajman, who has to pay it. But usually the charge is Rs. 5/- to Rs. 7.50 in cash for conducting a marriage or a death rite plus Sidha in kind. Similarly, the Dakshina for the Satyanaryan Katha varies from Rs. 2/- to Rs. 5/- in cash and Sidha. The priest expects Rs. 7/- to Rs. 11/- for casting the horoscope of a child in the family of his jajmans. A few jajmans give one sup (winnowing fan) of paddy to their family priest.

It has been mentioned earlier that Shri Parshuram

Mishra, the male head of the family, is the Mukhiya of the village and has sufficient laded property to be looked after. Moreover, he is the President of H.E. School at Toto, one of the Directors of the Central Coorperative Bank, Gumla, the Chariman of Agriculture, Animal Husbandry and Cooperative standing committee Gumla, and member of about half a dosen institutions of Gumla. He is an active politician and is even keen on visiting diferent parts of India and meeting the important persons of Bihar ad India. Now he has got a house constructed at Gumla and remains there most of the time. Hence he does not find time to give due attention to Jajmani. A man of multifarious activities he finds Jajmani the least paying and most time consuming. Naturally, he does not mind if any of his Jajmans calls a Brahmin from Toto to conduct a rite.

I met Shri Jagnnath Pandey to Toto who had come to officiate at a Katha at Anjan, and gathered from him that he use to visit Anjan very often Shri Parshuram Mishra was no longer interested in the traditional occupation of Virtiya. On the other hand I learnt from Shri Mishra that whenever he had leisure he did not mind conducting rite : but honestly speaking he seldom got an oppertunity for it. Similar is the case with Shri Laldeo Pandey the male head of the other Brahmin family. He is the post-master of Anjan Post office. Besides, he is a rich man of the village having sufficient land to till. He has a hobby to junting activites and has no interest in the Jajmani. He also does not mind if some Brahmin from Toto comes to officiate as a priest in the family of his Jajmans. Thus,, by way of summing up this can be safely said that the Brahmins of Anjan do not have to depend on Jajmani, thanks to their prosperous circumstances.

THE HASAM

At Anjan there are only two families of Hasams. They come next only to the Brahmins in the social scale of kamins. The villagers regard them to be chief of all the village menials. The Hasams hold a very important role in the ritual structure of the village. Their presence at all the rituals of life and sacred perfromances is deemed essential.

It is only the barber and his wife whose services are indispensible for all the communities of the village. The Harijans (the Dhobi and the Ghasi) of the village usually do not call a Brahmin to officiate at the ritual of birth, marriage and death. But the presence of Barber ad his wife is a must on all such occasions. The tribals also call the barber at all the purificatory rites and the Hindus of the village regard them as the second pandit in the sense the even the pandit has to depend upon the barber whereas the barber may not depend on the pandit.

I met Jarkoo Thakur, a responsible barber of the village and could gather from him the following information. "It is the Hasam who does all the arrangements for the Pandit. He collects the sacred fuel for the Homa. He arrives at the house of Jajman before the Pandit, and when all the necessary arrangements have been made by the Hasam, the pandit is informed about it. Generally, the Pandit is late, so it is the duty of the village barber to contact the Pandit and escort him to the place fixed for the ritural. Sometimes only for this the barber may have to visit the house of the Pandit times and again. On the other hand the Pandit comfortably presumes that everything must have been kept ready so that he does not have to waste his temper and scolds the poor barber, who being a subordinate has to bear everything with full cokposure. In fact, he must be praised for this gesture of restraints, as his remuneratin also is not much of an allurement, generally it is half of the Pandit's dakshina.

(1) The daily serivce of the Barber is to visit his Jajman for shaving and hair cutting. The Hasams cut the nails on being asked by the Jajman. Usually a Jajman expects his Hasam once a week for shaving and once a month for hair cutting. But in the case of death in the family of his Jajman he has to visit very frequently and stay much longer. Similarly, the Hasamin, the wife of Hasam, visits her Jajmans once a week, cuts the nails and applies red colour to the nails and the feet of the women folk. But the barber does not get immediate payment for shaving or hair cutting. It is done annually and in kind. A Barber gets annually one kath (40 pailas) of paddy per adult male and one Khanrai (20

pailas) male child in the family of his Jajman. His wife gets the Sidha for cutting the nails of the women folk. In addition to this payment, during the harvesting season every year, he goes to the field of his Jajmans once, and gets and bundle of paddy stalks, free of cost.

(2) The ceremonial or ritual service : The ceremonial serivices rendered by the Barber is no less important. It has been mentioned earlier that a barber is required either to assist or officiate at all the rituals connected with all the major events in the course of life-birth, marriage and death.

Birth : It is the Barber who cuts the hair of the baby soon after birth, while his wife cuts the nails of the mother. They get Rs. 1/- to Rs. 2/- and Sidha for this.

Marriage : The services of the Barber in connection with a marriage have two aspects : (i) The Sociological function of the Barber is to act as a Dootee (a go-between) for carrying the message from one party to another, and settling the marriage with the help of a Pandit. This office of the broker is very important. He is the first person who visits the house of the groom and officially opens negotation. Sometimes a Brahmin Pandit can go alongwith the Barber. But at Anjan, as it is, the barber is all in all as the Brahmins of Anjan seldom find the leisure for going long with the Barber and negotating a marriage. The Barber gets one piece of Dhoti and Rs. 2/- to Rs. 5/- for this. When the marriage has been finally settled it is the barber's duty to distribute the invitation cards among the friends and relatives for which he gets Sidha and a few paise.

On the day of marriage, both the Barber and his wife are busy with various social and ritual perfromances. He collects the scared fuel for the Homes and makes all the necessary arrangments required near the vedi. He has to shave the relations and friends of his Jajman who assemble on the eve of the marriage. For all these services he gets food or sidha. As for the cash, it is always half of the amount paid to the Pandit. His wife is kept busy for distributing sweets and taking care of the bride. She gets food or Sidha and also some paise.

Death : The Barber has to shave and do the hair cutting of all the male members of the family. His wife cuts the nails of women folk. For this they get sidha. On the day of shradha either for officiating or for helping the Brahmin priest as the case may be, he gets half of the amount given to the Pandit.

It the barber is called for assisting the Pandit on the eve of Satya Narayan Katha, he gets sidha in kind and in cash half of the amount paid to the Pandit.

(3) The Kumhar (Potter)

The potters of Anjan have a floating Jajmani system in the sense that neither kamin nor jajmans are permanent. Any member can purchase the earthen vessels from any potter, similarly on the eve of marriage and death any potter can supply earthen pots on payment in cash or kind. According to Mahli Mahto about twenty year ago they had a Jajmani system in the true sense when no other potter could supply earthen pots in the family of his jajmans. But due to the immigration of two more families of potters in addition to the three families which were very old the system had to be changed. When these two families immigrated to Anjan they wanted some Jajmans in the village but the three kamin families of the potters would not spare even a single family to the new settlers. The new settlers, in revenge started supplying vessels at a much lower rate and Thus, attracted most of the village customers. The old familes of the potter had to suffer because the immigrants got public support in the village. For a pretty longtime there was a very tense relation between the old and new potter families in the village. Eventually, a compromise was possible. They decided to sell the vessels at a fixed rate and no one would increase or decrease it without a prior metting of all the five families of potters. Again, they decided that any potter could supply vessels to any one and Thus, the old standing Jajmani relation disappeared. Now every potter has a fixed price for every pot, so a customer can purchase pots from any one.

As regards the payment to the potter, in all cases it has to be made immediately. On the occasion of marriage or death, when the potters have to supply vessels on a large scale and deliver them at the house of the customer, they charge sidha or free meals. For manufacturing the earthen tiles, the potters are empolyed on the daily wage basis and the payment can be made in cash or kind.

(4) The Ahir : The cows and the bulls of the village are generally in charge of the village-Ahir. At about sun-rise, the Ahir takes out the cattle to the village jungle for grasing. Such cows, as have recently calved are miked by the Ahir. At about 10 a. m. the Ahir returns with the cattle to Bathan or a resting place for the cattle, This Bathan at Anjan is situated towards the extreme western part of the village. The Ahir goes to take his mid-day meal, leaving some boy of his family to look after the cattle. On his return to the Bathan after the mid-day meal, he takes a little rest. He then goes out again with the cattle and returns home at about sun-set. During the cultivation season, the plough bullocks are generally looked after by the owner itself. The Ahir does not graze the goat and the buffalo of the village.

As regards the remuneration paid to the Ahir, each of the Jajmans has to pay one kath (40 palias) of paddy for one pair of oxen and one khannai (20 pailas) per cow every years.

(5) The Dhobi : There are two families of Dhobis at Anjan. Lal Mani Baitha is the original settler of the village whereas, Gujua Dhobi, the maternal uncle of Lal Mani is an immigrant at Anjan. Bujua has no Jajman whereas Lal Mani has Jajmans all over the seven villages namely, Anjan, Barinakhar, Kutuma, Marwa, Gortoli, Gani, and Dumurla. Lal Mani Bhaitha is a school teacher in the village night school and has 4.10 acres of cultivable land. He does not wash the dirty clothes of the daily use because he is educated and considers it disgraceful to wash the dirty and blood stained clothes of all communities of the village. But his mother with the help of her brother (Gujua) washes the polluted clothes of her jajmans on the eve of birth and death. She gets one seer of rice and Rs. 1.50 to Rs. 3/- varying with the econmic condition of the jajman. Lal Mani has very little interest in his traditional trade of brooming, but he is a hardly cultivators and a good teacher at the village night-school.

(6) The Lohar : The 12 families of Lohars are regarded as chief among the essential artisans in the village. Their service are very important from the economic point of view. It is the Lohras who make plough, spadle, axe, harrow, sickle, hand-hoe and plough share for agricultural purpose. Similarly, for the mud houses of the village they make the door, window and wall pegs. For the household they make the cot, small charpai (rope bed) pestles for crushing grain, folder cutting stumps, arrow head and several other small sharp weapons for hunting proposes. The Lohras are paid one maund of paddy annually for making and repairing the plough and sharpening the plough share. They charge the payment in cash or kind for making all other agricultural or household articles and mentioned above. A Jajman may require the service of a Lohra for making the repairing houses. In that case, payment has to be made on the daily basis.

Thus, from the perusal of the working of the Jajmani system of Anjan it is evident that the tribals of the village have also welcomed the Hindu institution of Jajmani system. The Hindu co-villagers also did not resist their incorporation rather, they gladly extended the Jajmani facilities to the tribals. But it has been the common experience of all the Hindu kamins that their tribal Jajmans do not have as much faith in this system as the Hindus. This lack of faith in Hindu kamins by the Tribal Jajman may be due to the recent incorporation of the Tribals into the midstream of the Hindu Jajmani system. Now it is entirely upto the tribal jajmans of Anjan as to how they maintain the tie of the Jajmani system.

VIII
The Leadership Pattern of a Tribal Village : Anjan a Case Study

Anjan is a mixed tribal village because as many 14 communities both of the tribal and Hindu castes live in the village. The details are given in the following table :

Sl. No.	*Caste / Tribe*	*Male*	*Female*	*Total*	*Percentage*
1.	Oraon	400	404	804	65.7
2.	Ghasi	59	57	116	9.8
3.	Chik- Baraik	35	30	65	5.3
4.	Lohra	30	32	62	5.0
5.	Kharwar	20	29	49	4.0
6.	Kumhar	24	15	39	3.0
7.	Munda	8	15	23	1.8
8.	Brahmin	6	8	14	1.1
9.	Rajput	6	8	14	1.1
10.	Hajam	5	9	14	1.1
11.	Dhobi	2	5	7	0.6
12.	Mahli	4	4	8	0.6
13.	Bania	4	2	6	0.5
14.	Ahir	2	2	4	0.3
Total		605	620	1,225	100.00

The Leadership Pattern of the Village

The term leadership designates role behaviour of a dominant, influencing, and directing character. It is provided by an individual who stands in a superordinate status position to one or more individuals. These individuals, by nature of their interaction, comprise a social group whose collective behaviour is more or less goal-oriented. Thus a leader is one who stands in a superordinate relationship to one or more other individuals.

Similarly, Krech and Crutchfield have given thirteen characteristics of a leader which are given below :

(1) Executive, (2) Planner, (3) Policy maker, (4) Expert (5) External group representatives, (6) Control of internal relationship (7) Giver of reward and punishment (8) Arbitrator and mediator, (9) Examplar, (10) Symbol of group, (11) Idealist, (12) Father figure, and (13) Scape goat. 2

Now, obviously, these definitions and Characteristics of leader and leadership appear to be Utopain ideas in the Present context of the study of leaders of a village. At Anjan any one who has some followers is regarded as a leader. Thus quite a large number of leaders can be seen in the village who have support of a particular caste, group or entire village. Thus the leaders of Anjan can be grouped under three heads.

(i) Leader of a particular community.

(ii) Traditional leaders of the village.

(iii) Modern Hindu leader of the village.

(i) Leader of a particular community Since Anjan is inhabited by a mixed population of fourteen communities, and each community is led by one leader the number of these leaders come to fourteen in the village. These leaders are the polotical heads of their respective communities and represent their specific tribe or caste in a meeting of the village.

The following chart bears the names of these community leaders :

	Name of the Community	*Name of the leader*
1.	Brahmin	Shri Prarashuram Mishra
2.	Rajpur	Shri Kastu Soy
3.	Hazam	Shri Jareku Thakur
4.	Kumhar	Shri Bina Mahto
5.	Baniya	Shri Triloki Sahu
6.	Ahir	Mrs. Sobraina Ahirin
7.	Ghasi	Kanglu Ram Ghasi
8.	Dhobi	Shri Lalmani Baitha
9.	Kharwar	Shri Khudi Singh
10	Baraik	Shri Bandhu Baraik
11.	Munda	Shri Harkhu Baiga
12	Oraon	Shri Punia Oraon Ex-M.L. A
13.	Lohra	Shri Sokha Lohra
14.	Mahli	Shri Gandal Mahli

Anjan is facing crisis of the community leadership because of an emergent group of Bhagats. These Oraon Bhagats do not believe in Punia Oraon and they have selected Shri Bhikhiya Oraon, the Guru of Kamroo Kamakhya Bhagat sect, to be the leader of all Hinduised Bhagats of Anjan.

(ii) The Traditional Leaders of Anjan : Pahan and Mahto are the two traditional leaders at Anjan. The Pahan is the ritual head of the village who makes sacrifices and offers worship on behalf of the villagers. The pahan is regarged to be mediator between the earth and the people whose interests lie in that particular locality. The Pahan offers special sacrifice on behalf of the people during the sarhul festival which occurs in April. A mimic marriage of Pahan and his wife takes place on this eve. The mother earth is married to the sun God, and the Pahan represents the Sun and his wife the earth.

Till recently the ritual and religious leadership of Pahan

was a matter of monopoly. But after the Bhagat movement in the village of Anjan, his status has been adversely affected. The Bhagats have adopted Hindu god deities and their faith in the Pahan has shaken. They consult their respective Gurus whereas in the past they used to consult the Pahan. But even after the advent of Gurus the Pahan is respected by all.

Mahto : The mahto is the secular head of the village. who decides on disputes and looks after the traditional laws of the village. There is a common proverb in all the tribal villages that "Pahan gaon Banata Hai our Mahto gaon chalata Hai" meaning therby that the Pahan makes the village whereas the Mahto runs it.

After the Zamindari abolition, and the inception of the State-sponsored Gram Panchayat at Anjan in 1952, the powers and functions of the Mahto have been affected considerably. Now most of the cases are tried and decided by the Mukhiya and Serpancha of a Panchayat, while only a few orthodox Oraons of the village would go to the Mahto for the trial of case or some legal advice.

(iii) The Hindu leaders of the village

The Hindu constitute 17.6 percent of the total population of the village which includes 9.8 per cent of the Chasi population. It is really strange that the village is led by the Hindus, who are clearly a minority group in the village. Nor it is true that the tribals who Constitute 82.4 per cent of the total population are politically unconcious. In fact, Shri Punai Oraon, an ex-M.L. A of Anjan is a seasoned politician of this locality and is a permanent formidable rival of any Hindu leader of the village, but in the trial of strength in the Gram Panchayat election of 1960 Shri Punia Oraon lost to Shri Parashuram Mishra for the post of Mukhiya.

The history of Anjan preserves some very important data on the conflicts of the tribals with he Hindus. They reveal that whenever there has been conflict, the tribal group has been defeated by the Hindus. It is also seen that the Hindus, provoked by the tribals, have opened institution on the tribals modal and have established their separate Akhara in the village.

Some twenty years ago there was only one village Akhara on which both the tribals and the Hindus of the villalge used to dance. But one day it so happened that an Oraon insulted a Hindu boy on the Akhara. The news spred like wild fire among the Hindus of Anjan and they prevented their boys from going to dance on the tribals Akharas. Later on they established an independent Akhara reserved for the Hindus. To make the Akhara attractive they kept a Nachni, a professional dancing girl, who used to be the only female, dancing in the centre of Akhara. The Nachni was maintained on the subscription of the Hindus of village. They gave her some ornaments and a few good saris, but she fled awaya from Anjan one dark night with all the clothes and ornaments. Since then this Akhara has been without a Nachni. now only the male members of Hindu group dance on this Akhara.

Before 1958, the village leadership appeared to be a bit confused mainly for want of a person who has initiative and energy for such a job which was then not paying. The Pahan and the Mahto were the religious and secular heads of the village : Similarly the Brahmins and the Hazams were the Purificatory leaders. But then this concept of leadership was very narrow and the progeny of these persons had not to worry for the followers, because they inherited their heir by the accident of birth in a particular family. They might not possess even a single quality for leadership, but even then they held the office.

The history of the modern leadership of Anjan dates back to 1948. When an educated, young Brahmin appeared on the political scene of the village Shri Parashuram Mishra, the leader under study, could not pass Matriculation Examination in the year 1946 and went to Orissa in search of a job. He got an appointment in the Gangapur Estate of Orissa where he served for about a year. He came back to Anjan in the year 1948 as his father was not keeping well. Later, he decided to remain at Anjan.

He was not happy with the then village life of Anjan, and wanted a revolutionary change, by introducing the current ideas of welfare among the tribals and Hazams of the village. He established a "Gram Sudhar Sangh" in the year 1947 and made a few young fellows its members. They started preaching among the villagers the values of cleanliness and education in human life. They cleaned the Harijan and Adivasi streets and trained the villagers to maintian them. The "Gram Seva Kendra" was established in the year 1949 with Shri Parashuram Mishra as its president. The Seva Kendra was recognised by " the Kasturba Trust" and a post of Gram Sevika was sanctioned for the Anjan Gram Seva Kendra. One Gramsevika trained at Madhubani was posted to the Seva Kendra of Anjan on the condition that the Trust would bear 75 per cent of the total expense of the Seva Kendra for the first year and the contribution of the trust would come down to 50 per cent and 25 per cent on the second and third year. From the fourth year the financial help would be stopped and the villagers had to bear the entire expense after that. The Seva Kendra could not run more than 1951 because it had to face the economic problems in which the villagers did not share much.

The father of Shri Parashuram Mishra died in 1950. and Shri Mishra was a bit disturbed due to his domestic problems. But as a devoted social worker, Shri Mishra started his social service work afresh in the year 1952 by establishing Anjan Harijan Balika Vidalaya with the facility of co-education. His wife Mrs. Raj Kumari Mishra was appointed an honorary teacher of the school and Shri Mishra also engaged a few classes in the School. This was the first institution in the village which made so many tribals and Harijan literate and the people of Anjan began paying due respect to Shri Mishra for his noble role.

Harijan Seva Ashram

Harijans form the second numerous group in the village. The Ghasi has the second largest population of about 10 per cent in the village, but they are very backward, economically. The Ghasi tola even to-day is full of filth about which these people are careless. The term Harijan was an award of late Mahatma Gnadhi to the untouchables of India , who were so backward that their touch was sufficient to pollute the persons of clean castes. Mahatma Gandhi did not like this idea, and he started the Harijan movement. Shri Parashuram Mishra of Anjan was very much impressed by the arguments of Mahatma Gandhi and decide to do his little best for the Harijans of Anjan.

The Harijan seva Ashrama was established at Anjan on the 2nd October, 1953. Shri Parashuram Mishra raised some subscription from the villagers and demanded shramdan from Harijans of the village. Thus with the cooperation of the Harijans of the village a small thatched house was built for the office of Harijan seva Ashrama. Shri Kanglu Ram Ghasi was elected president of the Ashrama, who nominated shri Parashuram Mishra as its Secretary. Seven members were also nominated by the president. Its functions.

This institutions was an improvement on the Gram Seva Kendra. While it decided to continue the programmes as were followed earlier, it did attach special importance to the following four functions

I. To remove illiteracy from the Harijan Community was the main aim of this Ashrama. Harijan Lower Primary School was opened in the year 1953, and since then it has made a very large number of villagers literate. In fact, some of them are highly educated.

II. The second important function of this Ashrama has been to remove litigation from Harijan Soceity. Litigation is an intoxicant which spoils from the root. The simple and illiterate people of the village are befooled by the clever pleaders and their brokers. The litigation affair is reported to be one of the major reasons of the Ghasis backwardness. This Ashrama has done great help by warning the Harijans against the evils of litigation. If some one requires justice, the Gram Panchayat's court is open for them.

III. The third function of this Ashrama has been to remove extravagance from the Harijan Society. Generally, they are very fond of spending beyond their means of the eve of marriage and other festivals.

IV. The last but most important function of this Ashrama has been to remove all the dirt from the Ghasi Tola. The Ghasis are taught about the importance of cleanliness in every sphere of human life. The Harijans are shown by the practical, demonstration as to how to clean roads, streets, houses, clothes and utensils. As reported they have shown considerble improvement in this crusade against dirt; but of course, much remains to be done.

Adivasi Seva : Ashrama

Since it started functioning in 1953 , hte Harijan Seva Ashrama began to give benefits to the Harijans of the village. The tribals saw that the Harijans were so few in number, but with the help of Shri Parashuram Mishra they had organised such a nice institution, whereas they constituted about 82 per cent of the total population of the village and had no institution of that type. They required an institution where they could assemebl to discuss some problems of the tribal life but did not know the ways and means to establish it. A few enthusiastic Oraon young men went to Bithu Bhagat, the then Mukhiya of the Gram Panchayat, and presented before him the problems of establishing an institution for Adivasis on the pattern of Harijan Seva Ashrama. Shri Bithu Bhagat also felt the need for having one, but he was not clear about the ways and means. Then the deligation went to Shri Parashuram Mishra and told him that they also wanted an institution like Harijan Seva Ashrama, but had neither the fund nor an organising capacity for the same. Shri Mishra was very glad to note that the tribals had also felt the need for an institution of modern nature. He assured them all coopertion.

Shri Parashuram Mishra with the help of Bithu Bhagat Started collecting subscription from each household of the village. Thus within one year they collected about twenty maunds of paddy in the village. Those who were poor and landless were asked for bringing timber from the forest. Thus a two roomed house with a thatched roof was built.

A sum of Rs. 200/- was given from the old Panchayat fund of village. (This sum was realised as a fine from an Oraon who had premarital sex-relation with a girl of the same killi-(clan) which was also spent in the construction work of the house. Thus when the building was ready for use. Adivasi Seva Ashrama was established in the year 1955 and the newly constructed building was used as its office.

The functions of Adivasi Seva Ashrama

1. It serves as a meeting hall.
2. It is a guest house for the strangers.
3. It is very useful in keeping the marriage party in this house.
4. It is an ideal place where the villagers can conduct their cultural programmes.
5. Parashuram Mishra helped the tribals of the village to establish a Night school in hte year 1953, but for want of a separate Building the Night School runs in this very Ashrama.

In the year 1960 when Shri Mishra was elected Mukhiya of Anjan Panchayat, he wanted to improve the condition of this Ashrma . He Managed to obtain a grant of Rs. 500/- from the Welfare Department. This sum was spent over the cement plastring of the floor and white washing of the walls of the Ashrama. A small amount of the grant was spent over the purchase of a few chairs, tables, and date-mats and one carpet. Now the Adivasis of Anjan have become great admirers of the character and capability of Shri Parashuram mishra.

Harijan Upper Primary School, Anjan

From the aforesaid examles of the establishment of institutions of Anjan it is evident that all the modern institutions of the village own to Shri Parashuram Mishra for their inception. The history of the inception of Harijan U.P. School takes us back to 1952 when Anjani Balika Vidyalaya was established with Mrs.Raj Kumar Mishra,W/o Shri Parashuram Mishra as the only teacher of the School. It may be added that she did not accept any salary.

The Harijan Upper Primary School may be regarded as

an improvement on the Anjani Balika Vidyala. This Upper Primary School came into being in 1957 when the Government took the charge of the School under the Educational improvement Project. Sicne them it is being maintained by the State Government . It has more then a hundred students, both boys and girls, and two teachers Mrs. Raj Kumari Mishra as the Head-Mistress and Shri Dukhi Chanda singh as assistant Teacher of the school. They get their salary from the Block office, Gumla, payable from te E.I.P. Scheme of Bihar Government.

Anjan Post Office

The innocent vilagers of Anjan owe to Shri Parshuram Mishra for having been able to open a post office in the village, prior to this the villagers had to got o Toto, about three miles from Anjan to purchase a post card or to drop a letter. But thanks to the sincere effort of Shri Mishra, the postal authority was compelled to sanction a post offie for the village in the year 1955 on the condition that the Villagers had to provide a room for the post office. Shri parashuram Mishra gladly gave a room for the same and post office was established the same year (1955), and since then it has been serving the villagers in various ways, Shri Laldeo Pandey is the present post Master and Shri Pula Bhagat is the working post man of the village post ofice. The villagers both kol and sadan feel greatly benefited from the Jansevak and one of the School techers have to send money to their village home every month. Similarly, a few guardians of the village send mony to their wards by money orders but those who are outside Anjan either in Bhutan or Assam send letters and money orders to the members of their family at Anjan.

Anjan Multipurpose Co-operative Society

This Cooperative Society was established in the year 1956 with Shri Manik Nath Pandey as the president and Shri Parashuram Mishra as its Secretary. It has been doing various good things to the members of the Co-operative by advancing Loan, Supplying fertilizer at subsidised price and the like.

The following is the list of the office bearers of the Co-operative :

1. Shri Biru Bhagat	President
2. Shri Laideo Pandey	Secretary
3. Gauri Oraon	Treasurer
4. Shri parashuram	Member of the Executive
5. Shri Bhikhu Bhagat	-do-
6. Shri Kanglu Ram Ghasi	-do-
7. Shri Jagannath Baraik	-do-
8. Shri Bithu Bhagat	-do-
9. Shri Gauri Sanker Bhagat	-do-
10. Mrs. Rajkumari Mishra	-do-
11 .Shri Kastu Soy	-do-

Par shuram Mishra has become a village hero because of his deep insight into the problems of the people and his sympathetic understanding of their needs.

Anjani Public Library

The Present Anjani Public Library was established in the year 1947 as a personal library of Shri Mishra and it was known to the Mishra for Library. This library also owes to Shri Parashuram Mishra for its establishment. He purchased about fifty books dealing with the alphabet and pahara which were useful for the beginners. He collected about forty more books from his friends and relations and donated a few personal books to this library. Thus in the year 1947 when the library was incepted it had about one hundred books.

After the establishment of Harijan Seva Ashrama, Night School and upper Primary School in the village its function was acclerated and in the year 1955 it was converted into a Public Library. Now it has about 400 (four hundred) books of the following order.

90 Books on the alphabet and pahara in Hindi.

30 Books on English alphabet etc.

95 Books on Hindi novel.

70 Copies of Hindi Magazines.

50 Books on the short stories and poems in Hindi.

65 Books of different classes prescribed for the students of Upper Primary School.

The villagers of Anjan owe to Shri Mishra for having established a health centre at Kulhi under Anjan Gram panchayat, and for connecting Anjan with Toto a distance of three miles by a Kachcha road.

Now, all these services are very important and valuable. What the Government , with its well organised machinery and huge funds of money wants to do was done by the initiative and leadership of a single individual Parashuram Mishra of Anjan. He has become such a popular and affectionate in the village that for all political and economic matters people of all the communities go to him with the confidence that nothing is beyond the reach of "Parshu".

The popularity of Shri Mishra can be very well understood by the perusal of the following case :

Shri Parashuram Mishra for the first time contested Shri Punai Oraon in the election of Mukhiya of the Panchayat in 1960. Shri Punai Oraon was also known to be a very popular leader of that locality and he was an elected M.L.A from 1962-67. This Panchayat has more than 80 per cent of tribal population but even then Shri Shir Punai Oraon was defeated by Parashuram Mishra, and since 1960 he has been working as a successful Mukhiya of the Panchayat. Now Sri Parashuram Mishra is considered to be one of the most active and efficient leaders of Gumla Thana and holds the following chairs in various capacity :

1. He is one of the directors of the Central Co-operative Bank, Gumala.
2. He is the Chairman of the standing committee for Agriculture, Animal husbandary and copoperation, Gumala.
3. He is the President of H.E. Schol, Toto.

4. He is a member of Panchayat Samity, Gumla.
5. Secretary of the Cooperative Society for the Dairy, Gumla.
6. He is an active member of the working committee of the Vyapar Mandal, Gumala.

So far as the results of Shri Mishra's leadership for Anjan are concerned, it can be judged for the welfare services which he has done for the betterment of the village. The people of Anjan will always remember Shri Mishra for having established Harijan Seva Ashrama, Upper Primary School. Adivasi Seva Ashrama, Night School, Public Library and post ofice in the village. The Poor cultivators of Anjan bless him for having so many irrigation wells dug and the Khatwa dam constructed at the cost of Rs. 35,000/-

The villagers in general are very happy with their popular leader. they have cause to believe that the Brahmins are very kind by nature. Their "Parshu" is really a supreme instance in point.

Thus, to sum up it may be noted that in the preceding pages an attempt has been made to study the changing and persistent pattern of leadership in the village. The Parha Panchayat, caste- Panchayats and State sponsored Gram panchayat and their powers and functions have been discussed in brief. A few case studies of the inception of institutions have also been examined. leadership, both traditional and Hindu have also been analysed and the impact of Hindu leadership particularly led by Mr. Mishra on the tribal culture has been evaluated . Anjan offers a rare opportunity where the Hindu leadership has delivered a good number of welfare institutions to cater the need of poor Harijan and Adivasi. If the model of Anjan is followed by the other tribal villages having mixed population like the village in question, much of their welfare problems could be solved by the villagers themselves.

IX
The Sacred Specialists of a Tribal Village

Anjan is inhabited by 14 communities.Both the tribal and Hindu castes live in the village. The details are given in the following table:

SI. No.	*Caste / Tribe*	*Male*	*Female*	*Total*	*Percentage*
1.	Oraon	400	404	804	65.7
2.	Ghasi	59	57	116	9.8
3.	Chik- Baraik	35	30	65	5.3
4.	Lohra	30	32	62	5.0
5.	Kharwar	20	29	49	4.0
6.	Kumhar	24	15	39	3.0
7.	Munda	8	15	23	1.8
8.	Brahmin	6	8	14	1.1
9.	Rajput	6	8	14	1.1
10.	Hajam	5	9	14	1.1
11.	Dhobi	2	5	7	0.6
12.	Mahli	4	4	8	0.6
13.	Bania	4	2	6	0.5
14.	Ahir	2	2	4	0.3
Total		605	620	1,225	100.00

Religion is still one of the most vital factors, responsible for guiding the fate of villagers of Anjan. The modern atheistic tendencies have not yet touched the village. The villagers have a strong belief in the existence of deities and spirits. They believe that there are spirits behind all evils and miseries that befall them. Though auster Purity in thought, word and deed is not the ideal. numerous beliefs and ceremonies observed by the various communities of the village portrary the villagers as dedicated devotees of their respective gods and deities, with one common belief that the liges of human beings are at the mercy of various deities. Wealth, good health and peace of mind, all depend on the grace of these deities. Some of these deities are benevolent while others are malevolent. The villagers have reverential owe for them and they know that the benevolent spirits have to be approached with prayers and offerings, where as the malevolent spirits have to be controll and avert4ed by spell and magic. Everyone does not know the secret of religion and magic, hence there are a few specialist to help the people in every village the details of Anjan are given below :-

The Sacred Specialists of Anjan

The Pahan

The religious life at Anjan is mainly regulated by a set of sacred specialists who have become indispensible for the various sacred perfromances. The Pahan is the recognised religious head of the village, whose powers know no limit in the specified locality, The Present Pahan of Anjan-Lohra Baiga comes of a Pahan Khunt, Munda family, which is said to be the earliest settler of Anjan. people believe that the ancestor of Lohara Baiga came and settled first after cleaning the forest.

It is common feature of an Oraon village that it prefers have a Munda as its Pahan because of the Mundas being the earliest settlers on the Chotanagpur Plateau have better knowledge of the deities and spirits of the land and also of the proper methods of propitiating them. The office of the Pahan at Anjan is hereditary and has come to the present Baiga after Chhandu Baiga, Khedan Baiga, respectively expired. The Pahan holds his office as a matter of right by birth and the “Pahnoiti” land measuring about annas of rentfree land given by the ex-Maharaja of Ratu is also hereditary and goes to the Pahan while he in the office. This "Pahnoiti" land is exclusively given to the Pahan on a clear understanding that the Pahan will have no right to sell the land.

It has been mentioned earlier that the post of the Pahan at Anjan is hereditary and must go to the next elder married person of the 'Pahankhunt'.

According to S.C. Roy" In village where the office of the Pahan is not hereditary, the method of electing a new pahan is as follows. All the Adult male villagers assemble at the Sarna on the full moon (15th) day of Magh (January-Februrary) and in a few villages (e.G. Tingria, thana Bero) in Aghan (December-January) bringing with them from the outgoing Pahan's house the Sarna Sup or the winnowing basket upon which the Sarna deity or Chala-Pachcho is believed to sit, and which has been the emblem of the pahan's office and has been used at every Puja at the Sarna and carefully and religiously kept up from a beam of a compartment in his house known as chala Kutti or compartment sacred to the Sarna spirit. They also bring alongwith them a sal (Shorea-robusta) pole split into two at one end and attached in the manner of a fork to this sup. The outgoing Pahan also comes from his house ot the Sarna cariying a new sup on which he brings some Arua rice from his own house. A young bachelor, known particular sensitive to supernatural influences, has his eyes blind-folded with a piece of cloth, and the old Sarna sup is put in hands. Each one present takes up a few grains of rice from the new sup, and throws the rice on the old sup, saying "Do enter Chala Pachcho, the house of the man with who thou art well pleased". Now the blind-folded young man or paichalabana as he is styled, proceeeds to the village, holding one end of the Sal Pole, at a other forked end of which the old Sarna sup is attached. The outgoing Pahan follows with the new sup, scattering as few grains of rice along the road ater every few steps, and with jug which he goes on dropping water. Only three or four other men accompany them, the other villagers waiting at the Sarna. The blind-folded boy is supposed to be led by the Sarna spirit seated on the Sup to the house of the person to whom the deity takes a fancy. On arrival at the door of house of such a person, the blind-folded young man places the old sarna sup at the threshold o f his house. The party will then go back to the Sarna, the newly elected Pahan carrying his new sup and the Paichalbana carrying the old Sarna Sup.

Even in villages, where the Pahanship is hereditary, should the family of the Pahan be extinct or converted to Christianity or some ohter religion (such as Tana-ism) thereby necessitation the election of a new Pahan, the above procedure has to be followed for election of a new Pahan. The above procedure has to be followed for the election of a Pahan".

The Pahan is assisted by the Pujar in the perfromances of his duties and the latter may officiate for him in his absence. The Pahan is the sole incharge of all the major public sacrifices and religious responsibilities. He is the key figure round whom all the sacred rites revolve. It is he, who sacrifices to Gods on behalf of the villagers and represents the entire village in all rituals.

As a representative of the village, the Pahan sacrifices a white cock in the name of 'Dharmes', who is the supreme body in the Oraon religion. Normally the sacrifices made by the Pahan for the community are propitiatory whereas the Mati sacrifices for appeasing an angry spirit. The circumstances in which the Pahan offers sacrifices can be summed up as follows : He offers sacrifices when epidemic either of man or of cattle breaks out in the village. He offers sacrifices at the beginning of a fair. When an individual wants to cut a tree in the Sarna he has to make necessary arrangement for offering sacrifices to the 'Sarna Bruhia' (the lady of the Sarna grove) . It is the Pahan who decides as to what and when should be sacrificed. The sacrifice is offered by the Pahan himself in the Sarna after which the intending person is allowed to cut a tree. The Pahan who is the mediator between the earth and the people has to offer special sacrifice on behalf of the people during the Sarhul festival which occurs in April. on the day of Sarhul, a mimic marriage of the Pahan an his wife takes place. This function is a symbolic representation of the fact that the mother earth is married to the Sun Godm, the Pahan represents, the Sun and his wife the earth. The earth's blessing is sought by offering a basketful of rice by the Pahan and this sacrificial rice is set aside for the use at sowing.

The Pahan is universally respected by all the members of each community living at Anjan. Even the Brahmins of the village pay due respect to the village Pahan. In the maintenance of all the religious shrines of the village and in case of any conflict the verdict of the Pahan is regarded to be final, But below is a very interesting case story in which the order of the Mukhia of Anjan Gram Panchayat was challenged by the Pahan and the fromer had to submit.

Let it be mentioned here that Anjan is full of siblingas and the popular belief connected with the Siblingas is that those are of Anjani's days because she used to worship Lord Shiva daily and thus would worship all the 365 siblingas every year in the process of rotation. But now most of the siblingas are uncared for, unattended and forlent. The author, while in the field (Anjan) thought to carry one Siblinga to Ranchi to assess the approximate age of the lingas and to keep one in the departmental museum for further investigation. The author expressed his desire to the mukhia who welcomed his view and showed the author one Siblinga which was aloof from and outside the village under a termerind tree. The author was told that the Mukhia was all powerful in the village administration, and hence he need not ask any one else for the Same. Naturally he did not seek the permission either of the Pahan or of the Pujar for uprooting the Siblinga. In the evening of the 30th May, 1965, the author alongwith a few friends went to uproot the said siblinga. while the author with his friends was busy in the excavation work some Oraons of the village infromed the matter to the pahan of the village. The Pahan alongwith a few dozens of villagers rushed to the spot and forced him to stop the excavation work at once. The author in the beginning did not care and kept on with the excavation work but in the meantime about two hundred persons reached there and questioned the author whether he had sought fromal permission of the Pahan for uprooting the

Mahadeo. The author replied int he negative and argued that the Mukhia had given him the permission. The Mob started scolding the Mukhia and the author was told that the Mukhia was not the religious head of the village, hence it was beyondf his power to give him a Mahadeo. The author left the spot without taking the desired thing.

From the case described above it is evident that in spite of a heavy impact of Hinduism the traditional role of the Pahan has been very little affected. Talking about the honourable office of the Pahan, one Bhawan Oraon about 70 year old man of Anjan told the author that the pahan, in his jurisdiction was superior even to the King. He further said that the Pahan of Anjan had never gone either to Ratu or to Palkot Raja. When a Raja wants to see the pahan it is the Raja who comes to the village and then the Pahan see him. The Pahan cares only for the "Dharmas" who is the supreme power; the king is a negligible creature and has to keep the Pahan pleased.

The Pujar

References of the Pujar have been made earlier wherer it was mentioned that the Pahan is always assisted by an assisted by an assistant whom the villagers address as Pujar or Panbhara. The Panbhara name of Pujar is a functional one because he is supposed to fetch water on all the occasions of worship and sacrifice.

Chatu Baiga, the then Pujar of the village, took over in the year 1964 from Atwa Munda when the latter was forced to relinquish the office on the charges of 'Matwari" (drunkness). The office of the Pujar at Anjan is not herediary. Whenever the Pahan finds anything wrong with the Pujar he first warns him to mend his ways , failing which a new Pujar is selected on the Sarhul day by the magic Sarna sup in the same manner as told above in connection with the selection of the Pahan, with the difference that this tiem everyone present at Sarna invokes the 'Sarna Burhaia' by throwing a few grains of rice from the new sup to the old and saying "Now Sarna Burhia go and choose the new Pujar or Panbhara".

The duty of the Pujar is to assist the Pahan during the

sacred perfromances. It is the sacred duty of the Pujar to fetch water an make all the necessary arrangements for the worship and sacrifice at sarna. If there be a community feast at Sarna either on the eve of Sarhul or on some other occasion, the Pujar has to act and collect the sacrificial materials from the villagers. He is sole incharge for the maintenance and repairs of all the religious shrines within the village. On every Tuesday when the Pahan offers prayer and worship and 'Devi' of the village in the ' Devi mandap' situated in the heart of the village, the Pujar is kept busy in cleaning the mandap and washing it with cowdung mixed with clay and making all the necessary arrangement for the worship.

The ex-Raja of Ratu had donated 'one Anna' of land to the Pujar of Anjan which always goes to the Pujar while in the office. It is not always necessary that the Pujar must be of a Munda ribe. In the past even the Oraons had held the office of the Pujar and the villagers remember one Sawna Orraon as a very competent ex-Pujar of Anjan.

The Brahmin and the Barber

As the Pahan and the Pujar play a very important role in the religious life of the tribal population of the village. So the Brahmin and his assistant, barber, are indispensible for most of the sacred perfromances made by the Hinus in general and tribals i particular. The Bhagats, who are comparatively an emergent group, and believe in the Hindu way of life, need the services of the Brahmin very often. Similarly the Kharwar and the Baraiks who claim a Hindu origin always invite a Brahmin for conducting all the important sacred perfromances. To cut short and to sum up the important functions of the Brahmin Pandit it can be said that he perfroms the various religious and ceremonial rituals. Again the religious teaching like the 'path' of Ramayan and Geeta or of Satyanarayan Katha is conducted and supervised by him. He is invited to note the time of birth of a child. He decides the date and time for chatthi. the presence of a Brahmin Pandit and his assistant Barber is a must for the marriage and Sardhya in Hindu family, and now many tribal people also, both Bhagats and non-

Bhagats, call a Brahmin because they feel a bit elevated in doing so.

The Hinduized Bhagats

The fourth type of sacred specialist at Anjan may be regarded the various groups of Hinduized Bhagats. To Roy, "The Bhagat cult among the Oraons may be taken to have originated in the latter half of the 18th century of Christian Era, if not earlier".

The study of the Bhagat cult in the villages of chotanagpur is very interesting and Anjan is a very suitable place for the same because one can find as many as six categories of Bhagats in the village.

The term ' Bhagat' appears to be the corrupt from of a Hindi word 'Bhakti' or devotion. The term Bhakti has been defined as "ardent and hopeful devotion to a particular deity in grateful recognition of aid received or promised" (Noss. 1949 :28). The Hindus who believe in salvation through "Bhakti Marga' or the way of devotion, are known as Bhagats. To carpenter, in the early years of the Muslim period a remarkble sect of the Bhagwats came into view (about 1100) with important scriptures of their own, who developed what was known as the Bhakti Marga or the path of devotion over against the ritualistic cults known as the karma Marga or the Path of work (rituals) and Jnan Marga or the path of knowledge.

Since the days of Sankaracharya (ninth century), the South had given birth to great Hindu Acharyas who substantiated Hindusim with a sound philosophical and metaphysical basis. In spite of their differences, they succeeded in holding the intelligentsia and they also initiated the great Bhakti cult. Ramanuja (1070-1137) Madhwa (13th Century). Nimbarka and Vallabha (1479-1531) were all Brahmans from the south. Jayadeva, the author of Gita Govinda, Chaitanya (1445-1553) and other great leaders of the Bhakti Marga were the spiritual descendants of these Acharayas. Ramananda, another very great Bhakta, was the follower of Ramanuja who popularised and liberalised Hinduism.

Caste was regarded only as a social distinction and not as an impediment to spiritual progresss. He laid greater emphasis on freedom in the mater of food and acknowledged that even sudras the outcaste, and women could attain salvation. Among his twelve disciples was a Muslim weaver (Kabir), a cobbler (Rai Das) and barber (Sena). The Ramanandi Vairagis (ascetics) are found in large numbers is North India Bihar. Rai Das is said to have belonged to Arrah.

The teachings of Ramanand led to the creation of two distinct schools. One school was represented by Nabha Das and Tulsi Das, contemporaries of Akbar and respective authors of Bhakta mala and the immortal Ramayan (Ram-Charita manasa). They safeguarded the authority of the Vedas and did not break with the past socially or religiously. They enriched Hinduism by popularising the cult of Ram and by elevating the moral level of the people. The other and no less important school followed the lead of Kabir, Rai Das, Nanak, Dadu and other mystics who preached strict monotheism and refused to acknowledge Gods and demi-gods. They denounced the caste system and rituals as absurd and futile, and attempted to ridge the gulf between Hinduism and Islam by synthesizing the best elements of both. Kahir's following was rather small but his influence has been widespread.

With regard to the spread of the Bhagat movement in chotanagpur in general and Anjan in particular the following is important. The fact that Hindu influence has been at work in developing and giving a shape to the Bhagat cult cannot be denied. Moreover the ancient tribal tradition and certain tribal customs would appear to indicate that the germs of the Bhakti cult had been long present in the tribal soul. Contact with Hindu ideas, beliefs and practices in time stimulated and fructified the Oraon's original barren belief in Dharmes as a Supreme spirit. And slowly the Bhakti cult spread among the tribals.

That Chaitanya had visited Chotanagpur is supported by a few following lines : "In Shri Chaitanya Cariamarita we find a mention of Jharkhand. Lord Chaitanaya on his way from Vrindaban to Puri Jagannath passed through the

Jharkhand area. (1916 A.D.) The Panch Paragana and the sub-division of Khunti are still the strong hold of Vaishnavism. Bundu, Tamar and Jaria in Khunti sub-division are supposed to have received visit of Lord Chaitanya."

It has been mentioned earlier that the village is very old and the Hindu influence has been operative even in the past again the popular Hindu myths and sacred shrine have always been a place of attraction for the Hindus from outside the village. The relations of the Hindus living at Anjan have also paid several visits to the village and have contributed in the intensification of the Bhagat movement in the village. "Whether due to the historical antiquity of the village or any other reason, there is a fairly good concentration fo Hinduized Bhagats. These Bhagats have a large following and, in the case of any strange ofr extraordinary phenomena, people invariably seek the assistance of these Bhagats."

It has been a common feature of the Bhakti cult that every Bhagat has to choose one Devata (deity) who is popularly known as his Ista Devata (chosen deity) for special worship and contemplation. The Ista Devatas are many, but Lord Shiva, Lord Vishnu and Goddess Durga and Kali are some of the distinct Personalities for giving rise to three distinct systems-Shaivism, Vaishnavism, and Shaktism. Shaivism and Shaktism are partly interchangeable and complementary. But in the end a realised Bhakta may not find any difference between Hari (i.e.Lord Vishnu) and Har (i.e.Shiva) because the very name Hari-Har Kshetra given to the great Sonepur temple in Bihar, involves joint worship of Vishnu and Shiva.

As it is, one finds more of Shiva temples than Vaishnava temple in Chotanagpur in general and Anjan in particular. The arguments which come in the favour of Shiva temples are as follows :

(a) If any harm occurs to the presiding deity in a Vishnu temple, it requires a far more elaborate ceremony to replace it, than in the case of a Shiva temple. (b) Shiva temples are accessible to all, but women and Sudras are forbidden to worship in Vaishnava temples. (c) Worship in Shiva temple is similar, sometimes even mere water is sufficient to worship the Lord Shiva : People believe that Shiva is Asutosh (easily pleased). But many things, such as Akshat, sandal, flower and prasadi and so on are needed in Vaishnava temple. (d) Shiva is a God of all classes and Shavisim does not impose restrictions in taking meat and fish, (e) There is a very close connection between the Shaivis, and the Shaktism.

It is high time to make it clear that in other parts of Bihar the term Bhagat is often employed to designate sorceres and magicians. "But among the Oraons of Chotanagpur the name Bhagat has come to be applied as the distinctive name of a section of the tribe which subscribes to the cult of Bhakti or loving trust in and adoration of the deity and observes certain rules of ceremonial purity." The entire Bhagat movement, attempting as it does to raise the status of its members in the eyes of the surrounding Hindu society, is characterised by a large scale incorporation into its ideology of Hindu beliefs and practice.

The field study of Anjan revels that it has as many as six varities of Bhagats, the details of which are given below:

1. Kamru Bhagat.
2. Mati Bhagat.
3. Nagmatia Bhagat.
4. Nemha Bhagat.
5. Vishnu Bhagat.
6. Tana Bhagat.

Kamru Bhagat

Bhikhua Bhagat, a resident of Anjan and one of the Gurus of Kamru cult had his initation there at Kamrup-Kamakhya in Assam. So when he came back to his village (Anjan) people began to call him Kamru Bhagat. Bhikhua had learnt a few effective mantras from his guru. He gained popularity very soon and his success brought home a large number of Chelas (deciples) from all over Chotanagpur. At

Anjan also he has a few dozens of Chelas who are always at his command.

In spirit Kamru Bhagat are Shaktas and offer their prayers and sacrifices to Shakti (Durg and Kali) They offer the sacrifice of black he-goat during the Durg Puja Path (lesson).

The Gurus of Kamru Bhagats are very much particular about the initation of Chela. A newly initiated Chela is very closely guarded by his Guru. The Guru orders him not to take ordinary meat and wine, however a Chela can take the meat of a he-goat or peigeon sacrificed to Devi.

From the day chela is initiated and given a path (lesson) he has to see his Guru every evening to know the details of the path. One path continues for one year and then the Guru examines the Chela about the path and when the fromer is pleased with the answers of the latter, another path is given for another year. The power or so to say, the quality of a Bhagat depends upon the number of paths he has taken from the Guru. The Guru, who is believed to know in detail the nature of spirit both good and bad, explains the Bhagats under training the various symptoms to recognise them. He may take his chelas to the jungle and explain them about various herbs and their use. Somtimes he may take a few chelas with him to demonstrate to them the actual procedure of driving an evil spirit. A chela, while in training may give occasional gifts of rice, he-goat and piegon th his Guru. A rich chela may offer even money to the Guru.

Mati Bhagat

There are four Mati Bhagats at Anjan and none of them holds the Status of a Guru. In spirit there is hardly any difference between kamru and Mati Bhagat except that in Mati cult the Bhagats worship Mahjadeo first and Devi next. But in kamru cult Devi is taken to be all powerful. To Roy "The Matis or Deonraj are black magicians who, besides playing the role of witchfinders and witch -doctors, spirit-finders and exercisers, practise anti-social magic for their own ends." It is a fact t hat the matis are black-magicians but at Anjan there was never an occasion when a Mati wanted to harm one. he feared that Bhikhua Bhagat, the Guru of Kamru cult would cure him and might harm the Mati inn revenge by his strong Mantras which were infallable.

Nagmati Bhagat

Nagmatia Bhagats or sanke -doctors are specialized in btringing down the position of a snake. When anybody suspects that he has been bitten by a snake he rushed to a Nagmati Bhagat. At Anjan there are only two Nagmati Bhagats i.e. Lohra Baiga and Thakur Bhagat. When the suspected person reaches the house of a Nag-Mati he invokes goddess 'Mansa' and after establishing communication with her he can say wheather the suspected person has actually been bitten or it is just a suspicion. It takes only a few minutes to decide it and if at all the person in question is bitten by a poisonous snake the Bhagat starts beating the portions of body which have been affected by the poison of snake. This process of bring down the poison is known as 'Jharna' in the village.

Nag-Mati Bhagats offer worship and sacrifice to goddess 'Mansa' collectively on three occasions, once in the month of Jeth, again in Asarh and lastly on the eve of Deothan. They believe that if the Goddess is not pleased with any Nag-mati Bhagat on any ground she can take away his power of setting down the poison of a snake.

Nemha Bhagat

Nemha Bhagat or ordinary Bhagats at Anjan are represented by only two Bhagat i.e. Phagua Bhagat and Bari Bhagat. These Bhagats in this village are of later origin. It was reported that when any rich person wanted to raise his social status he invited a Gosain (Brahmin of inferior stock) for his initiation and after the function was fromally observed he was declared a Bhagat. To generally observe the same rules of ceremonial purity in diet and habits are known as Nembha Bhagats. They abstain from eating beef and pork and the meat of fowls, but may take fish and the meat of other birds and animals particularly goats."

They worship Lord Mahadeo and Devi Mai and offer

sacrifices of he-goats and she-goats or seep respectively to them. It appears that among most of the Bhagats, specially among the ordinary of Nemha Bhagats, tribal ideas have generally been fused with than it is among orthodox Hindus.

Vishnu Bhagat

It is clear from the very name that a Vishnu Bhagat is one who has taken the path of Lord Vishnu (the one who maintains the universe) and has become Vaishnav, a staunch vegetarian. It may be mentioned that of these semi-Hinduised Bhagats who take vaishnav Gosains as their Gurus, call themeselves Vishnu Bhagat as they adopt Vishnu or Sri Krishna as their Tutelary deity and abstain from fish and flesh of all kinds including goat's flesh.

Mahil was the only Vishnu Bhagat at Anjan who believed that the Vaishnav was the best cult and the argument he had in its favour is given below :

"The Vaishnavas do not kill any living creature nor do they eat the flesh of any bird or animal. A true Vaishnava does not harm anyone and considers every object a part of Lord Vaishnu who is omnipotent. The Kamru and the Mati Bhagat offer sacrifice in the name of deity but the reality is that they themselves relish the meat. Everyone knows that all the living creatures are the various parts of one almighty God and to sacrifice an innocent animal to make available the blood to God is to offer. His very blood to Him and how can it please him. We offer fruits and sweets to God and this keeps him happy and satisfied."

Tana Bhagat

The Tana Bhagat are some what different from the other Bhagats of Anjan because they have included social and economic activities within their course of action. In the beginning Tana Bhagat movement was known as the "Kurukh Dharma" the original religion of the Kurukhs or Oraons.

It was one Jatra Bhagat who initiated the Tana Bhagat movement in the year 1914. One fine morning he proclaimed to his tribes men that in a dream Dharmes (the Supreme God of Oraon) told him to give up Matia (Ghost finding) and belief in spirits, to adjure all animal sacrifices, animal food and liquor and to give up ploughing their fields which entailed cruelty to cows and oxes but failed to save the tribe from famine and poverty, and no more to work as coolies or labour under men of other castes and tribes.

Roughly in the same period when jatra was preaching the new religion, a woman who was a popular leader of local Tana religion also had a vision from Lord Mahadeo and began preaching the Bhakti faith which eventually become known as Tana Bhagat. The leaders of the movement maintained that the tribal deities whom they had been worshipping were not helping them ameliote the social and economic ills to which they had fallen victims and indeed affirmed that these deities were responsible for the present state of degradation. proceeding, according to the rationale that those Gods were in reality not Oraon, but alien that has been imported from Munda religion, the originators of the Tana Bhagat movement embarked on a program of proselytisation and agitation for the exorcim of the foreign spirit. The cult emphasized a return to the original, or real, Oraon religion and consequently become known as the Kurukh Dharma.'

In the village of Anjan there was one Guru Tana Bhagat namely Budha Ram Bhagat who had twelve obedient disciples to preach and practise the following ideologies :

(i) Exorcism of evil ghosts and spirits and alien deities.

(ii) Abolition of all the following; drinking liquor, eating meat, sacrificing hens and pigs, worshipping at the sacred grove, the carrying on of sorcery, the playing of musical instruments, dancing on festivals, the wearing f elaborate jewellery and head dress, the continuing of the customs of premarital sex-relations, the institution of Dhumkuria or dormitories for young men and women, certain kinds of ceremonial friendship, and the fromer custom of marriage.

(iii) Return to the pre-religion of the original Oraons.

(iv) Recognition of one God, Mahadeo or Bhagwan and worhsip him by Bhakti, devotion.

(v) Learning how to mediate and pray with deep

(vi) Love and good-will towards fellowmen, kindness to all living beings, and purity in good and habits.

To sum up it can be safely said that all the Bhagats, irrespective of their sects have to maintain the rules of ceremonial purity in food, drink and other habits. In general, all the Bhagats of Anjan have emulated the religion and culture of the Hindus of the village. Only Kamru Bhagat, headed by Bhikhua may be regarded as an exception to this because he had his initiati in a cult which originated in Assam. Namha Bhagats who are comparatively an emergent group of rich person have little to do with the Bhakti in the true sense; rather, they seem to have adopted this cult only to raise their social status among the tribesmen. As it has already been said that there were six from of Bhagats who had their independent ideologies, there has not been a case of serious difference between two or more groups of Bhagats on any issue, and it is reported that all the Bhagats were Bhagats first and followers of a particular sect only afterwards.

X

Wild Animals as a Source of Joy and Sorrow for the Natives of Palamu Betla a Case Study

The district of Palamu forms the north-west corner of the Chotanagpur division. It contains a big area of about 4900 square miles which is inhabited by Hindus, Muslims, Christians and Adivasis. Among Adivasis Chero, Kisan, Birjia, Parhaiya and Korwa are the special tribes of the district. Daltonganj is the district administrative headquarter which is named after Colonel Dalton.

Forests predominate in the district of Palamu. According to the figure of 1961 out of the total area of 4916 square miles of the district 2146 square miles are covered with forests. The economy of the district bears a very intimate correlation with the forests which covered 43.6 per cent of the total area of the district. There has been huge destruction of forest in the recent past, but even today the district of Palamu preseres some very dense government managed forests. Generally the forests of the area have Khair, Asan, karam, Guri, Mahua, Semal, Kedar, Kusum, Sissam and several other trees and bamboos of various types. There are several ranges of forest of Palamu, but a few of them namely Garu, Latehar, Mahuadanr, Chhipadohar and Betla are very famous for several reasons.

The present study is based on a field work at Betla. Betla was once a small forest village, situated about 25 k.m. from Daltongonj with the passage of time, it witnessed so many changes and now Betla is known as palamu Tiger Reserve.

This is one of the 15 reserves specially established under Project Tiger in 1947. In 1962 an area of 249 Sq. Kilometers received attention and some water points and watch towers were constructed, but the habitat was not protected and falling of trees and bamboos continued till the creation of Tiger Reserve.

The Tiger Reserve as now constituted comprises most of the forest of Daltonganj south forest division and is 1026 Sq. kilometers in area. The basic concept of Project Tiger is total environmental conservation in an adequately large faunal area, as far as possible from human disturbance and for this, core area of 201 square kilometre was carved out which is primitive forests almost in the middle of the Reserve.

The location of Betla is very beautiful because it is surrounded by the Auranga River from the East and the North koel river from the west and the south. Thus, it has rivers from three sides and only a narrow strip of land from the East.

Betla National Park is one of the best developed parks in India, and unlike most reserves has a very long season for the visitors. Wild elephants, gaur, chital and Sambhar and various types of monkeys are in abundance here. The tiger and leapord are seen at dawn and dark. Leopards are expert at climbing trees and prey on a great many animals. Wolf is another predator which mostly prey on young ones of Chital, Sambhar and wild pig. Though this is a dreaded animal of Hazaribagh area but is also found in good number at Betla. The sloth bear is also seen, soon after the first rains. There are a few antelopes and innumerable deers and rabbits. Besides these a large number of pond tortoise, the pathon and poisonous snakes like the karaits, the Cobras and the Russel vipers are also found. Thus, Betla with its beautiful surrounding green forest full of wild life has become a very important tourist centre of Chotanagpur where people go for picnic, view of wild animal and a few for change also. There are several tourist rest houses and cottages a few of them are owned and maintained by the forest department or tourism department and others run by private owners.

The rapid urbanisation and industrialisation have resulted in taking us away from nature. This on the other hand resulted into our great awarness or carving for the nature in from of plant and wild life. Today with the rise of standards of living and spiration of people, there is more of education, leisure and recreation, mass communication and easy transport system. All these have resulted into more people to know more about wild life.

By wild life we generally mean the animals and birds of the wild, but the term wild life with respect to a locality as region will denote the entire animal community therein covering all froms. The conservation of wild life assume new dimensions, directly influencing the human enviroment and can hardly be viewed part from the conservation of forests.

Now we have to examine first, as to what are the sources of joy from wild life. Let us take the case of Betla alone. The wild life of Betla attracts thousands of visitors every week. The local people of Betla help the visitors as guide for which they get renumeration. If some guide has shown tiger to a generous family he may get Rs. 50/- to Rs.100/- as reward. In normal case also a guide may earn Rs.50 /- per day during busy seasons. The natives are engaged in the up deep of the park. There is huge demand of labour for the repair of roads and burning the dried leaves on both side of the road. Sometimes new roads have to be constructed for which local people are given jobs. The forest department of Government. of Bihar also appoints local people as seasonal and causal labourers. There are several rest houses, guest houses, cottages each of them have some watch-men, cook and other supporting staff, most of them are the natives of Betla. The natives have established some small tea-stalls betla shop and grocery to serve the tourists and they earn their livelihood thereby. The natives get the skin of dead animal for making drums and other leather goods. Thus, they get a lot from the wild animal for which they are happy.

We find that mostly things that are useful for us we take them as faultless, but on close examination we find that nothing expect God is absolutely good and helpful. The same wild life that is source of joy for so many becomes sorrowful for their neighbouring villagers. Major sad and sorrowful part of these wild animals are the killing and injury of men and domestic pet animals by wolf, elephant, tiger, leopard and snakes etc. These wild animals are not governed by the weak fencing of the forests, very often demarcated by some pillars here and there and seldom by barbwire. Hence, these demarcation which is normally symbollical hardly restricts the wild animals within boundary limit. Very often these animals come out of the forest and invade the neighbouring villages of Betla, Kerz, Munda and the like. Very often the wild elephants go on rampant and damage the standing crop and creat havoc for the poor farmers of the locality. These poor villagers are mostly helpless in *chagrin* the group of elephants which is generally in large number of ten to fifteen. The villagers are provided with kerosin oil and cracker by the forest department to frighten the elephant and to chagrin them, but all these fail, when they are in a big group. it is also believed that once a single elephant has seen any favourite crop the other day a herd of elephant will come over there silently and would consume and destroy the standing crop. If they are disturbed in this they attack the villagers. They damage the houses also. The villagers believe that these animals have a very long and strong memory and take revenge of each harm does to them. This animal has a very strong sense of identfication, it can identify its human enemy even in the crowd of thousands and may kill him then and there. Thus, elephant memory is a very common proverb here. Every year there is huge loos of crops and lives. The villagers narrate so many cases of killing in and around Betla forest and damages done vehicle by these wild elephants. There is provision for the payment of compensation of Rs. 10.000 (Rupees ten thousend) only in case of killing by wild elephant, but people say that there is lot of fromalities which these poor and simple people fail to do. The herd of deer and monkeys are also permanent source of anxiety for the natives. They are such in large number that they finish the standing crops within hours. They have comparatively lesser problem with wild bear, wolf, leopard and tiger as they do not damage their crop, but every year the natives have to bear the loss of several of their pet animals, which fall prey to these carnivorous animals while grazing in and around the forests. Similarly every year so many pet animals and human beings die of snake bite in the forest at Betla.

God has made kind and rational. It is this quality of man which has awaken him to his duty of preserving the nature and wild life. In the South Bihar, Chotanagpur in general and the district of Palamu in particular has remarkable floral wealth which is home of innumerable wild animals. The thick forests along with the water resources of the North Koel and the Auranga rivers make Betla a wild animal's paradise, because this is one of most suitable area for their peaceful living and survival of their progeny. Betla has now been given the staturs of a National Park. The natives of Betla are very much anamoured of the wild life of Betla because it has helped them in many ways. They get jobs in the upkeep of the birds and animals in the forests. They are also engaged as labourers for the fencing and road making around the forest. Some of them work as guides to tourists who throng from various parts of India and others earn their loves and fishes in so many cottages, guest houses, rest houses and establishments of the departments of forest and tourism. These are all jouous part of Betla. It has certain sad and sorrowful effects on the natives as well. Very often the wild naimals particularly elephants go rampant and creat havoc for the villagers. The herd of elephants not only consume the standing crops and damage them but also injure the natives and kill them. Similarly deer and monkeys also harm their crops. The carnivorous animals kill their pet animals in and around forest and every year a few persons die of snake bite. Thus, Betla is source of both joy and sorrow for its natives.

XI
Problems of Rural Area in Chotanagpur : Its Reconstruction and Welfare

Chotanagpur has long been neglected. If one examines the reasons of this neglect, one learns that the physical conditions of this area have contributed a lot in its retarded development. Due to rich natural resources available in this area a few industries have come up, but rural areas are still underdeveloped. The Chotanagpur plateau with its elevation ranging from 1,000 to 3,000 feet above sea level froms the north-eastern part of the great plateau of Ranchi and plateau of Hazaribagh from the central part of this Chotanagpur plateau, and are seperated by the basin of Damador. The pat area of these two plateaus, rise above 3,000 feet and the general elevation is about 2,000 feet. Parasnath, the highest hill in Bihar, is 4,480 feet high and is situated at the eastern part of the Hazaribagh plateau. The southern part of Singhbhum is comprised of hills and valleys, have no level land can be found except those of the river valleys of South Kole and Subarnarckha. Thus unlike the northern gangetic plain. the chotanagpur plateau consists of a large number of hills and valleys, which make the surface very uneven.

A look into the administrative history of Chotanagpur reveals that the traditional king Phani Mukut Raj was the founder of the Chutia village from which Chotanagpur derives its name. During British rule this area was a part of South-west Frontier Agency which was later on abolished in 1854, after this Chotanagpur became a non-regulation Province under a Commissioner and the same year one Mr. W.J. Allen was appointed as the first commissioner of Chotanagpur commissionery.

The commissionery of Chotanagpur had five districts namely Ranchi, Palamu, Singhbhum, Hazaribagh and Dhanbad. Only a few years ago the old Commissonery of Chotanagpur located at Hazaribagh and the South Chotanagpur located ar Ranchi. Similarly so many districts were also born out or old five districts and all of them were attached to either of the two. The creation of new districts has helped in the efficient and effective administration but main ecological and economic problems of the area have not been solved.

Hilly and Forest Land

As has been mentioned earlier that lion's share of land of Chotanagpur are full of hills and forests therefore Aryans called this area as Jharkhand or the 'forested territory'. It will not be out of place to mention here that out of 14,638 sq. miles, the total forest are of Bihar (20 per cent of the total area of the state) more than 12,000 sq, miles which is about 75 per cent of the total forest area of the state occur in Chotanagpur alone. Forest has various utility but forested and hilly land ate not cultivable, nor the local people can use the forest products as they like. Though the plateau was thickly covered by forest, yet as a result of urbanisation, growth of population and industrialisation, recless extermination has been carried on for a long-time. This extermination of forest has facilitated the erosion of soil over large areas in the districts of Ranchi and Hazaribagh. This plateau also froms th catchment basin of several streams. These streams dry up in the summer months and cause serious floods during rainy season to West Bengal and Orissa.

Marginal Land Use

Besides the forested land of this area, remaining lands are mostly full of rocks, boulders and reabbles of various size. Also lands are mostly full of rocks, boulders and slope which allows rain water to rush out of the field. If it is stopped it trickles down hence these plots are also not cultivable. Thus only a marginal fraction of total lands remain cultivable. The district-wise land sown annually is given below

District	Land Sown Annually
Palamu	11.5 %
Hazaribagh	18.2 %
Singhbhum	22.4 %
Dhanbad	35.6 %
Ranchi	39 %

Poor Fertility of Land

The soil of Chotanagpur is very poor in productivity, more over thick forests cover the greater part of the plateau and elevations of hills make irrigation and agriculture difficult. This is why the area of land sown annually is comparatively far less than in the North Bihar where it is about 90 per cent annually. Also in the Chotanagpur plateau due to lack of fertility of the soil and other natural inconveniences, double cropping is not possible to the extent it is done in the northern parts of Bihar.

Poor Irrigation Facility

Irrigation facilities, which depend upon factors like rainfall, topography and rivers and lands very considerably from one area to another. The highly irrigated part of the state is in the south gangetic plains where about 70 per cent of the total irrigated area of the state is to be found. As contrast to this area, the Chotanagpur high, i.e. about 50 inches annually, yet due to elevation of the hills the rain water drained out quickly. Irrigation is therefore, comparatively difficult. Dams are constructed in the valleys to store water for irrigation, but this cannot be a common source of irrigation.

No Choice of Principal Crops

The main crop of five districts of Chotanagpur is rice. Rice is grown in the low-lands known as Dong during the rainy season. Other crops of pulses and oil seed of mustard,till and surguja are also grown for the self consumption, But other cash crops like jute, oil-seeds, sugar-cane etc. are not cultivated for want of irrigation facilities. Chotanagpur had monopoly in lac cultivation it use to produce 60 per cent of lac, but recently this trade has been affected adversely due to various problems one being gramophane records not manufactured in the same scale s they cesed to be manufactured 20 years ago. Also indiscriminate cutting of forest has adversely affected this crop as this is cultivated mostly on palas, Kusum, Bair, trees which are known as the host trees have disappeared from the forests.

Heavy Soil Erosion

The problems of soil erosion is very serious in Chotanagpur. It has been mentioned earlier that the cultivable fields are located at different levels. During rainy season when there is heavy rain soft soil gets eroded and it is washed down to lower level. Similarly the hilly streams also erode the soft soil of the banks thus there is huge lose of fertile soil each year.

Huge Damage by the Wild Animals

The hills and forests of Chotanagpur are full of wild animals of various types and sizes. Elephant is the biggest and rabbit the smallest wild animal and in between the two are the tiger, the monkey, the leopard, the wolf, the bear, the Nilgay and others. The native of Chotanagpur, particularly those living in and around the forest have to suffer the loss of both man and material each year. In Netarhat area wild bear damages the crop nd injure and kill the natives. Similarly in the Betla area damages done to crops by the monkeys, the Nilgay, and the elephant huge. Rats also eat and spoil the grains. Tigers of Betla project have killed so many domestic animals of the farmers of this area. In Hazaribagh area every year so many children are killed by the wolf. In Palamu area every year so many domestic animals are killed and eaten away by the tigers. The problem of elephant damages has menacingly increased in last five years. As many sixteen persons in the district of Ranchi were killed by the elephants only in three months June to September 1989 for which the compensation were paid, similarly seven persons of Gumla and three of Singhbhum districts were killed by the angry elephants in the year 1989. These are recorded facts of Government may be many more persons might have been killed by the elephants and these cases were not recorded. Similarly unnatural death by snake-bite is not negligible in this area.

White Ant and Earth Worm Infestation

The whole of Chotanagpur plateau is infested with white ants and earth-worms. These serious problems to the poor farmers of the area. Storage of any material is problem here because white ant can consume anything stealthly without any sound. It can devastate not only grain but hamp. husk, and any other fodder for animal. Therefore, the natives keep these materials on a natural platfrom on the junction of trunks of branches of trees more commonly on Karanj of Neem bark is bitter hence not fit to be consumed by these white ants and earth worms.

Poor and Weak Breed of Cattle

The cattle of Chotanagpur are small and undersized which is due to weak breed of cattle and lack of proper and good pasturage and nutritions fodder available here. The size of the cows and oxes of Palamu is not bigger than those of common sheep. In the plains of Bihar buffalows are mainly kept for their large amount of milk yield having more cream while in Chotanagpur they are used for ploughing because weak oxes are not able to cope with the hard soil of this area. The tribals, particularly the Mundas considered it almost a crime to drink the milk of a cow which they considered proper to leave entirely to the calf.

Poor Chain of Communication

Chotanagpur plateau has been communicationally neglected since remote past. There are fewer roads in this area as compared to north Bihar. There has been some physical comstraints due to high hills and steep valleys, which are impedement in the roads construction. Thus, natural delimitations are very common in the construction of road. A few roads have been constructed but most parts of this area are not connected with pucca roads. Rail communications is very nominal here in this part of Bihar. The natural handicaps are challenging in the construction of railway lines in this part of country. Most of the districts head quarters are far away from the railway station. Thus Hazaribagh, Gumla, Simdaga and the like are not connected with railways lines. It is matter of sock and surprise that most people of Hazaribagh have not even seen the train. Similarly Chotanagpur has no navigable rivers or canals, hence no wonder that most of the natives may not have seen a boat. There is only one aerodrome at Hinoo in Ranchi from where people of entire Chotanagpur can avail of the air-travel to Patna, Delhi and Calcutta. Thus Chotanagpur continues to be backward communicationally also.

Problems of Digging the Past

Chotanagpur is a meeting-point of Pre-history. This area possesses relic and remnants of numerous prehistoric stone implements. Its monuments, some of which are related to the Asuras by the Mundas, yielded such a mixed assortment of finds as polished stone tools, carnalian beads and several other pottery of pre-historic days. Although relic of Palaeolithic period are not so well marked here in Chotanagpur, of there appears to be abundant relic of the Neolithic period, particularly in the southern and south-eastern part of Ranchi district and I places of Singhbhum district. Archaeological excavation and exploration of all the ancient sites including those of Anjan and Tanginath may furnish valuable data for pre-historic period. The discovery of solitary stone celt of by professor Valentine at the foot hill of a small hill near village Burhadihi in Tamar P.S in 1867 and subsequent finds by S.C. Roy between 1915 and 1920 at Majhgon in Chainpur and a few places of Singhbhum support the view that Chotanagpur which possess invaluable materials of prehistoric importance, one of them at Anjan in the district of Gumla is facing the danger of erosion by the swift current of Khatwa river. Each year this inundates this mound nd damages some preserved antiquitic remains of Chotanagpur. All these call for an urgent step to protect them now or never.

Thus in a few foregoing pages, an attempt has been made

to enlist some very important problems related with the physical conditions of this area. The problems highlighted had their roots in nature and the constraints were also not human, but physical. Now we have to study and examine how economic problems of this area have made the life of the people of Chotanagpur miserable. Therefore, in few forth coming paragraphs some very important and common economic problems of the people of rural Chotanagpur merits attention.

Before the economic problems are highlighted something about the people of this area there population composition and enthnicity etc are given below - The total population of five districts of Chotanagpur area divided in four categories and their respective distributions are discussed separately in a tabulor from. The four categories are (i) Scheduled Tribes, (ii) Scheduled Castes, (iii) Backward class (iv) other upper castes.

Precentage of Population Districtwise in four Categories

District	*SC.*	*ST.*	*BC.*	*Other Upper Castes*
Ranchi	60.49	11.14	5.10	30.62
Hazaribagh	13.91	3.79	10.73	64.72
Palamu	13.50	23.34	10.43	52.72
Singhbhum	44.44	4.72	6.90	43.94
Dhanbad	17.07	15.43	10.61	57.99

Economic Problems

Economic problems of rural Chotanagpur are different from rest of the country for various reasons. Till a comparatively recent period in history, the plateau of Chotanagpur mainly because of its dense forests and steep landscape, remained isolated. The difficulities of communication and transport mde virtually impossible for the impact of the outside world to be felt by the local inhabitants. This continued till 16th century, thereafter it was slowly exposed during the reign of Akbar and than British rule. The Chotanagpur Tenacy Act of 1859 did not allow an outsider to purchase land in this area. Then there started money-lending in from of Zarpeshgi among the Raiyats themselves and then new Raiyats started transferring land ot outsider as gift or on lease and slowly with the passage of time as the number of outisde increased in this area most of the land of local people had already passed into the hands of alien pepople. Thus local people were deprived of their ancestoral lands. Another serious economic problem of this area has been the illeffects of industrialisation. Recently Chotanagpur has become the industrial heart of India. So many heavy industries have come up on the lands of Chotanagpur. Thus Ranchi which was a village town has so many heavy and small industries. Jamshedpur is famous for Tata Steel, Bokaro has been renamed s Steel City, Similarly whole of Hazaribagh and Dhanbad ae full of coal mines and other industries like thermal power plants, cement factories and an chains of ancillary industries. Needless to mention, these projects have brought in great changes in the life of the natives of Chotanagpur, particularly those of tribals. From the point of view of the tribal people, perhaps immediate effect of Industrialisation has been displacement. The land that they had been tilling for their livelihood for generations have been taken away from them for industries. A large number of people got jobs in these industries, but only a few tribals were given jobs and those who were taken in were the lowest paid. Industrialisation played havoc in the social set up of the tribal village life. As we know that a tribal village is a more corporate and almost a self-sufficient social unit which was disturbed by the outside which were previously made by the local artisan Chik-Baraiks were the traditional weavers of Chotanagpur, who made Barik and Karaya a very durable sari for the ladies, but when the mill made sari was introduced in this area those Chik-Baraiks had to close down their traditional looms as they failed to compete with the mill made cloths. There was problems of unemployment for those weavers who were forced to be a casual agricultural labour afterward. The problem of culture contact proved more of curse than blessing for the natives. A new type of moneylender was introduced to this area who lent on an exorbitant rate of interest and whose calculations of interest was so complicated that the poor and innocent natives failed to understand the trick of the moneylenders. Thus, the rural Chotanagpur is badly in the clutch of these moneylenders who have exploited the natives to their best.

There are several other economic problems of this area like those of poor storage facility, poor knowledge of the market where their agricultural product can be sold at proper price, home-sickness of the natives restricts them to migrate where they can find jobs, faulty economic planning and wasteful expenditure on festivals particularly after liquor and drinks etc.

Problems of Health and Hygiene

The people of Chotanagpur share most of the problems of health and hygiene with those of the people of North-Bihar, but over and above there are certain local problems which have to be highlighted. There are some pockets where there are huge cases of leprosy and other skin diseases, similarly in other part cases of T.B., Jaundice and bone diseases are rampant. The forested areas of Chotanagpur are highly Malerious. There are general scarcity of drinking water in the hilly areas and due to heavy industrialisation of this area all the rivers of Chotanagpur are polluted with the resuse of factories. The coal washeries are another source of pollution of river water. There is lack of proper up-keep of filter plants which supply drinking water. Thus by and large people are used to drink unbleached and impure water full of germs and poisonous chemicals which affects the health of natives badly.

There is a prevalent belief among the tribal folk of Chotanagpur that if windows or ventilators are given in the living rooms, evil spirit may enter the room through that therefore, no hole is left in the room due to the superstitious belief and this is harmful to health. Similarly sanitary condition of this area is far from being satisfactory. A serious problems of this area is the extremely poor and improverished condition of health of the people. The birth rate and death rate ae very high in this area and cases of infant mortality are also very high. There is general scarcity of medical centres and people ae also not so medical minded. The people believe in the Jhar-Phook and thus they go to a doctor when the condition of patient has reached the terminal stage. Again due to inadequate and undernourished food there is hardly any resistance to epidemics which are very common in this area and there are no means to eradicate them. Another problem related to their health is that the medical centres and hospitals managed by the government remain without qualified doctors. The doctors posted in this hilly and forested area are not seen willing to stay here, because they do not find many patients who would go the private clinic of these doctors. Thus unwillingess of the doctors to serve these poor people complicates the problems of health all the more.

The problem of health is related to the problem of housing also, because in the villages the problem of housing is very accute nor that in a villages are not available but their construction is haphazard and unhygienic. Most of the housses are kacha and facility of good drainage system is under-rated. Similarly it is commonly believed that if a house holder lives in the vicinity of cattle they are better looked after and are more productive. Therefore it is found that human beings and cattle live in the same room.

Traditional Political System in the Melting Pot

The traditional Parha Panchayat system of Chotanagpur was very effective and powerful institution which controlled the political and economic life of the people of this area. Similarly at the village level there used to be a village Panchayat which used to maintain law and order in the village. Cases of incest and other village disputes were referred to the Paraha Panchayat with the introduction of state sponsored gream-panchayat system the traditional system suffered set back and gradually got weakened. Thus people who used to get justice for no cost in the villages have to go to court of law for the justice and have to pay the lawer and his helpers heavily.

Although the modern Gram Panchayat have been given tremendous administrative power over the village community, in practice they have achived little. Lack of education lack of spirit, lack of proper guidance and funds, the self-interest of the members and the misuse of power account for their failure.

Problem of Education

Under a Directive Principles of State Policy free and compulsory education is to be provided for all children upto the age of 14, but even today mass of rural folk of Chotanagpur are illiterate despite so many schemes of government offering incentives such as mid-day meals, free books and unifroms. There are various barriers for the growth of education-some of them are economic, cultural, ecological and the like. The disinterested students and inefficient teachers make the problem all the more worse.

Problems of Exploitation

The problems of exploitation of the local people by the civil contractors, forest contractors, Mahajans and money-lenders, petty Excise and forest officials and others engaged in the development work of this area call for an early attention. The simple people of this area have been deceived so vigoriously that they refuse to believe even in the bonafide persons who really mean and wish the welfare of these down-trodden people.

Inadequacy of Welfare Scheme

The problems of this area are so numerous and cronic that they have to be cared for a longer period of time. The people are uninnovative and suspicious about the conduct of outsiders who come to excute the welfare schemes. The welfare need is so big and help which would actually reach the needy people so little like a drop in the ocean that there is hardly any visible effect of the welfare scheme. Also there is lot of adhocism in the nature and type of scheme, hence most of them are charged before they become popular among the natives. Most of the schemes go by five years plan priority and it appears that the planners feel that by allocating a certain sum if money over a particular problem for a certain period they have solved the problem, but the fact is that only a nominal fraction of resource are made available on spot due to reavy pilferage at various levels.

Another problem with the welfare is the multiplicity of

finding agency having huge over-laping. There are some schemes of Government. of India a few of state Government. of Bihar, some by voluntary organisation, hence there are possibility of duplicacy and local people get bewilder as to who should be approached for what and if per chance one approaches a wrong person who would like to redirect the person to the right man, one loses interest and would sit idle there after, presuming that again he would be sent to the third person and this is how these persons avoid work.

Thus, from the persual of the discussion about the problem of Chotanagpur's rural areas presented in a few foregoing pages it is evident that this area has been long neglected through this is the backbone of industries in India which has mines and minrals of all the raw materials needed for industries. Now this has taken a political colour and natives want a seperate state of Chotanagpur which of they expect will come for the all-round development of the people of this area.

XII
Village Studies in India : An Anthropological Appraisal

Our epics and classics are full of various illuminating accounts of the then village life and Dube's observation is very correct that "From time immemorial the village has been a basic and important unit in the organisation of Indian social polity. It finds prominent mention in the classical texts of the land. For example, according to Rig-Veda (generally dated in the latter half of the 2nd millennium B.C.) society developed in a series of ascending formations, starting from the family (Griha or Kula) and gradually extended to the village (grama) the clan (vis) the people (jana) and the country (rastra). The term grama, still largely used in India for village, denoted an aggregate of several families sharing the same habitation. Besides mentioning that the village was headed by the gramini, the chief of the village............ The Mahabharata (2nd century B.C.- 2nd century A.D.) mentions several types of habitations and settlements, such as catele farm (ghosh of Vraja), small barbarn hamlets (Pali), forts to protect surrounding settlements (durga) village developing around the forts (grama), town (kharvata of pattan) and city (Nagara)" (1955, pp. 1).

Although the mention of a few aspects of the village life in the classics of India is regarded as the earliest writing, but while analysing these studies on the line of socio-logical writings one finds that those have hardly to do any thing in describing the society as a system. Again they lack a systematic and detail description about the structure, interrelationship, unity and extension etc. of a village which is regarded as the core of the modern village studies. Coming to the modern history of the village study in India, one would find that even before the fromer half of the 19th century a few works, dealing with the village life, either in connection with the land revenue or forest right, were published by the administrators, economists, geographers missionaries, visitors and the social workers. Although these had nothing to do with the anthropological in creating a favourable atmosphere for further study in this dimension.

In the latter half of the 19th century village study was initiated by the publication of few book namely "Ancient Law" (1861), and "Village Communities in the East and West" (1871) by Sir Henry Maine, “Ancient Law” was mainly devoted to the study of the land system in India with the argument that land was originally commonly held by groups of people, "Village communities in the East and West" was collection of six papers dealing with land tenure, legal codes and the evolution of village communities. As is commonly known that Maine was an evolutionist, therefore his works had an evolutionary bias.

The publication of "Indian Village Community" (1896) by Baden Powell was an outstanding work for dealing with many new aspects like "Severalty Village", "Joint Village" and the like. But as the sources of infromation were the settlement reports, manuals, gazetteers and like, the human element which is the core of the village life could not be proportionately represented.

The year 1936 deserves specific mention for the publication of the "Hindu Jajmani System" by W.H. Wisher. This was an excellent work ever done in the history of the village studies. Wisher stayed in the village of Karimpur in U.P. for a considerable period of time and collected empirical date on the economic aspect of the village. This was the first work of its kind in which economic interdependence of twenty four different castes was very nicely depicted. Again the use of two terms i.e. kamin (employee) and jajaman (employer) and their interractions on the various occasions were some of the beautious aspects of the book. Although Wisher deserves congratulation for this work of such a high order the main pit falls which perhaps escaped his vision were the inclusion of the Muslims and the Christians in this system (which should have restricted only the Hindus as per title of the work) and his total negligence about the concept of purity and pollution.

In addition to these important books mentioned above, the sporadic accounts of the village life presented by the British administrators, posted in different parts of India are many. Risley, Dalton and O'Malley in East India, Russell in Mikkle India, Thurton in South India, Crook in Northern India wrote encylopeadic account about the tribes and castes and their village.

Vidyarthi has very nicely summarised some of the salient features of the village done till the first half of the 20th century, which he termed as the "Fromulatory period", in the following lines :-

"Firstly, all the village studies were of generalised nature. Secondly, in case of the survey of a specific village only the economic variable were taken into consideration. Thirdly, in some these economic survey of the villages the need for emphsising the social aspect of the village were also realised. Fourthly, with the passage of time the need for empirical studies was realised and several village studies were conducted by University department, Government. institution and missionaries. Fifthly, in addition ot these socio-economic surveys and empirical studies of the villages Wiser made an outstanding contribution to the field of village studies by studying it in an intensive and analytical manner. Sixthly, with the nationalistic spirits for rural reconstruction in India, Gandhijee pointed out the need for social and economic development of the villages, and a number of economists and social reformers collected data about the rural problems." (1966)

The village studies in India felt somewhate an excellent leap roughly from 1984. Though there were various factors responsible for the leap; India's independence had an vital role in this regard. The dreams of Gandhi jee for the establishment of Ram Rajaya in post independent India was gaining popularity and his slogan to go back to villages was well realised by the social workers. The newly established India Government. was also desirous to improve the lot of rural communities. The community Development Programmes were carried to the villages and the Programme Evaluation Schemes were chalked out. All these activities had a direct bearing on the interest of social scientists to rush to the village for intensive researches in the village communities.

After the second global war and specially after India's independence, there was a positive increase in contact of the American social anthropologists with India. Some American Anthropologists like Morris Opler of Cornell University, Oscar Lewis of the University of Illionois, David Mandelbaum of the University of California and many of their students came to India with their research teams and created an atmosphere for the systematic study of Indian villages. These American scholars not only produced valuable, theoretically oriented village studies, but also inspired the Indian anthropologoists to take up researches on the rural and village studies. It goes without saying that it was Opler who inaugurated his large scale village study in the village of Senapur in the Eastern U.P. in the year 1951. in the same year Oscar Lewis had taken up a similar study in Rampur, a village in the Western U.P. and Mandelbaum was already engaged in his village studies in the Nilgiri.

The Indian Social Anthropologist also did not lag behind Dube and Shrinivas were busy in studying Shamirpeth a Deccan village and Rampura a Mysore village, respectively, roughly during the same period. Vidyarthi (!966) has very nicely ovserved that "All these studies brought to Indian social anthropology an area of village studies as a number of social anthropologists were attracted to this study. The different aspects of India's village i.e. caste, marriage and family, village social organisation etc. On the pattern of American village studies of Redfield, Oscar Lewis etc. become fashionable".

With all the developments mentioned above, the village studies in India were getting popularity. Social anthropologists from India and abroad (America and U.K.) took up several very useful researches in India; as a result of which there was a boom in the publication of the village studies in and around 1955. "Indian Village" by S.C. Dube, "Village India' edited by Mckim Marriott. "Indias Village" edited by M.N. Srinivas and "Rural Profile" edited by D.N. Majumdar were all published in the year 1955.

'Indian Village' by Dube was the first complete village study which was widely welcomed and accepted as model study of an Indian Village. This book guides the young research scholars like the 'Palar Star' and provides a standard model for the similar studies in different parts of India. Morris Opler while writing the 'Foreword' to this book has correctly observed. "In a number of ways this volume is especially valuable and challanging and is a tonic to present day research into Indian village life.. Dube's book does much to dispel doubt and raise hope". (1955 p. IX)

Mackim Marriott's (1955) "Village India" had eight brilliant papers of which except one (Srinivas were written by the American anthropologists (Beals, Cohn, Cough, Lewis. Marriott, Mandelbaum and Steed.) All the papers of this book had a definite and vivid theoretical orientation and proved very useful for the research world.

India's Village by Srinivas (1955), a collection of excellent papers written by five American (Bailey, Collin, Castairs, Miller and Newell) and three Indian scholars (Dube, Srinivas and Sarma) was really a very valuable contribution. In addition to various theoretical dimensions shown by the British and American anthropologists, a few concepts of Srinivas-namely the concepts of "Sanskritisation", "Dominat caste", The village Unity and Extension", and the like brought a revolution in the annal of village studies in India.

Majumdar's Rural Profiles" (1955) had eleven scholarly papers devoted to the various aspects of village life, of which six papers were written by the Indian Social Scientists (Reddy, Majumdar, Dube, Srinivas, Pradhan, Sen, Mishra and Puri) and remaining five were written by the foreigeners

(Hopper, Ryan, Eames, Rallis and Goodall). Though each of the papers the book contained had its own value. "Demographic structure in a polyandrous village" by Majumdar, "Ranking of castes in Telangana villages" by Dube, 'Village Studies and their significance' by Srinivas and an excellent introduction of the book by D. N. Majumdar have been "A thing of beauty" hence a "Joy of ever".

Thus, to sum up the works published in 1955, it can be said that while Dube's 'Indian village' is a master piece total study of a caste village which will be a model for the research scholars for century to come, the three invaluable edited volumes of Marriott, Srinivas and Majumdar have brilliant papers by the vateran scholars from India and abroad. Each of the papers included in these books opens a new dimension, unknown in the history of anthropology and the theorectical contributions of these invaluable papers for their yeomans service render for enriching this branch of research. The only comment which one has about these papers is that each of the papers separately deals with only one or two aspects of a society but this comment also does not carry much wait because of the fact a paper has many inherent limitations and space factor is one of these whichdoes not allow it to cover all aspects of life in detail. These four major publications on the Indian village studies were followed by several other important publications mention among them may be made of "Caste and Communication in an Indian Village" by D.N. Majumdar (1958) which is the result of an intensive study of 'Mohana' a multi-caste village in U.P. It is an excellent contribution which deals in the inter-caste relationship, the economy, religion, leadership, factionalism, recreation etc. The last chapter, under the title "Village : A concept, a way of life" is the outcome of a systematic thinking by a seasoned scholar, where the author has accepted a village as a concept. He writes 'An Indian village is not merely a way of life, it is also a concept it is a constellation of values and so long as our value system does not change, or changes slowly and not abruptly, the village will retain its identity, and so it has done till today" (Mazumdar, 1958).

Oscar Lewis, an expert in Maxican village studies, with

the assistance of Victor Barnouw, published Village life in Northern India on a Delhi village in the same year. It was Rampur, the fictitious name for village of 1095 inhabitants located near Delhi. This is a very beautiful full-length book on a north Indian village which serves as a model for research scholars (H.S. Dhillon, I.P. Singh, R.S. Rathee, R.N. Bansal.Venu hamdas, P.Gorge, Kamal Prakash and others) who later on did some very useful village studies in India.

F.G. Bailey also published his celebrated book "Caste and the Economic Frontier" in the year 1958. This was study of Bisipara a village in highland Orissa M.N. Srinivas while writing an excellent foreword to the book has correctly observed "In brief, the field-anthropologist has found that in studying the microcosm he is also studying the macrocosm and that some knowledge of the latter is essential in order thunderstand the fromer. That his work sheds new light on the macrocosm is not only a valuable by product of his research, but it also opens up new avenues of social anthropology itself. This book which is based on an intensive field work is very rich in the analysis of the peasant economy and social change in the village of bisipara not only from synchronic point of view but also diochronically taking a time perspective of hundred years. His keen interest in understanding the problems of the villagers and subtle obsevation can be very easily seen in Chapter IV of the books, under title "Why does land come into the Market" where he furnishes the various reasons for selling the land. Thus to sum up it can be said that this is a unique and refreshing book of its own type, which provides us a prespective to understand the change in the economic and political structure of the village, which to Bailey, 'are not marginal but fundamental'.

The year 1960 deserves specific mention for the publication of a celebrated book "Caste And Kinship in Central India" by A.C. Mayer, a British Scholar of repute. This book, which is a study in a village (Ramkheri) and its region is very significant because it is the only village study which is exclusively devoted to the study of castesystem as such. Mayer's view that for study of caste system on needs a more wider convas than a single village, has been very emphatically put forward. This means both that the village, has been very emphatically put forward. This means both that the village is a social unit to be studied, and also that in any analysis of either cast or kinship, the data from single village are not enough, and the influence of the wider locality must be assessed" (1960). His concepts of caste and sub-caste is also very important and to him "On the whole, caste membership is significant for relations with other castes, and subcaste membership for activities within the caste" 1960. Thus to sum up it can be safely said that this book, which highlights the structural network of caste and lays emphasis on the concepts of caste and subcaste, is very useful for the research work on this line. "When Caste Barriers Fall" by D Sivartsen was published in 1963. This is the study of a village Thyagasamuthriram in Tanjor district of Madras Province. The author has very aptly tried to show as to how the villages have defied the working of caste system in the social aspect but it still has a very important role to play in the matter of village politics. Again his emphasis on the importance of economy in the process of decay of traditional ties among the persons of various castes is some of the very subtle observations in the field. It goes without saying that his observation on the conflicts and tension between the Brahmins of the village on one hand and lower caste people on the other is a universal problem all over in India.

Berreman's "Hindus of the Himalayas" was also published in 1963. This is study of Sirkanda, a village in the central Pahari area, and deals with the hill people of Himalays. The aims of the book are both ethnographic and analytic. At ethnographic level he talks of the various festivals and ceremonies celebrated by the Hindus and then he describes as to how the villagers go on pilgrimage where they contact with the Sankritised Hindus of the Great Tradition, at analytic level also the book is very fascinating. Thus Berreman has done a great service to anthoropology world by writing such an excellent book which deals with the life and culture of such people who are very little know. K.S. Mathur's "Caste and Ritual in a Malwa Village" was published in 1964. This is a full length book dealing with the religious life of the village of Potlod. This book is unique for its penetrating analysis of the function of Hindu religion in the intergration of caste Society-and the author has very clearly explained "The task I have set to myself in the present study is an analysis of the function of Hindu religion in the integration of caste society". 1964. This book, which opens with the discussion of the geographical enviroment of the region, describes the social structure next and is followed by a careful examination of the Hindu belief system among the rural folk and concludes with the impact of the pattern of beliefs and values on the day-to-day life of the villagers, is a model for the arrangement of materials in a very orderly manner. Dube while writing the foreward to this book has very rightly observed "Simple and unpretentions, this book is rich in ethnographic detail, displays bright analytical insights, and throwas up important leads for the further work to be taken up in this field."

Ranjana : A village in west Bengal was published by G. Chhattopadhyay in 1964. This is the first village study from West Bengal in which the author has tried to show the changes brought home by Zamindari abolition, Independence and General election and the like. The author observes "After the Zamindari system was abolished, the landlords were gone and thus a great unifying factor was removed from the life of the villagers. True, this unifying factor was an imposed one, but still it was there in the past and now it was there no more in the present. With the abolition of this system and the intermediary rights over lands there came a great change in the economic field'. (1964). It is study of a village, which has lost its traditional solidarity and has adopted a new set of ideas to from a new solidarity. This is a study of a Bengal village and as the author also comes of the same linguistic area, the book is very rich in ethnographic details.

Thanks to the census operation Department Government of India, for studying about eight hundred villages from the various part of India. The investigators and the officers of census operation have been studying these villages since 1960-61 and have published many monographs based on the field study of the selected villages. while talking about the monograph published by the Census of India, our attention is at once attracted towards vidyarthi's work on "Ghaghara" (1966). This is the first full-fledged account of a tribal village in Bihar, studies by a seasoned anthropologist trained at Lucknow and Chicago. This study has surpassed all the moinographs published by the Census of India (1961) in collection of abundance of empirical enthnographic data. And the scientific treatment of these data have given birth to a number of interesting and useful theoretical and methodological ideas and concepts. This study has received warm welcome due ot the fact that this is the first total study of a tribal village in Chotanagpur. The author of the book, an inborn anthropologist by nature, has as very soft corner for the tribals and their villages, has rightly observed "while we talk about "Village studies" or "Village India" our attention is mainly drawn to the dozens of studies of rural villages and we almost seem to forget that the "tribals" also live in Indian villages". On the methodological ground he comments"........that in tribal studies, the tribal as such, and not its villages have usually been the unit of". He further recommends "such empirical and specific studies of tribal villages of the various types, if adopted, will lead to effective comparisons of culture of villages in tribal and non-tribal areas, and will also help the applied anthropologists and administrators in identifying the problems of tribal villages of different levels of ecological, economic, technological and cultural developments against the background of concrete quantitative data". This book which is very rich in enthnographic data, has studied every aspect of the village life and culture, and the persual of the exhaustive table of contents is indicative about the thoroughness of the work. The author of the book deserves congratulation for publishing such an excellent work, which serves a model for the further study of a tribal village.

Yogesh Atal's "The changing Frontiers of Caste" (1968) which is a study in change in two villages-Kheri and Khiria (the fromer fails within Rajasthan and the latter in the Saugar District of Madhya Pradesh) is a masterpiece work. This is a valuable contribution to the growing volume of sophisticated discussion on caste, living in two different villages in India. This book aims at describing the structure and working of the caste system in a comparative framework evolved for the purpose. The author's attempt to a critical review of the theories of casts ranking and his empirical examination of the concept of the 'Dominant Case' are really praiseworthy, Dube while writing an excellent forward to this book has very aptly concluded "Dr. Atal merits commendation on this useful piece of research. It represents honest fieldwork and faithful reporting. Some of its analytical insights ae also penetrating. It definitely helps us to understand the phenomenon of caste better, and illuminate some significant aspects of change in village India". (1968).

In addition to these full-length books, a number of other important papers. both descriptive and analytical, have been published by the scholars of India and abroad which have helped in understanding the life and culture of Indian villages. Morris Opler occasionally in collaboration with D.R. Singh, has written a number of excellent papers (Opler 1950, 1952, 1956; Opler and Singh 1948, 1952 and Singh 1956) on the village life of U.P. It goes without saying that Singh's paper on unity of a village (1956) and that of Opler's on the extension of a village (1956) are very useful works for the use of a research scholar, Scholarly papers of Srinivas (1952, 1954, 1956 and 1959), Dube (1958 and 1965), and Mazumdar (1955 nd 1956) deserve specific mention in connection with the history of the village studies in India.

XIII
Theoretical Anthropology and E.B. Tylor

Edward Burnet Tylor was born in 1832. While he was only 24 years old, he found his health far from being satisfactory, and he arranged for a tour. He did not join a University. While on tour he met Henry Christy who was a banker, was going to Mexico, where he had been working in a bone cave. He requested Tylor to accompany him and the later did so. Tylor was with him for about ten years where he developed interest towads Anthropology. He gained good knowledge of ethnology and prehistory from Christy, and thus dedicated his life for the cause of Anthropology which was so little known at that time.

He was a British classical evolutionist but not so dogmatic as his contemporaries. Although there where some anthropologists even before Tylor but the mere fact that he was so often been called as the "father" of theoritical Anthropology indicates that his contributions were so great and important. Among so many his concept of Culture is most outstanding.

The word "culture" itself was not new. This was in circulation even befor Tylor. Originally it was a biological term, related to breeding and improvement of animals and plants, surviving in words like "agriculture" and "horticulture".

Its application to its human societies occured first in Germany in the 18th. century (Krober and Kluckhon 1963:13) and that time it still carried the connotation of improvement,

Long before that the idea of culture had been recognised under different terms such as "customs", "traditions" or social habits of peoples. Thus the term "culture" had been used right from Herodotus onward in various general and partial usages which led to several confusions before Tylor.

Tylor's definition of culture obviated all erroneous explanations. The very first sentence to his primitive Culture (1871) reads "Culture or civilization, taken in its wide ethnographic sence, is that complex whole which includes knowledge, belief, art morals, law custom and any other capabilities and habits acquired by man as member of society" (Tylor, 1958; 1:1).

If we analyse his definition of culture we find some very useful terms therein. For example the terms "acquired" appears to be the key word of this difinition, because it meant that culture was the product of social learning rather than of biological heredity. Again Tylor's insistence that culture was a "complex whole" implied that it included all socially learned behaviour.

As a classical evolutionist he believed in the "psychic unity" of man kind and held that all people were equally capable of progress. The differences between cultures were those of development rather than of origin various groups of people would eventually progress along similar lines, because their minds were unifromar. He regarded independent inventions as a strong argument for psychic unity does not mean that he regarded diffusion as strong argument against psychic unity. His evolutionary scheme of progress consisted of well-known stages of Savagery barbarism and civilization but his ws not a dogmatic system. Whenever he mentioned these developments he was careful to note that it was an ideal scheme, presenting a possible order of evolution, that there was a tendency in this direction, that the course of progress was not always unifrom, and that evolution could take place along different lines (Tylor 1958, 1:6,27). He did not attempt to force specific cultures into savagery or barbarism. But by and large he was nore inclined to reconstruct the evolution of particular culture tralt of institutions than to establish overal stages.

Tylor, however, deserves still greater credit for his treatment of statistics human institutions. Using a sample between 300 and 400 societies, he placed the comparative method on a statistical basis. He calculated percentages of probabilities of associations between post-marital residence, descent, taken onmy, and couvade and thereby advanced toward an understanding of exogamy, endogamy and the origin of crosscousin marriage and incest prohibition. He has taken help of certain statistics to prove the precedence of maternal societies to paternal. He begins by defining three social systems. In the maternal type matrilineal descent in coupled with avuncular authority and nepotic inheritence, at the opposite pole the paternal society has patritineal descent, paternal authority, filial succession; in the intermediate condition the features of the two extremes are varously blended. Tylor inqires how certain selected usages, such as the couvade, arew correlated with these three types. The couvade is absent from the maternal stage occurs twenty times in the intervening and only eight times in the pure paternal systems. This he argues, shows the priority of the maternal stage.

Although Tylor contributed a lot in the various spheres of anthropology but to me his contribution in the field of religion is unique in comprehension and analysis. He began with defining religion as "the belief in spiritual Beings". He firmly stated that religion was a cultural universal fact, because no culture was without such belief. Next he sought for an explanation of how the belief in spirits could have arisen.

Picturing early men as rationalis who did not possess the necessry knowledge to reason scientifically (he called them "savage philosophers") they must have noted the difference between a living being and a dead one. They pondered about this as well as phenomena of sleep, trance and visions, and concluded that every man possessed not only a meterial body but also a life and a phantom. Life enabled the body to think and act and the phantom was its image or second self. Both were separable from the body. Life went away after death, the phantom could appear to people at a distance, as in dreams. Soon enough, the savages began to consider the two identical and conceived of the idea of soul. After death the soul left the body permanently, but it sometimes appeared in dreams, acting as if it were alive. Thus the belief grew up that souls continued to exist after the death of the body. Early man thus began to believe that every one possessed a life and a soul, and this early stage of religion Tylor has called as "animism". He went on to explain that early man soon recognised that soul was superior to the body because of its greater mobility and durability of existence, first merely admiring the souls of the dead, earlyman later on ascribed additional powers to them. It was believed that they protected their own families and tribes, and watched over their moral behaviour. Attempts to communicate with these souls led to prayer and worship. The idea that souls and spirits must reside somewhere gave rise to belief in an afterlife, while their freedom to move about and to appear everywhere led to the idea that they could enter into the bodies of the living, and thus also the notion of "possession : and the practice of exorcism. Since spirits could also take up residence in material objects these would acquire special powers and thus idolatory was born, elevating spirits to the rank of Gods. Each god controlled a specific aspect of nature or of life. This gave rise to the stage of polysteism. The various Gods had different importance, and hierarchy emerged, with one God as supreme deity. Later on all minor gods receded into the background, and when they disappeared altogether, the final stage of monotheism was reached.

Anthropologists often blend Tylor as unilinear evolutionist. But to me Tylor was far from being a unilinear evolutionist, with a simple and universal scheme of development. He would refuse to go beyond his data and would not believe in sweeping generalisation and mere speculation. The question of diffusion and independent invention was always in his mind. First we note ghis introducing diffusion into a discussion of prehistoric technology. After pointing out the amazing similarity of stone fools in different parts of the world, he argues that with all due allowance for psychic unity "it is very doubtful whether it can be stretched far enough to account for even the greater proportion of the facts in question : (Tylor 1865). Again while not ruling out independent origins, he concluded that the observed unifromity "may some day be successfully brought in with other lines of argument.... which tend to centralize the early history of races of every unlike appearance and living in widely distant ages and countries" (Tylor 1865).

Now, after it has been examined as to what for Tylor stood, let us analyse the views of some leading anthropologists for the same. I would like to quote Lowie who observes "As Professor Elliot Smith is compelled to admit, Tylor himself was constantly producing proof of contact. He was in fact the very antithesis of a strict paralleslist even if he viewed the facts with scientific pose instead of falling prey to cheap diffusionist dogmatism. In short, he was thoroughly convinced of the force of borrowing in human history and expressed his faith both abstractly and with strict to special cases "civilization", we read "is a plant much more often propagated than developed" (Lowie 1937).

It has been mentioned earlier that Tylor is regarded as the father of modern British Anthropology hence a few paragraphs about his research works and publications deserve mention.

Tylor's first book "Mexico and the Mexicans" was published from London in the year 1861. This book was based on the study of caves in company of Henery Christy a prehistorian friend of Tylor.

"Researches into the Early History of mankind and the Development of Vivilization" was another very important book of Tylor which was published in the year 1865 from London. This work can be taken as representative of a very high scholarly standards of these times. Concerned with the question of general evolutionary directions and the origin of language, writing, naming, tools marriage, fire and myths, this book contains in embroyonlic from most of the themes developed in Tylor's more muture writings. This work may once again serve to demonstrate the importance of pre-Darvian archaeological achievements for the theories of the period 1860-90. It may be said without exaggeration that archaeological evidences are atleast as important as ethnographic evidences for Tylor's conclusions concerning the overall unifromity of evolutionary change.

Tylor's greatest contribution was "primitive culture" the publication of published in the year 1871 from London. Soon after the publication of this monumental work Tylor appeared as the foremost of English Anthropologists. For about next thiry years there was hardly any theory to hold the field, here or in America or on the continent. His solid array of accurately attested facts, his common sense in interpreting them and beautiful simplicity in style in dealing with vast amount of evidences, a style and power of organisation akin to darwin's won a permanent place in th history or religion. "Primitive Culture" carries extra ordinary recognition for Tylor used several terms and concepts for the first time here in this very book some of them given below : The concept of "survival" was first used in this book where Tylor emphasised the value of survivals for the reconstuction of history by means of the comparative method and he observes. These are processes customs, opinion and so forth which have been carried on by force of habit into a new state of society different from that in which they had their original home, and they thus remain as proofs and examples of an older condition of culture out of which as never had been evolved (Tylor, 1871).

Again, the concept of "Animism" which is the minimum definition of Tylor's religion, is perhaps the central theme in "primitive culture" Animism exists wherever there is belief in souls, ghosts, demons, devils, gods or similar categories of phenomena. The root of all these concepts is traced by Tylor to the belief in the human soul about which he observes the conception of human soul once attained by man, served as atype or model on which he framed only his ideas of other soulds of lower grade, but also his ideas of spiritual beigans in general from the tiniest elf that sports in the long grass up to the heavenly creator and Rural of the would, the Great spirit" (Tylor 1871).

Explaning why he devoted so much of "primitive culture" to traits that are "worn out, worthtless, or even had with down right harmful fooling" Tylor rejoiced "that in such inquiries we have continual reason to be thankful to fools." In this context he observes" it is quite wounderful, even if hardly go 'below the surface of the Subject to see how large a share stupidity and upractical consrvatism and dogged superstition have had in preserving for us traces of the history of our race, which practical utilitarianism would have remorselessly swept away "(Tylor 1871).

After "primitive culture" (1871) Tylor did not write any complete book except "Anthropology" (1881) in which he displayed his characte ristic insight and understanding of humanity. This book included chapters on the antiqity of man, his relationship to other animals, on the races of mankind, on language, and he often referred to archeology. His examination of communication among deaf-mute provides a model for the sudy of exotic systems of communications, and his insights into the nature of symbolization and its importance to human life are crucial for an understanding of the nature of culture and of man.

In addition to his several monumental books, he contributed many serious and scientific articles some of which were published in the Journal of the Anthropological Institute.

He was the editor of "Notes and Queries on Anthropology" and as many an eighteen sections of them were drawn up by him for the year 1874 and 1892 editions. He was very much interested for the foundation of many research institutes.

It has been mentioned earlier that Tylor did not join the University and hence was not a university graduate. He was associated with Oxford University as a Keeper of the University Museum. He became a reader in the year 1884 and then a University professor in Oxford in 1896. By then he had long enjoyed an international reputation, his, principal books having been translated into several languages of the world. But long before his death his became far from satisfactory as a result of which he could not contribute any book thereafter, and he died in 1971.

As a teacher of Oxford he produced many good and

serious Anthropologists. One of his close students R.R. Marett (1866 -1943) wrote Tylor's biography which was published in 1936. He summed up the theoretical contributions of Tylor as".... his concept of animism, his inclusive definitions of culture and of religion his use of comparative method, his attempts at statistical corelations, his stress on material culture, his historical reconstructions, and so forth perhaps, none of these was netirely original with Tylor, but he brought them together in a coherent whole. In his hands; anthropology became "the science of culture' (Marett 1936) I am very much in agreement with Marett about his summary of the contributions of Tylor.

Bibliography

1. Atal Yogesh 1968 The Changing Frontiers of Caste : National Publishing House Delhi.
2. Bailey, F.G. 1955 An Oriya Hill village (Ed.) Srinivas, M.N.
3. Beals, A.R. 1955 Change in Leadership of Mysore Village Ed. Srinivas.
4. Bhowmick P.K. 1978 Occultism in Fringe Bengal.
5. Dube. S.C. 1955 Indian Village, London.

   1958 India's Changing Village, London.
6. Levis Oscar 1958 Village Life in Northern India, Illinois.
7. Mariott, M. 1955 Village India, Asia Publishing House.
8. Mathur, K.S. 1964 Caste and Rituals in Malwa village, Asia Publishing House, Bombay.
9. Mazumdar, D.N. 1958 Caste and Communication and Indian Village, Asia Publishing House, Bombay.
10. Mishra, N. 1978 Cultural Persistence and Change, Classical Publication New Delhi.
11. Opler Morris 1956 Extension of an Indian village, Journal of Asian Studies.

12. Roy, S. C.	1915	The Oraons of Chotanagpur, Man in India.
13. Roy, S. C.	1928	Oraon Religion and Custom, Man in India.
14. Sachchidanand	1968	The Tribal Village in Bihar, Munsiram Manohar Lal,
15. Singh, I.P.	1962	Religion in Deloka : A Sikh Village.
16. Srinivas, M.N.	1952	Religion and Society among the Coorgs of South India, The Clevendon Press, Oxford.
17. "	1955	Indian's Village, Asia Publishing House, Bombay.
18. Vidyarthi, L.P.	1963	The Maler, Bookland Ltd.
19. "	1964	Cultural Contours of Tribal Bihar, Punthi Pustak, Calcutta.
20. "	1966	Ghaghara, A Village in Chotanagpur, Government of India Press.
21. Wiser, W.H.	1936	The Hindu Jajmani System, Lucknow Publishing House.

Index

C

R

S